LEARNING and SOCIETY

Further details about the series are at the end of the book.

EXITS AND ENTRANCES:

Political Research as a Creative Art

Lewis Minkin

Sheffield Hallam University Press
Learning Centre
City Campus
Pond Street
Sheffield S1 1WB

First published 1997

Designed and typeset by Design Studio, Learning Centre, Sheffield Hallam University

Cover designed by Stefan Boberek, Nothern College

 ISBN 0 086339 6364

ABOUT THE AUTHOR

Lewis Minkin left school at the age of 15 and went to work in what was then the world's largest tailoring factory. At the age of 26 he went to Leeds University on a Mature Matriculation scholarship. He was the first student to gain First Class Honours in Political Studies at that university. Later he received a Doctorate from York University and then for twenty years lectured in Government at Manchester University.

He has published extensively in the study of the British Labour Movement and since the mid 1980s has acted in various advisory positions to the Labour Party. In 1992 he became the academic adviser to, and a full member of, the Review Group of trade union and party leaders which produced the historic constitutional changes in relations between the Labour Party and the trade unions in 1993. From 1996-7 he was co-adviser to the National Executive Committee "Party into Power" project on relations between the Labour Party and a future Labour Government.

For a period in the 1970s and early 1980s he acted as political adviser to a range of television documentaries and plays, including the acclaimed series "Bill Brand" and the Prix-Italia award winning play "Spongers".

In recent years he has been a Visiting Professor at the Leeds Metropolitan University with responsibility for encouraging a research culture. He has always been committed to the development of adult education and since 1984 has been associated with the Northern College. After its partnership with the new Sheffield Hallam University he became Professorial Research Fellow at the new Northern Institute for Continuing Education based at the College, and Visiting Professor at the University.

ANALECTA

When at the the first I took my pen in hand,
Thus for to write, I did not understand
That I at all should make a little book,
In such a mode; nay, I had undertook
To make another, which when almost done,
Before I was aware, I this begun.

from "The Author's Apology for His Book"
John Bunyan *The Pilgrim's Progress*

One does not discover new lands without consenting to lose sight of the shore for a very long time.

André Gide
quoted in Julia Cameron *The Artists Way* 1994

. . . architect, bricklayer and painter, moving from drawing board to attic to brick yard, discarding a foundation here, an upright there, then suddenly hurrying off for more bricks. It seems far removed from the cool flowing logic of completed texts and never destined to get there. Also very much at the mercy of the weather. What begins as one theme is blown to one side and becomes another. The structure changes purpose, the sections change shape. Over time, the whole thing even subtly changes colour.

Lewis Minkin
Introduction to *The Contentious Alliance: trade unions and the Labour party, 1991*

. . . look on every exit being an entrance to somewhere else.

Tom Stoppard
Rosencrantz and Guildenstern are Dead Act I

ACKNOWLEDGEMENTS

For me, this has been an immensely rewarding project to think about and to discuss with a variety of people working in different fields.

I am grateful to Chris Price for a car journey across Cyprus to my old RAF base and a discussion which led to my revisiting some of the themes in this study.

I would also like to thank all those who participated in the seminars on *The Realpolitik of Research* held at Leeds Metropolitan University on 9th February 1993 and on *Thinking About Thinking About Research* at the Leeds Business School on 2nd December 1993; on *Research and the Creative Process* held at the Northern Institute for Continuing Education, on 31st May 1995, and *Thinking About Thinking About Research* with scientists at Sheffield Hallam University on 20th September 1995. Those discussions were all very supportive in the development of this study.

I am particularly indebted to some very busy friends who gave their time to read and discuss the ideas contained in some very rough early drafts. The comments and suggestions of Peter Ashworth, Huw Beynon, Michael Birch, Bob Britton, Ros Driver, Maria Edmondson, Gill Griffiths, Trevor Griffiths, David Howell, Jude Kelly, Jean McCrindle, Susanne McGregor, Jim Morgan, Jane Pillinger, Patrick Seyd, Eric Shaw, and Fiona Williams, have been of great value.

Over a long period, Arthur Lipow has always been available to give encouragement to this project and was, as ever, a provocative source of intellectual stimulation.

I am most greatly indebted to Bob Fryer, the Director of the Northern Institute for Continuing Education and a close personal friend, who gave this project enthusiastic support and provided a regular stimulus to the process of meeting myself afresh - periodically also providing a very illuminating methodological mirror. What I have to say here has gained enormously from his critical and creative reading of several drafts of this text, parts of which are the direct product of our dialogue. I personally have been enormously enriched by the mutual education and companionship, and the book would have been much the poorer without both.

I am, as always, very grateful to Liz Minkin for her comments on the draft, and her general sustenance, and I apologise for the piles of paper and the demented behaviour.

I thank Jean Goodridge and Elizabeth Jackson for their assistance with typing and tidying the manuscript and their struggles to get presentable copies out of various recalcitrant machines. Also, Stefan Boberek for his patient creativity with the cover, and the staff at Northern College Library for their assistance in securing various books.

I also thank Bernard Jones acting as proof reader/editor, and the staff of Sheffield Hallam University Press, with their colleagues in the Design Studio and Print Unit for moving the book from typescript to final product with heartening speed and efficiency

And I thank also all those who, in conversation, discussion and interview, have contributed over the years to the creative process described here.

Of course, I hasten to point out that responsibility for the judgements expressed here, and any inadequacies, are mine alone.

Lewis Minkin

TABLE OF CONTENTS

About the Author iii

Analecta v

Acknowledgements vi

Table of Contents ix

Introduction xv
- Why? xv
- Who and how? xviii
- For whom? xxiv
- Where is it going? xxvi
- The mosaic of experience xxviii

Chapter 1: The Research Experience 1
- The spinal cord 1
- Reflections 1
- Diagnosis 4
  - Learning about creativity: the limited dialogue 4
  - Learning about creativity: the personal experience 4
  - The creative and the scientific 8
  - Reconstruction and analysis 10
- Reflexivity and metacognition 12
- Demystification 15
- Specialism and style 18
  - The varieties of research 18
  - Specialism 19
  - Style 21
- The art of the researcher 24

Chapter 2: Research Creativity: Characteristics 33
The elusive definition 33
The creative player 34
Relevant attributes 35
The forms of creativity 36
Enhancing creativity 37
Approaches to creativity enhancement 39
Awareness of creativity 39
Self-awareness 39
Self-help and self-image 40
Applied creativity 41
Exploring, playing and using time 42
Exploring 42
Playing 44
Using time 46
Solitude 51
"The flow" 52

Chapter 3: Creativity and Problem-seeking 61
Problems and distinctiveness 61
Examination, peculiarities and problems 64
Critical Examination 64
Peculiarities 66
Problem focus 68
Problems, solutions and problems again 71
Purpose, preoccupations and peculiarities 71
Purpose 71
Peculiarity: the agenda management 74
Peculiarity: the union leaders 78

Chapter 4: The Psychology of Creative Research 85
The intellectual and the psychological 85
Creativity and personality 86
Motivation 88
Deferment and risk-taking 91
Emotions, moods and self-management 93
Persistence and effort 95
Anxiety 96
Community, showbusiness, market and "courage of mind" 97
Resilience, confidence and the Destructive Critic 100
The delicate balance 102
Self-image 104
The helter-skelter 105
Success and the use of failure 107
Fulfilment, "the Pilgrim" and Faust 109

Chapter 5: Role Playing and Creative Research: "The Detective" 117
The secret life of Walter Mitty 117
The Detective 119
Image and reality 119
From the past, to the present as past 121
Watching, questioning, listening, sensing 121
Responsibilities of observational vigilance 124
Discovery 126
Enlarging the possibilities 128
Following the peculiar 130
Peculiarities and the politics of the block vote 132
Context and perspectives 133
Empathy 136
Pitfalls and pratfalls of detection 137

Interviews, conversations, joint enquiries and the creative dialogue 138
Interviewing and recording 138
The interview as a conversation 140
The interview as a joint enquiry 144
The interview as a creative dialogue 147
Problems and dangers 151
Serendipity and the prepared mind 154
The case of the missing link 156
Enquiries and signposts 158
The observer-insider and creative research 161
The style of the detective 164
Heuristics and the role of the Detective 165

Chapter 6: Role Playing and Creative Research: "Juggler", "Patternmaker" and Company 171
The Juggler 171
The process of production 171
Frameworks 173
Juggling, writing and the creative process 175
The Patternmaker 179
Reorientation 179
Patterning: divergence and convergence 182
Images and the drama of politics 183
Creative patternmaking and symbolic representation 184
The dialogue with the Detective 186
The Patternmaker's tasks 188
The search for appropriate strangeness 190
Analysis and chronology: problems of presentational patterning 192
The deferred-judgement principle and the battle of the Patternmakers 194
Potency and fallibility 198
Allies, educators and models 202

Chapter 7: Creative Research and Heuristic Thinking 211
Contrasts of the creative mind 211
The Chattering Monkey 211
From heuristics to heuristic thinking 215
The modes of heuristic thinking 217
The creative critic 217
Working backwards from the end state 221
The Awkward Sod 224
Experimental mind-games 230
death, chance and murder 230
human choice and the 50/50 decision 233
re-dating a historical development 234
removing the typical 236
Analogies and metaphors 237
Presentation as creativity-generation 243
aesthetics, order and focus 244
the end of the beginning 249
Confronting the Vicious Circle 250
talking as thinking 250
the theatrical drama 252
scrutiny and creativity 253
and verification 255
the Vienna panic 257
Meeting the challenge 259

Chapter 8: The Creative Development of Ideas 265
The association of ideas 266
Back to the problem 270
Phase I: entrances 271
Phase II: peculiarities and inhibitions 272
Phase III: crisis 276
Phase IV: relations, rules and roles 278
Phase V: analogy and metaphor 282

Phase VI: problem re-framing and the challenge to the settlement 284
Phase VII: values 286
Phase VIII: the framework 289

Chapter 9: Instability, Autonomy and the Creative Process 293
Transmutations 293
Destabilising Forces 296
Shifting sands 296
Varying levels of generality and complexity 297
Generating problems 298
Stages of discovery and interpretation 300
Outside interventions 300
Conceptual development 301
Changing researcher 302
Asserting Control 302
Focusing and prioritising 305
The Dynamic Process: Implications 307
Discipline and Constraint 308
The Changing Culture: Implications 310

Chapter 10: Overviews and Afterthoughts 317
Entrances and exits 317
The perspective and the context 322
The creative era? 323
A creative research culture 326
The significance of failure 328

Bibliographies 333

Index of cited authors 357

Subject index 363

INTRODUCTION

WHY?

"Why are you doing this?", asked a puzzled friend who had presumably expected me to have set out on another long voyage into the oceans of British Labour politics.

My answer to this is fundamentally the same answer as I have given in relation to all my research. I had been working on it in my head, I was interested, indeed gripped by the subject, and I thought that it was important enough to explore further. Important for me and useful, I hope, for those who read it.

Useful, because it attempts to respond to a curious limitation in the literature and academic discourse about the empirical study of politics. Whilst methods of investigation are endlessly explored, individual creativity and the thinking which contributes to it are relatively neglected. Hence, my purpose here is to contribute towards an increased understanding of the creative process involved in research and to begin a dialogue about its forms and lessons.

As will soon become abundantly clear, this will be no abstract examination. It will involve an exploration of, and a reflection on, the way that my own thinking shaped a body of research projects over a long period, and it will attempt to relate the insights of that experience to the literature on the study of creativity. In this analysis of a mind-at-work, I will not attempt to engage with the totality of all the processes and problems involved in research, but I will cover the intellectual and psychological experience of some important dimensions, facets and activities of the research process which are not normally explored in detail and in public.

That then, is the objective. I know that this makes it an unorthodox project, both in its focus and its form. I also appreciate that it has produced a study which is not easy to categorise. But the fact that there is no synthesis quite like it in the research literature, (at least as far as I was aware in 1996) might be saying something about the value of what I am attempting.

It has, inevitably, a solipsistic flavour to it, with an equally inevitable emphasis on the personal pronoun - the "I"[1], but it is neither an arrogant nor an egocentric exercise. Indeed it runs counter to my usual practice where for self-effacing psychological, as well as conventional, academic reasons, I have in the past been reluctant to acknowledge my own presence in the work - even where I might marginally have had an influence on aspects of the behaviour or events under examination.

Here the bringing of the "I" to centre-stage is not simply a *mea culpa* rectification of that tendency. It is intended as an experiment: an attempt to illustrate the insights to be gained from detailed self-exploration - even if this is at the cost of opening a degree of vulnerability - and to share an experience of the creative process.

This sharing of the understanding to be gained by an in-depth study of the scholar's mental processes in relation to one body of work produced over a long period, involves a very serious commitment to the principle of mutual education. It represents my

[1] I have had difficulty with using the gender pronouns in a neutral way in this study, because at various points in Chapters Five and Six, the third person reference is to myself at work. Where this is the case, I have used "he". In the rest of the text I have used a range of neutral references, particularly "s/he".

answer to the fundamental question which underlies the whole book: how can we, the practitioners of research, learn more from each other's mode of work?

The approach I have taken here owes something to an old working class tradition of self-improvement, mutual support and the articulation of knowledge gained through experience. [Vincent 1981, pp 133-165] There is throughout my study, a necessary concentration upon the individual mind, and also, as a lone scholar, on the processes of individual production. But the latter - my favoured style - is a contingent not a necessary feature of creative expression. There are circumstances where creative collaboration or collective creativity can be both necesssary and add up to more than the sum of the parts.

However expressed, in lone or joint production, the creativity of the individual is always, to some extent, a social product and a social activity. Although it is not my primary focus here, there is a sociology as well as a psychology of creativity.[1] No mind is an island; each takes from and contributes to the whole. Creative scholarship, as I have experienced it, requires a degree of isolation and mental space but it also needs perpetual nourishment from a tradition and commmunity of scholarship. The anxious perils of the research journey described here must, ultimately, be met by the individual, although they are best faced in practice in the context of mutual encouragement and assistance. Further, the individualism of my activity is heavily oriented to the solution of problems of social concern and directed towards an educational unveiling of power and process.

So, although the strongest evocation here is of the spirit of self-help and self-development, the *raison d'etre* of the entire study is a commitment to mutual education in the pursuit of shared social objectives. In that commitment I recognise how much my life has been enriched by my own experience of political research, and in these difficult times this is the moment, and the opportunity, to put something back and to pass something on. What follows is an expression of a social obligation, and an educational philosophy, whose credo is exemplified in a book by Brewster Ghiselin which excited me and enriched my work nearly thirty years ago:

> Every genuinely creative worker must attain in one way or another such full understanding of his(sic) medium and such skill, ingenuity, and flexibility in handling it that he can make fresh use of it to construct a device which, when used skilfully by others, will organise their experience in the way that his own experience was organised in the moment of expended insight, [Ghiselin 1954, p18]

WHO AND HOW?

We all come to our research by different routes, and as students of social science we draw from that life experience in the values, perspectives and understandings that we bring to bear upon our work. Given that fact, and given the interplay between academic scholarship, analysis, introspection and mental autobiography in this study, I think that it is useful to say something here about who I am and, so to speak, "where I'm coming from" in terms of my personal history and values.

I am a university academic with thirty years' experience of research into politics, working at the interface of contemporary history and political science. I think of myself sometimes as a political analyst, sometimes as an analytical historian. At times I describe myself simply as a historian, and at other times as a political scientist. One friend is convinced that I am a "Contemporary Historian", another that I am a "Political Anthropologist." Probably none of these labels are fully satisfactory in conveying quite what I do.

Whatever the description, the point here is that the vocation was not an obvious outcome of my early development. I had dropped out of grammar school at the age of 15 with no qualifications and a view of myself as a complete failure. This was after an educational experience that suggested to me that what was going on in my head was of no special quality[2]. I would certainly never have thought of comparing myself with the kind of people who went to University, let alone those who lectured and wrote books. Nor would I have thought of myself as at all creative, even if I had understood fully what that meant.

There was, as always in these matters, an individual and a sociological dimension to my experience. Anyone reading Jackson and Marsden on *Education and the Working Class* would find my school story and my psychological state very familiar.[3] Grammar school involved an alienating culture shock and an alarming set of new goals. They were strange goals too. I had, at that time, very limited personal expectations or ambitions; none of my friends aspired or went to University. As far as I knew, nobody in the family or neighbourhood ever had been.

There was also almost an immediate change in my feelings about my ability. The inner city primary school that I had attended was well behind others in its standards (not helped by a persistent teacher shortage and, for a period, as I recall, seventy to a class).[4] After passing an intelligence test to get into grammar school, I found that I was well behind everybody else in basic subjects, without understanding why.

The loss of confidence combined with a loss of belonging was profound, and the sense of personal incompetence went very deep. I sometimes felt dishearteningly thick. So, for much of the time, I responded with my own form of revolt: constant trouble-making, a very low level of academic interest and an unwillingness to make more than the most minimal effort. "You are an oaf, Minkin", one of the teachers told me - doubtless with good reason.

However, around the age of fourteen two inter-connected developments began to transform my perspective, my motivation, my attitude to learning, and to some extent my life. The first was that, for reasons which are unclear to me, I became attracted to the image of "doing research" and being seen as somebody who was good at it.

Where did this come from? I have only a hazy recollection that a story in a boys' book stimulated me to emulate one of the characters. Then again, though I do not recall it as an influence at all in that period of change, the socio-cultural influence of a Jewish milieu[5] may also have passed on a reverence for learning and the image of the esteemed scholar. Certainly I can now see that it arose out of a deepening need to find a sense of my own capability and out of a longing to show that I was good at something - anything. I was, I think, searching for an identity which gave me not only fulfilment but self-respect and the respect of others.

Be that as it may, I do remember, vividly, breaking away from my normal scruffy, one-side homework submissions, and, working hours in the public library, producing for my history teacher an eight- page paper on the dictators Stalin, Salazar and Attaturk.

After handing in the paper I waited eagerly to see what the history teacher would say, anticipating surprise, and who knows, maybe, for a change, even a compliment. He stormed in with not a glance at me and imposed a collective punishment, making the whole class stand to attention for ten minutes because the work we had submitted was so poor. The work was then handed back in silence. And that was that.

I must say that his performance did not do a lot for my confidence. Ah well. Sod him. Although my re-found interest in history continued,[6] I did not bother trying to do anything special in homework after that. "Research" passed from my mind. Only now can I see that various seeds had been sown.

The second development, and I have a very clear memory of this, was a long and animated discussion with a young Communist (about Stalin I think). I became interested in politics and involved in innumerable arguments about it. Subsequently, as a socialist and a trade unionist, I developed some passionately held convictions about equality, democracy, solidarity and the liberty of the poor and the oppressed. This stimulated a desperate yearning to understand (and change) the world. The search pulled me into the public library and into the deep love of books and knowledge. It also added a new dimension to what became a desperate yearning for self-improvement.

Thus, as I left school, I became involved in what I now see not only as a social and political project but, as it now appears, a kind of odyssey to develop the ability to think and work effectively. My study here is an expression of some of the lessons of that voyage. It was not an easy journey, as many others in a similar position have testified. Much of it was undertaken in snatched moments, in lunch breaks and evenings after working hours, and even in a tent in Cyprus between guard duties. There was a persistent struggle with a sense of ordinariness, and often a terrible loss of energy and self-respect when the self-improvement reading (*Pelmanism, Straight and Crooked Thinking*, etc. etc.) and the nightschool, trade union and postal courses, failed to produce the dramatic revolution that I yearned for.

Increasingly I began to be very alert to the complex relationship between the individual's psychological frame of mind and the potentiality for sustained intellectual attainment. Few people are more aware than I am about the problem of retaining confidence and an encouraging self-image. There was never the dreamed of sudden leap-forward in intellectual ability. And yet, something was stirring and growing out of all this effort. It flowered most noticeably within the encouragement of an academic-political circle of (to me) dazzlingly impressive thinkers in the *New Reasoner* group - a network that I had become part of after a discussion on an Aldermaston March.[7]

It was at this point that I began to notice something very heartening. I found that I had things to say which felt as though they were truly the product of my own thinking. The intellectual involvement that had been generated by hours in the public libraries since the age of fifteen began to be accompanied by an excitement that I could create something myself. And it was at this point also that I became aware that I had been closely monitoring my own thinking process - an exploration that continued after I became a mature student at Leeds University.

The mixture of mental self-awareness and academic skills grew significantly as an undergraduate and, particularly later, when I became involved in the curious process of doing research. I encountered then, problems "on the job" that neither instruction nor literature had really prepared me for. I went through psychological responses that threatened my nervous system and my personal life;

but I also found things happening in my mind that surprised and sometimes delighted me. At times, I even experienced what can only be described as a state of fundamental joy at the satisfactions of creativity. So entranced did I become by these developments, that my first seminar paper as a member of the staff of the Department of Government at Manchester University mixed an examination of the substantive problems of the policy process at the Labour Party Conference with an exploration of some of the mental processes and problems of dealing with it.

Ever since then, "thinking about thinking" in connection with research, and exploring the art involved in this thinking, have accompanied my substantive research activities. As I worked away at this project or that, so (with much less intensity) I worked at observing my own mental activities, noting a skill here and a quality there, an inadequacy here and a fault there, watching the ideas emerge and the patterns alter, blend and transform. In the process, I began to form the view that, in terms of raising the creative quality of our work, how we mentally manage our research (both psychologically and intellectually) was worthy of much more attention than was normally given to it in discussions of research methods. In spite of the undoubted development in the quality of research training, I still believe that to be the case.

With this in mind, at Leeds Metropolitan University I began to shape an agenda for a different kind of research dialogue. That project was then continued at the new Northern Institute for Continuing Education where I developed the analysis in this study by - in effect - researching my own head, my own working methods, and whatever relevant work had been done in the study of thinking and creativity.

I did this alongside the continuation of my specialist area research (examining the internal politics of the "new" Labour Party) testing back and forth the congruence of my reports of the mental process and the real practice. Until last year, there was no intention of producing a book on this process, but that is - surprisingly - what has now emerged.

FOR WHOM?

The book grew out of reflections on my experience of, and my past discussions about, the practice of research. Primarily, I am attempting here to encourage a broadening of the dialogue with my professional colleagues, particularly those involved in political research: to draw attention to some often-neglected questions, to explore an under-valued literature, to analyse a mental process and hopefully to compare, and learn from, our experiences. As will become clear, I hope it will be an assistive and fruitful dialogue, not only about the present limitations of the agenda of research discussions, but also about the problematic nature of the research culture within which academics are now operating.

At the same time I have another, more specific audience in mind. Much of the time, as I write, I can see people not unlike myself thirty years ago - eager, excited, nervous, uncertain. They are those third-year students of social science and the humanities, with an interest in empirical research, who are contemplating going into the field and wondering what it will be like.

They are also postgraduates and young academics in these disciplines, who are deep in the throes of struggling with a thesis or a book and finding that the process has many strange and unexpected features. Today such researchers face a complex of academic pressures and difficulties far more burdensome than when I began my own research. I think that they may find much of value to be learned from the experience described here, although its lessons will have to be evaluated and applied with care, bearing in mind the *realpolitik* of today's research culture and the present constraints and timetables of assessment.

The examples of research creativity that I will be giving here are all drawn from political research. That is my specialism, and that is my primary focus. But those involved in research into other germane areas - education, psychology, sociology, social anthropology, social policy, and so on, may well find that much of what I have to say strikes a chord, generates an understanding, or suggests new possibilities for the mind at work.

There may also be other audiences, interested in the various forms of creativity, who might peep in. Judging from the responses of the diverse people who I have talked to about the manuscript, it does engage in an unusual way with the mental activities of those engaged in a wide range of creative activity.

Last, but not least, what I have to say here may be instructive for those interested in how we, the concerned citizens, learn about politics. What it represents is an honest exposition of the creative process by which the political world is intellectually constructed, interpreted and reported. In this frankness, it is consistent with my previous work which was concerned with both the unveiling of the political process and the democratisation of political understanding.

Because of the form that I have adopted, and the purposes of the study, what I have to say varies in terms of its detail and in the way that it is expressed. It shifts as I move from the general to the particular, from the broader literature to the personal experience, from the analyst to the raconteur, and from the first person to the third person as I report my activities through a range of self-images. There are some sharp changes in tone, depth, and pace. These changes of my voice and presence may be disconcerting to some, but could be a welcome variation to others. Either way, it is, I think, inevitable in the kind of synthesis that I am seeking and the different audiences that I am addressing.

WHERE IS IT GOING?

In order for the reader to be clear about the general trajectory and content of the presentation, let me give a brief prècis here of its main features, chapter by chapter.

The study begins with a mood and scene-setting first chapter which introduces my experience of research, then reflects on some of the weaknesses in the research dialogue in relation to creativity. It concludes with an exploration of my specialism and style, and of the art of the researcher.

In Chapter Two the focus switches to the idea of creativity, seeking clarity of definition and suggesting some key characteristics of creativity in relation to research. My own experience is threaded through the sections on "exploring", "playing" and "using time". There is also an examination of my experience of the creative "flow".

Chapter Three begins the process of looking at the main focus of my own research interests and the problems that I have sought to address. This is introduced by an emphasis on the importance of problem-seeking and particularly the search for "peculiarities".

Chapter Four switches focus again, this time onto the psychology of the creative mind. Drawing from the literature on creativity, but relating it closely to my own experience, I examine a range of important attributes and qualities of the creative personality as reflected in the research process.

Chapter Five switches back to my experience of the intellectual activity involved in research. This, and the chapter that follows, are approached through a range of self-images of the creative researcher in action. In this chapter the focus is on the processes of empirical investigation and the creative role of the Detective.

Chapter Six focuses mainly upon what I call the Juggler and the Patternmaker in the construction of analytical and presentational frameworks. The writing process is also explored, as are some of the less rational contributions of the Detective and Patternmaker. Following this, there is an examination of the creative accompaniment to the individual scholar - the intellectual relationships involved in research.

Chapter Seven stands back from the actors described in the previous chapter and looks at the creative process from a different angle. It traces first the creative assistance received from the non-directed activity of the mind. It then offers a range of systematic ways of stimulating, and benefiting from, creative opportunities in research. These modes of intervention in the creative process draw from my own experience of the research process from conception to completion.

Chapter Eight picks up on problems discussed in Chapter Three. It takes us into an exploration of long-term changes in the way that a particular set of my research problems and solutions were developed, and into the experiences, influences and thought processes that contributed to the creative movement.

Chapter Nine focuses upon my experience of the shifting and unstable character of research projects. It looks at the causes and consequences of movement and transformation in the project, examining the various ways in which, in a creative process, it can take on unplanned directions and contours. There is an exploration of possible responses by the researcher, and an assessment of the implications of this experience for the management of research.

Finally, Chapter Ten offers some overviews and afterthoughts, drawing conclusions and suggesting some general implications of the analysis for the conduct and management of creative research.

THE MOSAIC OF EXPERIENCE

There is a careful rationale to this sequence of themes, topics and perspectives, but the mosaic of experience could have been patterned (and can be read) in various ways, and it could have followed a different order. Even the foundations - the diagnosis, the nature of creativity, and the fundamental concerns of my work - might have had an alternative arrangement. What the reader has to keep in mind is that the mental processes portrayed here are often virtually simultaneous in my thinking about research, although, in the analysis, they have had to be described sequentially.

END NOTES

[1] See on this for example [Brannigan 1981], [Csikszentmihalyi, M. 1988 pp 325-338]., Schaffer 'Making up discovery' in [Boden 1994]. This literature emphasises the occurrence of multiple and simultaneous discovery, and

draws particular attention to the social, environmental and cultural context in which judgements are made about the creativity of the products, and to the way that "discoveries" are credited by authoritative communities.

[2] This is no false humility. Just to give the flavour of it: I used to get less than 40 per cent in most subjects and it was not unusual to get less than 20 per cent. In the examination for mathematics in the year before I left I even managed no marks at all!

[3] [Jackson and Marsden 1966]. This book was a revelation to me in giving my personal story a sociological dimension, particularly pp 265 - 277 which describe the culture shock, the alienation, the demoralising effect of testing and streaming, and the hostility to authority experienced by the grammar school drop-out.

[4] Some understanding of the teacher shortage in this school can be gained from the autobiography of Cec Thompson (a moving and inspiring story of the first black person ever to play Rugby League for Great Britain), who attended the senior class just before I arrived amongst the juniors. "Sheepscar had an evil reputation, which it fully deserved. Future criminals did their training there, and the heroes were the gang leaders and pimps, characters out of Brighton Rock." [Thompson 1995, p. 13].

[5] For an analysis of "The Phenomenon of Creativity amongst Jews in Modern Times" and an explanation given in terms of socio-cultural factors prevailing in Jewish milieus, see [Arieti 1976 pp 325-336]. I have some hesitation here in even suggesting this influence. I came from a mixed marriage in which my mother (who had converted from Christianity to Judaism) was the one interested in history who occasionally read a book. I do not recall any particular knowledge of this scholarly element in the Jewish tradition. Also I was at this stage deeply anatagonistic to my religious experience, including anything to do with Talmudic learning.

[6] In the last year or so that I attended that school, there was a huge improvement in my examination performance in history from around 30 per cent to around 70 per cent. The history teacher appeared not to notice anything different.

[7] *The New Reasoner* was a journal of exceptionally talented ex-Communist intellectuals based mainly in and around Yorkshire. They sought to completely re-think their positions after the revelations of the 20th Congress of the Communist Party of the Soviet Union and after the suppression of the Hungarian Revolution.

CHAPTER ONE

THE RESEARCH EXPERIENCE

THE SPINAL CORD

Hard lessons of personal experience form the spinal cord of this study. My path through the exposition, and the guidelines for what is to be discussed here, have been influenced by a depth of understanding gained over years of working as a field researcher. So, as a foundation for the investigation that is to follow, I am beginning here by introducing the reader to some key features and expressions of that experience, before I move on to some important reflections upon the practice of research and its discourse.

REFLECTIONS

Much of my most important research was done in the period when I was lecturing in the Department of Government at Manchester University. It was for me, overall, an exciting and deeply rewarding experience and, I must say, a wonderfully evocative environment in which to do that work.

I used to park my car on the spot where Engels had his house during the period when he wrote *The Condition of the Working Class In England*. I walked into a University where Wittgenstein had done some of his thinking, where Rutherford had done some of his preparation, where the world's first stored-program digital computer had been invented and where, a few miles away, Lovell had his radio telescope. I walked through the door into the Faculty where (as I was to discover) a rightwing economist John Jewkes had written a now forgotten book Ordeal by Planning [Jewkes 1948] which had helped drive the 1945 Labour Government away from its economic policies. And I walked into a Department of Government where the doyen of my profession, Sammy Finer, was lecturing and dazzling everybody on the basis of a research expertise which seemed to stretch from Afghanistan to Zanzibar. All the time I was there the place was full of distinguished research scholars and high level research students.

It was in some ways daunting (who could live up to all of that?) and in others uplifting. But then, a similar point could be made about the conflicting states of mind provoked by research itself. Research is a deeply fulfilling but, at times, profoundly bewildering and disturbing experience. At its best, there is the adventure of risk, the pleasures of design and discovery, the satisfaction of personal accomplishment and a pride in participation in a great chain of scholarship. At its worst, there is the disappointment of the inevitable periods of "failure" and the constant struggle against fatigue. And at its most burdensome, there is the repeated sense of adversity and frustration, and the nagging self-doubt about the ability to handle a complexity and turbulence which sometimes feels as though it was just outside the capacity to manage it. At its most sublime, research is imaginative and artistic. At its most gruelling, it makes the highest demands on patience, persistence and mental stamina in the loneliness of the long-distance scholar. In its totality, this is a magnetic, engrossing and enriching engagement. It is a stimulating process to discuss, and it has been a fascinating mental experience to explore and to reflect upon.

What I produced as a result of my research did eventually make me feel that I had a right to be there as a "proper" academic researcher. My publications had a significant political impact, and my books gained welcoming reviews from across the political spectrum; reviews of a quality which exceeded anything in my most extravagant dreams about earning respect. Researching was, and is, overall, a wonderful way of life. I never stopped loving it or, for that matter, at its best, academia. But for a variety of reasons, some of them personal, some concerning those recent changes which have so adversely affected the conditions of research work in the Universities, I took the opportunity of a very early "early retirement".

Since then, I have been fortunate in being able to continue my research in much less pressurised circumstances than those faced by many in the Universities today. I have also had more time to reflect on the research experience itself. As I have thought about that experience, about the character of research dialogue, and about the larger canvass of the research agenda within our profession, I found myself re-examining some unfinished conversations and reflections on the period at Manchester. It now seems to me that the culture surrounding research activity exhibits a significant tension between the spirit of scientific enquiry and the demands of academic life.

Integral to the former are "the love of truth," "a contempt for lying," and a "disgust at evasion,"[1] the acceptance that experiment involves trial and error, and an expectation of honesty in research presentation and educational discourse. Generally amongst academics these are impressively honoured and lived by. Nevertheless, a marked feature of academic life (and this was true even in the more relaxed conditions of earlier times) is the wearing of public masks about ourselves at work. There is an area of our mental activity, judged to be personal, which is not often examined in a public dialogue.

Of course, these masks protect our vulnerability in an academic market in which we are constantly, and recently ever more systematically, judged by our performance. The masks are raised but, in most cases only privately raised, in the company of friends and colleagues whom we trust. This is not unusual in social relations: the wearing of protective masks is a feature of the human condition. However, in relation to academic research it produces some rather odd outcomes.

The intellectual origins of what I am about to present lie in some observations about those peculiarities of the culture of academic research and its discourse. They are, I think, disturbing peculiarities really, given the spirit of scientific enquiry. The peculiarities, in my view, limited, and still limit, the character of the dialogue of academic research in ways that I think we could do something about.

DIAGNOSIS

Learning about creativity: the limited dialogue

The first and central peculiarity that I want to explore is the limitation to which this book is centrally addressed: the relative lack of systematic dialogue about the personal creative process in academic research. I am, in the first instance, drawing attention to my own experience and my own discipline but this also appears to be a wider phenomenon.

Today there is a huge and growing literature of research into creative behaviour, and there is a more "popular" self-improvement literature on techniques which encourage creativity, sometimes aligned to theories of creativity and a justifying framework for the practical applications. It is a literature which, as a whole, is marked by some strong variations in focus and some marked disagreements over substance, but it is packed with insights relevant to the research process. Yet, there appears to be only a rather segmented and spasmodic interest in this literature across university disciplines, and there does not appear to be much discussion of how far it might be relevant to the generation of improved university research.[2]

Nor is creativity given much emphasis in the varied and high-quality literature for research students on "How to do Research." Indeed, sometimes it is not mentioned at all.[3] Where it does occur, the references to creativity are generally not explored in detail,[4] and rarely with reference to examples drawn from experience.[5] The one general research text that I have found which attempts the (admittedly difficult) task of paralleling the scientific with the creative components of social research, gives the creative process illuminating but relatively brief attention.[6]

I am not suggesting that this limitation is a pointer to the reality of academic practice. Just the opposite. I am very sure that many of the processes explored in my study here are, for most academics, part of the routine of their scholarship - without fuss or even particular note. Yet, in the materials that we provide for research students there is, overall, little concentration of focus on the creative process, and little in the way of detailed and systematic exploration of the mental processes of the researcher involved in this creativity. As far as I can ascertain, this situation is not challenged by the training authorities.[7]

There is, perhaps, one area however - the use of new "experimental representations" in social science writing genres,[8] and the process of writing in research[9] - where there is a growing academic interest in the creative and knowledge-transforming processes involved. Perhaps this is a harbinger of significant change which might broaden out into a new concern with creativity in the whole process of research.

In my own field - the study of political life - I have become increasingly aware from my discussions with colleagues and research students that they have virtually no recent literature from which to gain insight into the creative process in relation to research.[10] This is in spite of new graduate training programmes and a range of studies of the research process which in other respects have undergone a huge improvement over my working lifetime. The weakness here is particularly odd when you consider that one of the pathbreakers in the modern analysis of the mental processes and developmental stages in creative thinking, Graham Wallas,[Wallas 1926] was a professor of political science at the London School of Economics.

Learning about creativity: the personal experience

Personally, I was fortunate in that, in my first year as a student at Leeds University, somebody had thought to send out to new students a general booklist which included Brewster Ghiselin's symposium on *The Creative Process* [Ghiselin 1954]. This was a revelation to me, and an aid to recognition about some of the spontaneous activities of the creative mind.

It brought to the fore a variety of experiences of creative "inspiration," but also emphasised the "labour of invention" involved in creativity and the need for self-knowledge in the management of the creative mind. I now think that it was also influential in long-term ways that I was not fully aware of at the time. This is also probably true of the work of C.Wright Mills on the processes of "intellectual craftsmanship" and on the opening up of a dialogue on that craftsmanship.[11]

I was fortunate again that, in the late 1970s and early 1980s, I worked as a political adviser to a series of plays and documentaries, an experience which heightened my appreciation of the intellectual and psychological features of the creative process which were common to both the academic and dramatic spheres. Subsequently, from time to time, I did try to keep up with the literature on creativity.

I recall that occasionally, with colleagues and particularly post-graduate students, and sometimes chatting to people at conferences, there were informal discussions on the personal creative process and on the relevance for that process of ideas drawn from the study of creativity. Periodically, I also took part in discussions of the different ways in which the psychological dimension of our activities affected our intellectual effort. These conversations were often accompanied by a rapt fascination and an animated interest which suggested that we were talking about something absolutely fundamental in our research work. Yet the concerns of these discussions were not systematically addressed on the formal agenda of the research seminars of the profession. What seemed to be accepted - at least in my professional area - was, roughly speaking, a differentiation of the sphere of the personally creative from the sphere of the academic methodological process, and also a differentiation of the psychological experience from the intellectual contribution in research production.

I have since had to ask myself the question why I did not attempt to challenge these demarcations with their exclusions of the creative and the psychological, and why I did not attempt to move this discussion on to the formal research agenda of seminars at Manchester, as I later attempted under different circumstances at Leeds Metropolitan University.

It might have had something to do with not having the confidence to raise issues which were related to a half-explored literature. Or maybe I was not quite ready to raise the mask and expose my own weaknesses. Or perhaps again, there was another consideration: such discussions had to take their place alongside a mountain of other concerns, and raising this issue was perhaps a peripheral priority in my own academic activities. The fact was that there was always the pressing problem of time.

Here is a crucial sub-text of this study, the Janus-face of time. Time is a liberator and a facilitator. It is the easer of pain and the opportunity for the muse to speak. But rationed time is also an enforcer and a constraint. University time has become a precious commodity - and a tyrant. More duties, more students, more bureaucracy and an explosion of specialised academic literature encourage an economism with time and discourage what might appear wasteful diversions, even reflection.

So, like other busy, indeed these days increasingly pressurised, academics I had other things that I needed to discuss and it must be said that, more than most, I was always prone to dash away from discussions to get on with the practical job of plunging into deep immersion in my own research in the time available.

The creative and the scientific

Only in the past four years have I fully renewed my interest and given concentrated attention to exploring the insight that scholarly research of the political world can be a creative art, and that the art involves a psychological as well as an intellectual performance. I have also come to question much more vigorously why the creative and the scientific should not be seen more as a duality of the intellectual adventure of political science rather than as alternatives.

Five minutes acquaintance with the literature on creativity serves to show that to be scientific is not to preclude being creative - indeed the literature tends to be dominated by the work and thoughts of eminent scientists. One of those scientists has argued that "every variety of creative episode in the world of letters or of everyday life can find its equivalent in science."[12]

However, in the academic world, being described as "scientific" evokes the authoritative, gives status, and becomes to some extent a protective shield. In contrast, being described as "creative", though it has about it the suggestion of imagination and talent, also evokes a sense of the expressive and the unrigorous. There is enough anxiety about the status of social science disciplines, and enough controversy within the disciplines about appropriate methods, for an association with "creativity" to evoke a degree of ambivalence about the label.[13]

This is probably accentuated in the study of politics because of the reputation of the subject matter itself. To take one glaring example, in the recently published and prestigious *Faber Book of Science*, the editor, John Carey, tells us that, "The real antithesis of science seems to be not theology but politics." In a sweeping passage he continues, "Politics is constructed out of preferences which it strives to elevate, by the mere multiplication of words, to the status of truth."[Carey 1995, p xxiii]

This is a breathtakingly impoverished understanding of the activity of politics. However, in the face of views like this it would not be surprising if practitioners of political research became over-sensitive to the possibility that in doing "creative" political research, the enquirers themselves could be associated with the untruthful and with a not-to-be-trusted "multiplication of words." I shall try to illustrate that all this is far from being the case.

Reconstruction and analysis

In attempting to reconstruct and analyse my own creative process, I am aware of the doubts raised about this form of enterprise by those who have seen creativity as an intangible and mysterious process which, by its very nature, is inappropriate for such an exercise. This perception of creativity goes back a long way. There has been an emphasis on the divine and the humanly inexplicable character of creativity since at least the time of Plato. More recently, as scholars of creativity have noted [Boden 1994], there appears to be a substantial source of heavyweight intellectual support for these doubts in the methodological literature, in the views of Karl Popper.

In his magisterial study of *The Logic of Scientific Discovery*, [Popper 1959, p32] Popper emphasised that such is the "irrational" element in creativity that "there is no such thing as a logical method of having new ideas or a logical reconstruction of this process". Many of Popper's contemporaries also "came to associate discovery with irrationality and lucky guesses romanticised as fundamentally mysterious."[14] As it happens, Popper was not consistent on this point. At one stage, he developed his own theory of the role of rationality in the creation of new ideas [Bergson and Wettersten 1984 p76].

Be that as it may, personally I would not deny the, at times, non-directed and unexpected ways that ideas can emerge. I will be noting that experience at various points later; it is part of the wonder of it all. There are times when the creative process is indeed elusive and does feel mysterious. As for a reconstruction of the process, this is undoubtedly complicated by the difficulties of accurate retrospective introspection and reliable mental autobiography[15] (on which I will have more to say below and in Chapters Eight and Ten). Nevertheless, I shall attempt to show that there is much that can usefully be said about creativity in research, albeit on varying levels of generality.[16]

The broad process of generating new ideas in, and through, research - the creative process - does have many clear and rational features. I shall also show that it is possible to usefully discuss the characteristics of creative activity, and to produce an illuminating description of the creative scholar in action. Further, as I shall illustrate, it is possible to offer a systematic analysis of the mental attitudes, processes and behaviour conducive to stimulating and sustaining creativity in research.

In pursuing these objectives, I shall also attempt to relate my personal introspections and reflections on the evidence and perspectives which can be found in the literature on the study of creativity. The task here is not primarily to outline or judge between those differing perspectives. Rather is it to explore my own experience of creative research, and relate that (occasionally tentatively, sometimes confidently) to the wider theory and evidence in a way that best highlights, explains and extends the significance of my own testimony.

In that personal experience, I show that constructing a rich world of characters who perform their heroic and distinctive deeds in the theatre of the mind, has many creative functions. In particular, it helps us to understand precisely what it is that we are doing when we are involved in the process of creative activity, and, to some extent, it can also help us to invent ourselves.

I shall also focus attention on creativity-generating practices,[17] which I will link to heuristics. Heuristics was an ancient branch of study concerned with the methods and rules of discovery and invention.[Polya 1957, p112] These days heuristics are thought of as rules, strategies, tactics, or practical methods which assist problem-solving and discovery.[18]

The emphasis, particularly in Chapter Seven, will be on the notion of heuristic thinking. This involves precepts, reasoning, challenges, tactics and techniques oriented towards stimulating the creative process and taking creative opportunities in research. My exploration of this heuristic thinking is not an abstract exercise. It is an attempt to explore various modes of my own mental activities in such a way as to make them accessible and exchangeable. Where memory and my records allow (which sometimes they do and sometimes they do not, and when they do, they only do so with varying degrees of confidence) I will try to give relevant examples. These are offered not as a claim to be amongst the pantheon of creative scholars (although I have a more than decent track record in that respect as will become clear) but as an accessible exemplification of a process which is worth opening to view and sharing in a context of application and experience. Indeed, perhaps it can *only* be usefully shared in that context.

REFLEXIVITY AND METACOGNITION

This reference to sharing our mental experience brings me to a further peculiarity of academic discourse as I have encountered it. It is rather odd, to say the least, that as academics and researchers studying politics, we live, so to speak, in our heads and yet, in my experience, we do not talk to each other a great deal about what is going on there. In our work and the life around our work, we might talk a lot about our subjects and about our methodology. We might try jointly to discuss and solve problems. We might on occasions talk about the social context of our thinking and the social influences upon it. Indeed we might talk about many things, but my experience is that we do not often talk to each other about our own mental processes in relation to our research. Our thinking about our thinking remains a fairly private affair.

This may be a limitation of my own experience or even of my own discipline. It may even be changing[19] in the light of the broad influence of a variety of well-established intellectual currents within the Universities which might be expected to encourage a different disposition and frame of reference. These include philosophical introspection, psycho-analysis, and more recently feminist social science research which focuses on personal and direct experiences,[20] and also recent cross disciplinary exploration of reflexivity.[21]

But I am not aware of a literature in political science which opens up these matters in relation to research, and my discussions with colleagues confirm to me that there is little change in the substance of inter-personal research dialogue. Certainly - to focus on my concerns in this study - I have not been aware of much dialogue amongst those of us involved in this research in the past thirty years about questions like this:-

To what extent are we monitoring, and reflecting about, our thought processes as we think and write about our research? What has been learned from this self-awareness and experience of self-observation? What do we understand about our personal style of thinking and any mental devices, tactics, or techniques that we employ in our research, and how these develop?

What do we know of the way, modes and circumstances in which our ideas emerge and develop, sometimes described as the involving "subconscious" or "unconscious" processes?[22]. What is going on in our minds when we arrive at, and attempt to solve, our research problems? What do we know of how our personal intellectual performance is related to what is commonly thought of as our "psychological" state of mind - our motivations, emotions, attitudes and beliefs? What images do we have of ourselves in action in the creative process?

I have grown to appreciate that questions like these, and the answers that suggest themselves, are crucial to an understanding of my own creative research process and an important preliminary to any attempt at regulation and improvement. Reflexivity in the form of metacognition - thinking about our thinking process - can be a vital process in creative research, and is an undervalued element in much of our research dialogue.

This metacognition is necessarily retrospective, and it is not unproblematic in terms of its accuracy and truthfulness. True, there is the uniquely privileged access of the participant observer with endless opportunities to watch and detect. But all the normal problems of partial observation, biased interpretation and weak memory are, if anything, accentuated when they are switched to an internal focus. And there are many "blind" periods where the creative researcher comes out of the depths, refocuses on the environment and is not quite sure where s/he has been.

Nevertheless, this switch in attention can be systematically and usefully undertaken. It can be a valuable aid to enhancing the creative quality of our work and could be the source of a fruitful dialogue amongst researchers, deepening our understanding of the research process. So another task I have set myself here is to introduce that dialogue by attempting to portray and analyse my own research-thinking processes across the broad span of mental activities over time, emphasising particularly (but not exclusively) those that I consider to have been the most creative and the most productive.

DEMYSTIFICATION

Attempting to portray my own research thinking brings me to a third element in my diagnosis of peculiarities, and one much more widely acknowledged. The fact is that, as anybody who has ever published their research will recognise, the normal conventions of research presentation are not much help to us in respect of portraying our mental activities in research production. It is well attested that such presentations normally obscure the true experience of the research process in both thought and action.

Characteristically, the academic convention is that the research product is offered without any hint of its true and perhaps problematic genesis. The representation is always wise and coherent and suggests that the author was always absolutely clear about its shape and objectives, and utterly steadfast in the linear process. Yet the process of production as I (and virtually everybody else of my acquaintance) have experienced it since my early days as a PhD student has been very different. It has been full of uncertainties and hesitations, mistaken assumptions and wrongly taken paths, zigzags in approach and revisions of strategy in tackling problems. Such experience seems to be the normality of research. Being puzzled, being unsure, being mistaken, and changing tack and viewpoint through trial and error, seem to be both integral and conducive to creative research.

The convention of perfection in presentation, and the reconstructed logic of events that accompanies it, may be judged to be economical with writing time and publishing space, but it is probably heavily reinforced by a strong sense of self-protection in exposing weakness in a potentially critical environment. It is very difficult to confess one's errors and to put on public display examples of one's failure.[23]

Certainly it can leave one feeling very vulnerable. In 1981, in a paper given to a conference of postgraduate research students [Minkin 1980], I attempted to open up this dimension of research by focusing on the messy and error-strewn reality of my own research experience of creative patternmaking, conjoined with some of the psychological problems which affected my research productivity. (Fifteen years later, I can see that in a sense it was my first very rough outline of this book.)

My emphasis on realism, and particularly my admission of a variety of personal failings and misadventures, met instant recognition and a very positive response from the audience. Yet, afterwards (in part because at that time I was only dimly aware of what had been, and what was being, published on these themes in other fields) I remember feeling a sense of weakness and illegitimacy, as if I had been confessing to my singular inadequacy as well as somehow breaking the rules. Perhaps it threatened my sense of belonging.

However, since that time I have come to appreciate that some of my working methods and experiences were really not as maverick as they seemed to be. I have also come to consider that where they were unusual my, at times, wayward modes of thinking were integral to the creative quality of my process of working. As for the way our presentations obscure important elements of the research process, I later found that this had long been lamented in many other disciplines. The matter had been raised before and continues to be raised as an important academic and public issue. In the 1960s, in a BBC talk, the Noble Prizewinning scientist, Peter Medawar, had drawn attention to the misleading (fraudulent, he said) nature of scientific papers [Medawar 1963]. Recently on the BBC, Professor Peter Stewart focused on the same limitation in mathematical presentations, a feature likened by some, he said, to the fox erasing his tracks in the sand with its tail. (The counter metaphor was that you do not leave scaffolding up when the building is finished).[24]

Now, re-reading Ghiselin and others, I can see that the same point had often been made about a wide range of creative activity, not simply academic research. The finished product is not a portrait of the artist involved in the difficult process of invention, and it gives an impression of unlaboured force which is not to be trusted.[25] This is in some respects inevitable, but it is not much assistance to those who would seek to learn from the experience. As Robert Louis Stevenson notes, it is "on the surface" that we perceive the "beauty, fitness and significance" of "all our arts and occupations". "To pry below" is to be .."shocked by the coarseness of the strings and pulleys". [Stevenson 1920 p3] Yet it is these strings and pulleys which have to be understood in our effort to gain insight from each other.

In general, in the past twenty years, there has developed a much broader recognition of this feature of research publication. Since the mid-sixties in the United States and the mid-seventies in the United Kingdom, particularly amongst anthropologists and sociologists, the reality of the research process has been examined in a variety of autobiographical and reflective texts.[26] Some of these occasionally cover political areas or areas with political implications,[27] but I have yet to find a text which reflects in detail on the experience of doing research on any of Britain's national political institutions. Generally, in the field of British political science, although there has been a call by Peter Burnham for more "glasnost" in teaching political research [Burnham 1991], we have not moved far in the production of an analytical literature on this crucial dimension of the research process. By and large, the masks stay firmly in place. Consequently, our dialogue about our research is to that extent restricted in its mutual educational benefit.

I find this frustrating. For years I have chafed at the restraints of conventions in research presentation.[28] My books and papers have been produced, it seems, by a *Doppelgänger* who apparently operates with flawless logic, complete certainty as to his objectives, and a confident, straight-line, passionless rationality - as do we all in the academic community. As a result, we can learn almost nothing from each other about the processes involved. Well, here is an attempt to go beyond those conventions with as much finesse and honesty as I can muster.

To get to the heart of the real process of research, we have to go behind the tidied-up, smoothed-down, legitimising façade. So in what follows - and this is another task - I am going to try to offer examples of the generation of my own research and its creative processes with a determination to portray it as near as possible to how it really was in practice. There were, as I shall show, effective processes which led to successes and achievements. But there were also many "failures" of different kinds; uncertainties and confusions, misconceptions and errors of judgement, pratfalls as well as pitfalls.

In pursuit of this openness I have the qualification of being an expert in unremitting self-criticism and something of a connoisseur of my own mistakes. It is an expertise which is not to be underestimated in the history of intellectual progress.[29]

SPECIALISM AND STYLE

The varieties of research

Of course, the claim to be making an analysis of my real working practice is not a claim to be telling others that my way - at times a singular way - is the only way to do "proper" research. I am a pluralist and I agree with those who argue that over and above certain basic practices of rigorous scholarship, there is no one clear and certain way to do quality social science research.[30] So, "let a hundred flowers bloom".

Research takes many forms and involves a variety of objectives, methods and priorities. The quality of each has to be assessed in relation to its own purposes, as well as to the researcher's skill in managing the constraints and opportunities. I hope to illustrate that, to the extent that creativity is involved in this skill of the researcher, it can add value to the work. I also think that whatever the form, we can offer a lot more from descriptions of our activities than is normally on show. In particular, we have much to learn from sharing the best practice of our process of working and, to the degree that it is creative, indicating the way that we operate - "the strings and pulleys".

Specialism

In attempting to share that operation I do have many years of work to draw from - three decades of hands-on experience of empirical research. However, whilst that specialism and experience in research means there is a strength in depth from which to draw the lessons and examples, it also means that, like most professional research scholars, there is a limited expertise in breadth. I am a specialist in two sub-fields of two disciplines of the social sciences (although where relevant I do venture into other sub-fields and disciplines).

If the reader will bear with me a little, that specialism needs spelling out briefly here, especially as overall it probably involves a distinctive combination of method, personal style, area of of work and perspective on research. The most obvious characteristic of my research is that I have become a classic lone scholar. This has been a developing style rather than an immediately committed practice, but it has now become an entrenched feature.

My method of work is mainly qualitative rather than quantitative. And, although I keep an informed eye on international comparative developments, and the theories covering them, I now work generally within one national experience and culture. The focus is often idiographic (concerned with one phenomenon, or one single chain of events) but the main thrust of my work is concerned with explaining variabilities and regularities in relationships through time. Within this national setting, I seek to be nomothetic, accounting for all cases over a particular period.

Whilst drawing from any available relevant theory and concept in approaching an understanding of the field, I have developed a self-reliant process of theorising and concept formation. This is focused upon the problem in hand, grounded in nuanced empirical investigation and close observation of minutiae.[31]

My investigations involve long-term fieldwork and a long-term perspective in pursuit of the solutions to problems, often major problems in the field of politics. I research by observation combined with formal and informal interviewing, and by an examination of a wide range of primary source material. Some of the fieldwork is conducted in highly sensitive political areas, covering processes and issues of public interest often surrounded by considerable controversy. In these areas, where there are risks and dangers as well as opportunities, the gaining of acceptance, respect and trust is crucial to the availability of access and the depth of information that I can secure. These features have reinforced the tendency to act as a lone scholar.

Style

I did not come as a stranger to this political field of enquiry. In fact, wearing one hat, I have had an adult lifetime of being a participant within it. On occasions I draw from this subjectivity to generate the puzzles and problems that I pursue, and at times (wearing another hat) the prescriptions that I offer. I also draw insight and a strength of understanding from a familiarity with the particular culture. But I am all too aware of the dangers of this partisanship, and of the way that bias creeps in and understandings become embedded in an unquestioned frame of reference.[32] Thus I make a conscious effort to gain an appropriate mood of critical self-awareness and detachment in the role of observer.

In a pattern which is not too unusual amongst field workers, I have played the role of participant-observer with varying degrees and modes of participation although never making any secret of my academic identity and its purposes. Over the years, I have tended to move from being an observer who also participates in other areas of the field to being, on occasions, a participant in this area who observes as he participates. Latterly I have even occasionally participated in the formal as well as the informal policymaking process.

At the same time there has also been a long-term shift in my own political perspective from the Left to the Centre Left. Some of this was influenced by the understandings gained from working in the field, some of it by much wider considerations. The point here is that this shift had its effect on my interpretation of various political problems and my definition of them. Indeed it meant that the person beginning a long term project was not quite the same person who finished it.

These changes of role, position and perspective took me by surprise rather than being engineered or anticipated. But then, many things took me by surprise. These days, in a very welcome development, postgraduate students receive extensive and high quality training in research. My own training for this field of expertise, though solid in terms of the depth of knowledge of the area and relevant theoretical work, was very weak in terms of appropriate methods of investigation - particularly of fieldwork. I lacked (and still to some extent lack) an adequate understanding of the range of available methods and of the experience of others in similar work.

This understanding would obviously have been very valuable. I keep finding out that others had noticed years ago what I thought that I alone had discovered. On the other hand, perhaps as a result of the limited instruction, and of limited knowledge of a useful literature, the style of my research had to be experimental in the broadest sense. At a formative stage in the development of my expertise, I was thrown back upon the resources of my own mind. This accentuated the tendency to become, as good fieldworkers often have done, a methodological pragmatist,[33] flexibly adapting my approach to what worked best in terms of the exigencies and objectives of the fieldwork, but also to what worked best in terms of my own mental processes and the efforts to improve them.

My emphasis here on personal experience, and the idiosyncrasies of personal style, has another significance. It reflects my belief that, in general, an element of individuality and flexibility, together with a light touch of irreverence about the application of commonly accepted methodological procedures (particularly procedures perceived as being technocratically pursued to an end point) works well in partnership with a creative disposition.

This is not to undervalue the importance of rigour in research method. Nor, as will be made clear, is it a rejection of reason, logic and systematic procedures. But it is to recognise, as others have done, that there can be inhibitive consequences of a professional socialisation into what are thought to be normal and orthodox modes of work.[34] Michael Oakeshott has even argued that "Advance in scientific discovery was never achieved by merely following the rules." [Oakeshott 1962 p8]. I would not feel knowledgeable enough to agree or disagree with that (and much depends on what is meant by "merely following the rules") but I think that there is a lot to Ghiselin's prognosis that eccentricity and "tykeishness" are far more likely to show creativity than the faithful formalist [Ghiselin 1954 p9].

The emphasis on the personal in my research experience, in particular the attempt to give an honest sense of the motivations, feelings and distinctive mental quirks which accompany my work practice, is also a recognition of the inevitability, and the value of, individuality in the real practice of research. Although there are common features to mental, creative, and methodologically trained research activity - features which allow us to talk fruitfully to each other - there are also some very personal and even idiosyncratic singularities. No two personalities are alike, no two minds are alike, and mental self-government comes in multiple forms. Even the same scientific training, the same field experience and the same training does not necessarily leave the same imprint on different minds. As Watson reminds us about the scientists working in the field of DNA, "styles of scientific research vary almost as much as human personalities".[Watson 1968 p14]. That variation is itself an important contribution to the multiplicity of approaches which constitute the richness of the creative research process.

THE ART OF THE RESEARCHER

There is a final and very important point to be made about the experience of research. Over time I have come to appreciate that the development of personal expertise and style in research is also a development of a professional art.[35]

The full development of this art can involve a long apprenticeship. The length of these phases depends on the scale and complexity of the field of enquiry. In my case there was a lengthy period - about seven years - of regarding myself as a novice at research and in the production of publications. (I shall use this language of "the novice" in later descriptions of my work experience.) This was followed by a long period of mature and more confident scholarship which slowly involved adopting the role of an ad-hoc "expert" adviser to the organisations I was researching, as well as continuing with research in the field.

As a novice researcher researching sensitive political areas, and at times probing sensitive political questions, I faced situations and negotiations which I had not anticipated, met problems and dilemmas that I was not fully equipped to tackle, and was involved in a mental process of intellectual construction and problem-solving which I only partly understood. Out of a process of experiment and trial and error, there emerged an extension of competence which I now recognise as the art of a mature researcher. The art draws from, but also moves well past, formal methodological education,[36] or even relevant reading and advice from others. It involves, to use Oakeshott's term, "practical knowledge" [Oakeshott 1962 pp 7-8] learned and refined, essentially, "on the job". This includes a range of techniques, knacks and routines - what Captain Ahab called, "the wondrous devices and dexterities, the sleights of hand and countless subtleties" of the veteran. [Melville 1985 edn][37]

As a process, the professional art can be more or less creative within the constraints of scholarship and of particular methodologies. Thus it not only involves command over method and craft techniques, it can also involve the imaginative transcendence and emancipation from established patterns often associated with the work of the artist. In this sense, ways of research thinking and modes of research activity can constitute a creative art.

Each researcher's art will be distinctively his or her own. However, it is not an incommunicable skill. We can describe it(well or badly). We can read about it. We can reconstruct it in our imagination. And sometimes, if we are fortunate, we can, to some extent, watch the practitioner in action. In general, the more that we understand about each other's art the more we are able to learn, and the more we are in a position to adapt, improve and refine our own practices.

What follows in this study is an attempt to assist that understanding - to lower the mask and to open up my own research art to public scrutiny and discussion as I explore the creative process.

CHAPTER END NOTES

[1] Israel Scheffler 'In Praise of the Cognitive Emotions' quoted in [Perkins 1981, p 118].

[2] For example, a monograph published by the Society for Research into Higher Education [Freeman, Butcher and Christie 1968, 1971] is immensely helpful in understanding creativity but says little about its relevance to higher education. An excellent work on educational psychology by Noel Entwistle [Entwistle 1988] has a very relevant analysis of creativity and imaginative thinking on pp 152-160 but this is not related to the production of academic research.

[3] For example, three excellent Open University Press publications, [Bell 1987], [Blaxter, Hughes and Tight 1996] and [Phillips and Pugh 1987] make no reference to creativity in their indexes. A forthcoming Open University publication by Pat Cryer, *The Research Students Guide to Success* is advertised as including a section on "Developing Skills for Creative Thinking".

[4] For example in a very useful recent study [Booth, Colomb and Williams 1995] there are some four passing mentions of creativity, but I could find no discussion of the creative process.

[5] [Howard and Sharp 1985] is unusual in that it has an interesting and very suggestive section which draws from creativity and problem-solving theory in generating topics for research, (pp 28-33) but I could find no further references in their book to the use of this literature in generating creativity in the research process.

[6] [Baker 1994] particularly pp 36, 172, 208, 237 and 259. A recent study by the anthropologist Harry F. Wolcott [Wolcott 1995] though it is not principally about creativity, is comfortably in tune with my own approach in its emphasis on the "mindwork" which underscores the creative expansive side of fieldwork, p. 61.

[7] [E.S.R.C. 1995] and similar documents make no reference to stimulating creativity.

[8] For the range of "experimental representations" see the analysis by Laurel Richardson 'Writing: A method of inquiry' in [Denzin and Lincoln 1994 p 521]. Richardson also makes a range of suggestions for using writing as a means of serving the process of discovery. She links this discussion with some of the literature on creative writing.

[9] See on this [Becker with Richards 1986] which discusses the use of free expression in research writing p 54. Also Flowers' analysis [Flowers 1989] which offers examples of creativity generation pp 101-108. [Bereiter and Scardamalia 1987] distinguish knowledge-transforming (as opposed to knowledge-telling) writing strategy. A developing British academic

interest in different writing strategies in relation to research, is reflected in Torrance and Thomas 'The development of writing skills in doctoral research students' in [Burgess 1994] pp 105-123.

[10] [Shively 1980] refers to Arthur Koestler's *The Act of Creation* but does not explore its relevance. A further study, [Shively 1984] which is the best book I have read on the real process and gives many insights into creative activity in political research, does not discuss creativity *per se* nor refer to the literature. Amongst British political scientists, even the informative and innovative article by Peter Burnham [Burnham 1992] pp 3-8 makes no reference to creativity and its literature.

[11] C. Wright Mills Appendix: "On Intellectual Craftsmanship" in [Mills 1959]. Judging by my recent re-reading of this wonderful little essay it may well have left an important residue of ideas and influences, but unlike the Ghiselin book I did not remember much about it subsequently.

[12] [Medawar 1990 p 86]. For a discussion of the complementarity of art and science, see [Wolcott 1995] pp. 11-15.

[13] [Atkinson 1990 p10] makes a similar point in relation to sociologists' reluctance to acknowledge any affinities with the aesthetic.

[14] Gerd Gigerenzer 'Where do New Ideas Come From?' in [Boden 1994 pp 53-54]

[15] See on this the discussion in [Perkins 1981 pp 9-38] and [Boden 1990 pp 240-244].

[16] In his introduction to the pathbreaking study [Hammond 1964] Phillip E. Hammond notes that "though at some reaches the origins of ideas, the theoretical breakthroughs during the course of research, are to be described only as poetic, as mysterious or awesome, at some other level they can be understood, or at least described, as very human activities" p 3.

[17] I have found little reference in the literature on creativity and creativity-generating techniques to its specific application in research. One useful exception is [Bargar and Duncan 1990]. The most prolific writer on

creativity generation, Edward de Bono, rarely mentions the field of research. Nevertheless I have found his approach to creativity and problem-solving suggestive in a variety of ways.

[18] Heuristics are used in a variety of disciplines and activities but the most systematic use has been in mathematical problem solving. See [Polya 1957], [Newell and Simon 1972] and [Schonfield 1979 pp 173-87].

[19] I am told by colleagues that that this is true of anything touched by feminist influence, particularly within sociology. However I also note the comments by Alan Prout about the relative weakness of sociologists in critical self-reflection 'Splitting Image: Pure and Applied Research in the Culture of Sociology' in [Burgess 1990, p185]. Also, the introductory comment in [Atkinson 1990 p vi] that, "Sociologists are not usually introspective or self-conscious about what they read and write".

[20] See for example [Roberts 1981], [Stanley and Wise 1983 and 1993], [Harding 1987], [Stanley, 1990]. The work that I have seen which is closest to my own approach is Fiona Williams 'Thinking: Exploring the "I" in Ideas' pp 11-24 in [Shakespeare, Atkinson and French et al 1993]. In the introduction to their study which focuses on "self-disclosure and self-reflection", the editors comment that their work covers "aspects of research which usually remain concealed and undiscovered" p 1.

[21] Reflexivity can be understood as "a bending back on itself". It is a form of enquiry, mainly within sociology, in which an account or theory has the capacity to refer back to itself, or the mind has the capacity to turn back upon itself to examine its own mental process. Scholars focusing on reflexivity emphasise that the beliefs and behaviour of the researcher are inextricably bound into the construction of what is reported. Also, there is in some of the recent work done by sociologists on research and reflexivity "an acute awareness that doing research must be expanded to include those artist-like processes that are already there but filtered out of ordinary research writing" [Steir 1991 p 4]. On reflexivity see also [Woolgar 1988] and the feminist literature referred to in the previous note.

[22] For a critique of 'The Mystique of Unconscious Creation' see Forrest Williams in [Kagan 1967 pp 142-152]. Williams emphasises that examples reported of unconscious thought can be explained by "powers of intelligence in the full light of consciousness". Personally I have long believed that the creative work that I am describing in this study was assisted in important ways by "subconscious" or "unconscious" (there is no fully satisfactory language here) mental activity and, in general, that still seems to be a reasonable interpretation of my experience.

[23] Bob Fryer makes the point that candour over slips, errors and missed opportunities is rare in the dialogue of research and then only visible when it can be demonstrated that the failings led to new insights and discoveries. Bob Fryer 'Trade Unions and Social Research: the casualties and victims of social research' in [Forrester and Thorne 1993 p14]

[24] I am indebted to Professor Stewart for a very interesting telephone discussion following his comments on the BBC programme *Start the Week* on September 18th 1995. He shared my concern at the limited educational value for postgraduates of the conventions surrounding the publication of academic papers.

[25] [Ghiselin 1954 p 18]. An interesting exception here is improvisational jazz. Ted Gioia notes, "I feel confident that I am not alone in being willing to exchange - were such an exchange possible - half a dozen of his written works for just one recording of Beethoven improvising at the keyboard". [Gioia 1988 p54].

[26] The breakthrough in the United States came with the publication of [Hammond 1964]. In Britain it came with the study by Jennifer Platt [Platt 1976] (based on "how they did it" interviews) and Colin Bell and Howard Newby [Bell and Newby 1977] (based upon post-hoc accounts).

[27] These include S. Encel 'In Search of Power' and Hugh Stretton 'Capital Mistakes' in [Bell and Encel 1978]. Nigel Fielding 'Observational Research on the National Front' in [Bulmer 1982]. Huw Beynon 'Regulating research: politics and decision making in industrial organisations' in [Brymer 1987]. There is a volume of reflective elite studies which includes a range of

experiences of researching political elites across the world. [Moyser and Wagstaffe 1987]. A similar study [Hertz and Imber 1995] has chapters on local power and local politics.

[28] In the introduction to [Minkin 1991, 1992], I did attempt to alert the reader about the real process of production. See the quotation which appears at the front of this book.

[29] See on this Daniel C. Dennett 'How to Make Mistakes' in [Brockman and Matson 1995, pp 137-144].

[30] The point is emphasised in the case studies of political research put together by Phillips Shively and his assessment that, "There is no cut-and-dried way to do good work", [Shively 1984 p 1].

[31] I am not sure that my methods can easily be categorised but they share something with the approach of [Glaser and Strauss 1967] although my theorising is mainly within a restricted national range. (This may, of course, have wider implications and applications - as, for example, in the politics of agenda management in relation to policymaking and the role of unwritten rules in organisational cohesion). In style it also has much in common with what W. Baldamus describes as "a trial and error process by which conceptual frameworks become progressively more articulate" - 'The Role of Discoveries' in [Burgess 1982 p 220].

[32] On this see Alvin Gouldner 'The Sociologist as Partisan: Sociology and the Welfare State' in [Gouldner 1973, Chapter Two pp 27-68].

[33] Robert G. Burgess [Burgess 1984, p 5] taking the same view as L. Schatzman and A.L. Strauss [Schatzman and Strauss 1973 p 7].

[34] A similar point is made by John L. Sullivan 'On Students and Serendipity in Social Research', in [Shively 1984 p 45].

[35] I played for a long time with the words "craft" and "art" which are in some respects interchangeable here. I have adopted "art" because it was the original term used to describe any kind of skill [Williams 1976 p 32] but also because it can include an association with imaginative transcendence

and emancipation from established patterns - which are themes of this study of the creative process. As I completed this study, I came across a very sophisticated discussion of some of the issues involved in the distinction between "craft" and "art" in [Wolcott, 1995 pp. 16-22].

[36] On this see the comment of Irving Louis Horowitz in his editorial introduction to a collection of reflective pieces by distinguished sociologists, [Horowitz 1969 p 11], "What is so genuinely interesting is the wide consensus that there is in fact a subjective side to methodology, that the simple egalitarianism of the training process cannot in and of itself either describe or define the limits of intellectual endevour and creation".

[37] In the course of research for this study, I came across the work of Donald A. Schon on the reflective practitioner - particularly [Schon 1987]. His "practitioners" aim to change the situation they face rather than, as researchers, to understand it better (albeit perhaps as preliminary to changing it). But there is a lot to be learned from him and on the process of learning-in-action.

CHAPTER TWO

RESEARCH CREATIVITY: CHARACTERISTICS

THE ELUSIVE DEFINITION

For me to open up this creative process and to navigate the reader carefully into the exploration, requires a clarification of some fundamentals, including my understanding of the meaning and nature of creativity. At the outset, part of the problem of engaging in this exercise is that in the literature on creativity at least three different approaches can be found, emphasising either the person, the process, or the product.

Where it emphasises person(s), the literature on creativity, and the general folklore, tend to focus on the "great" men and women, the especially talented who have produced path-breaking inventions, discoveries and paradigm shifts widely acknowledged to be fundamental examples of creativity. By contrast, social usage often defines a whole area of human activity as "the creative arts" even if the work is imitative or stereotyped [Williams 1976]. And A.H.Maslow makes a persuasive case in saying that we could fruitfully approach creativeness as an aspect of any behaviour [Maslow 1976 p74] and occasionally social usage does extend its meaning to inventiveness in any field - even to "creative accountancy".

Thus, the word creativity has been given a variety of meanings. It has, in that sense, an "elusive definition"[1]. For my purposes here I am defining creativity as a process; the process of bringing something original and appropriate into being. This definition helps us by locating the general area of my investigation, although it still requires some further elaboration as a necessary preliminary to the examination of my personal experience of research.

THE CREATIVE PLAYER

To fill out this definition, and to explore what is involved in relation to the research process as I have experienced and observed it in my field, I want to focus on one illuminating social usage. It is the notion in various sports, including football, hockey and rugby of the "creative player" of the game. This description involves an assessment of a quality of the player's process and the fluent artistry that goes with it. The creative player of these sports has skills related to the particular type of activity. This is basic to creative achievement [Ochse 1991 p 337] . But the creative player has some other capabilities and qualities which add a creative dimension to the play. These include imaginative vision and the ability to generate alternatives which enlarge the possibilities of a situation. This artistry does not necessarily result in, say, goals or tries but is viewed as reasonably likely to generate them.

Drawing from this analogy, I want to pick out some of the principal features of the behaviour of the creative researcher. The extent of these features become the test that I set for the quality of my own research process. From this perspective, the creative researcher, in addition to utilising methodological procedures and the traditional skills of scholarship appropriate to the domain, also:-

- employs imaginative vision tempered by a realism grounded in evidence,

- perceives or generates alternatives which enlarge the possibilities of a situation,

- produces interpretations, explanations and configurations of ideas, which take novel forms for that context,

- brings about original and appropriate outcomes, or the opportunities for their emergence,

- seeks a presentation which is fluent and aesthetically appropriate.

In the pursuit of this originality, the responsibility of academic research is to seek transcendence of the existing social understanding of the field of enquiry. This has to be distinguished from personal originality, that which we produce which is original for us.[2] But as researchers and educators we always need to keep a sense of, and give full recognition to, personal development and the enhancement of individual potential. There is a long-term social benefit in nurturing this individual creativity and personal originality.

RELEVANT ATTRIBUTES

In this creative behaviour the researcher requires a range of creativity-relevant attributes. Scholars of creativity have recognised a wide range of such attributes. Here, commensurate with the features of the creative player, I want to emphasise three general combinations of attributes of the creative researcher. These combinations are an amalgam of cognitive abilities, traits of personality and aesthetic sensitivities.

They are :-

- observational vigilance accompanied by a deep curiosity in relation to peculiarities, puzzles and problems,
- open-mindedness, mobility of ideas, and flexibility of perspective in relation to the project and its problems (although this flexibility may be from within a set of very broad theoretical positions),
- sensitivity to connections and to underlying as well as surface patterning within and across fields of enquiry.

THE FORMS OF CREATIVITY

The "great" women and men who have generated what would be widely agreed to be specially creative outcomes, provide us with an important experience to understand, to investigate, to gain insight into, and to set our standards by. Certainly, what I have to say in this study has drawn heavily from studies of that experience. But, in the encouragement of a creatively vigorous research culture, we need to be able to view research creativity in terms which embrace degrees of creativity.

This creativity, which can be expressed at various stages of the research process, as well as in the original and appropriate outcomes that result, may take a range of forms appropriate to the problem and the methods for its solution. It can even be creative to point up a particular illuminating problem, to define a significant problem in a new way, or to generate a perspective which is very suggestive of fruitful new developments.

I emphasise also that to be unsuccessful in a particular application - to "fail" - does not necessarily undermine the general creative status of a process. Creativity is a process of reframing perspectives and establishing new opportunities. If in that process we make a full "score", all the better. But if we do not, something valuable may still have been generated and passed on, either to the researcher who has "failed" or to others. From this viewpoint, it makes perfect sense in judging any particular process, and the outcomes that constitute its present products, to talk of "a creative failure". Indeed for reasons to do with the constructively fallible nature of creative enterprise, and the encouragement of a creatively fertile research culture, it is essential that we are able so to do. All experience suggests that it is only by being prepared to risk the failure can we reach out in terms of enriching the creative process and enhancing the possibility of creative attainment.

This broader perspective on what constitutes "success" and "failure" is a vital part of a healthy research discourse. It is part of the contribution that we all make to sharing our experience of the creative process, to enhancing the quality of creative performance and, crucially, to understanding what it is that collectively we might do to learn from each other.

ENHANCING CREATIVITY

It must be said immediately that the belief that creative practice can be enhanced by some shared or learned process is not an uncontested view amongst scholars of creativity.[3] I am, in general, on the optimistic wing in some of the arguments which divide these scholars. This reflects my own life experience which indicates not only the possibility of a self-improvement which is linked to learning from the work of others, but also, with Maslow[4] and Roe[5] , that the creative process is not unique to a few, but a form of activity that all human beings are capable of to some degree.

Almost certainly, creativity involves the more efficient use of our ordinary abilities "not something profoundly different." [Boden 1990 p 259] It involves no special process, just special purposes for familiar mental operations.[6] It is best construed not as a single power which you either have or you do not have, but as multidimensional, involving a great many different mental functions and requiring a combination of skills and personality factors [7].

There is evidence from a variety of studies which suggests that some creative abilities can (to a degree at least) be facilitated and enhanced much like any other human activity[8]. In this process of enhancement, we can seek to make more productive use of our imagination. Alex Osborn, a pioneer in the field of applied imagination, has pointed out the existence of certain obvious universalities in this respect [Osborn 1993 p15 and pp2 27-36]. We dream, we fantasise or identify with characters in books and films, and most interesting of all, we laugh[9]. By no means all of this imagination is creatively usable or controllable, but it is indicative of an ability - what Maslow calls primary creativeness [Maslow 1976 p80] -which, in principle, could be engaged and brought into the productive play of research more often than it is. "Inspiration", Anthony Storr suggests, is an extreme example of a process which constantly goes on in the minds of all of us [Storr 1989 p 260].

None of this is to suggest that anybody can be a Beethoven or an Einstein, still less (as Nickerson, Perkins and Smith put it in their analysis of *The Teaching of Thinking*) can we envisage an assembly line of such people produced by "teaching" creativity [Nickerson, Perkins and Smith 1985 p 100]. Nevertheless, "moderate but useful improvements in creative work" appears an attainable goal.[10] Certainly, there is no reason why a community of research scholars and students of high intelligence[11] who are, by training, "methodology-sensitive," should not focus more attention on the enhancement of creative performance.

APPROACHES TO CREATIVITY ENHANCEMENT

It may be that there is no one direct approach to enhancing creativity in research which would work for everybody. Different entry points and a variety of methods exist, any combination of which may suit or benefit one person but not another. Underpinning what follows in this study are four assumptions about the best general approach to creativity enhancement for those involved in the complex processes of research.

Awareness of creativity

Enhancement is more likely to be encouraged if we value, understand and talk more about the creative process. The encouragement to "be creative" does encourage the occurrence of creative acts.[12]. It is important to raise the level of awareness of the creative process, both in its most universal characteristics and in its particular embodiment in the work of individual researchers. We have a lot to learn about what is known of the creative process and creative people, and in this we have also much to learn from each other.

Self-awareness

In this process we have, as always, more to learn about ourselves. In principle, any technique which will increase self-knowledge in depth, should increase creativity [Maslow 1976 p 89]. Awareness of inner life has been found to be a characteristic of creative people[13]. The research on problem-solving indicates that an expert in any field is more likely to monitor progress than a novice. "He (*sic*) works on solving the problems and watches himself critically as he does so" [Nickerson, Perkins and Smith, 1985 p69]. An extensive analysis of successful inventors shows them to be highly aware of their own process.[14]

Metacognitive self-monitoring can help in the development of a general process of self-regulation which enhances the potentiality of creative thinking[15]. It has, of course, to be recognised that improvements linking metacognition and creativity, like improvements in any other human ability, require motivation and application.

The most basic means of raising metacognitive insight is through a process of self-interrogation about our mental processes. Questions become pathways into the mind - its intellectual and psychological performance. What did I do then? How did I do that? Why did I do that? Where and when did I do it? Could I do that again? Can I avoid doing that again? What are the general patterns of my thinking when it is going well? What is happening when it is going badly?

Self-help and Self-image

This questioning takes us into the realms of motivation, values, attitudes, emotions, beliefs and expectations. All of these can affect our creative performance. The enhancement of creativity may well be triggered and reinforced by a process of psychological self-management, in which we attempt to make ourselves more effective.

This self-help process may usefully be attuned to what is known about the personal qualities of creative people (See Chapter Four). It can be especially beneficial if it is conducive to raising the individual's self-esteem and to creating a favourable self-image for the researcher as a creative performer[16].

Applied creativity

The notion of applied creativity is not a barbarism.[17] It is simply a recognition that we do not have to wait passively for "inspiration". For a start, there is much to be gained in utilising our metacognitive explorations to differentiate, and then to develop further, the forms of creative thinking that we already practise with some success. Developing our best practice, and managing our weaknesses, can work in relation to mental performance as well as in other human activities. We can build upon our growing practitioner's competence to enhance our creativity as we learn to develop what we have already experienced.

We can also gain a heightened understanding from the literature on creativity generation. As it happens, though a wide range of problem solving techniques and creativity-generating procedures are now on offer in the literature, few of these are presented with a direct application to research. But some of them produce valuable insights, and suggest systematic approaches which can be productively adapted and integrated into the stimulation and steering of the creative process. The word "integration" here is carefully chosen. We can gain creatively from learning useful new heuristic strategies,[18] but again, my experience suggests that what is learned is most useful when it involves processes that are mentally comfortable and connects with processes that are already some part of one's way of thinking[19].

EXPLORING, PLAYING, AND USING TIME

These activities become fused into other features of my mental performance which are essential to the development of the creative research process. Indeed, if I ask myself what was the professional "secret" at the heart of my own research, I would focus on two particular activities - the process of "exploring" and the process of "playing". To be effective, both involve sustained effort, and both have implications for the use of time.

Exploring

In exploring the field of my expertise, in preparing the groundwork for a project, and in pursuing the objectives, I seek the greatest possible command of its detailed elements, nuances and texture.

My creativity is based to a considerable extent on this exploration of my field of enquiry. To put it metaphorically and a bit crudely, I journey to investigate the field for myself, I try to dig in areas where no-one has been before, and, when journeying in the well-travelled areas, I try to dig much deeper than others. As a novice "explorer" (who is also an "archaeologist") I used to think of this as digging to get information or to find evidence. As I developed a deeper understanding of the creative process, so I came to see it as digging to find peculiarities, digging to discover problems, and digging to feed a mind that wants to play with possible patterns.

In terms of productive creativity, the play can only be as good as the preparation. Good preparation takes time - time to develop the artistry of investigation and interpretation, time in the field to develop a rich general understanding of the terrain, and time on the specific project to uncover the data that will form the substance of the enquiry.

Research creativity can be enhanced through deep immersion in, and mastery of, a field (or fields) of enquiry. It is widely accepted that creativity is linked to the development of domain-specific knowledge and competence.[20] Given the demands of specialisation in modern circumstances of knowledge acquisition, creative individuals and creative achievement are, nearly always, tied to a limited field of expertise[21], although it may help if this covers more than one specialist area.

On its own, this deepening knowledge of a field of enquiry guarantees nothing in terms of creative engagement. Indeed, if the researcher is not very careful, it is possible for in-depth exploration to follow mental grooves, or established ways of seeing problems. To that extent, being relatively new to an area may be liberating in terms of seeing something afresh. Fundamentally what is required is the preservation of an irreverent questioning disposition towards the knowledge (and the self). What is also required is a particular quality of analytical grasp where the knowledge can easily be brought into focus for the purposes of mental play.[22] It requires not only the knowledge but also expertise covering when and how to apply that knowledge in specific contexts [Nickerson, Perkins and Smith 1985 p 102].

However, in so far as deep immersion and an enlargement of knowledge gives us a more intricate grasp of the elements, nuances and texture of the domain, (and perhaps a rising confidence in handling it) we achieve also an enhanced creative potentiality. We can discern more clearly the variations and consistencies, the patterns, peculiarities, and puzzles. We are therefore in a richer position to play mentally with the elements of the project and to generate something new.

Playing

In this mental activity "playing" and "playfulness" are crucial concepts[23]. Imaginative mental play - serious play (and as Sigmund Freud pointed out that is not a contradiction[24]) - is a vital element in creative research thinking.

In creative play, the mind is engaged in toying and juggling with information, concepts, relationships and patterns. The mind's playful abilities - to tease out and change meanings, to compare and contrast, to assemble and break down, to divide and combine, to associate and differentiate, to mesh and juxtapose, to shape and design, to find puzzles and set challenges, to speculate and muse, to try this and test that, to experiment with strategies and tactics - are crucial in generating alternative perspectives, in reconstructing our understanding of the world, and in opening up new possibilities of achieving creative outcomes.

In practice, I exercise only varying degrees of direction over my own creative play of the mind, both in its occurrence and in its form. The playing is not confined to normal occupational hours. It is a process which knows no demarcations of work and leisure and it sometimes has little respect for frameworks of time dictated by other exigencies. In my experience, there are many occasions when there is a non-directed but fruitful mental process, which continues even after I have made a conscious decision to stop. Indeed much of the time, my own playing is spontaneous and childlike in its irrepressible meandering. It often follows paths which are not consciously set, and there are times when, if I command it, I can not always guarantee to be obeyed for other than a few moments. Just abandoning any attempt at control, giving time for something to emerge, and letting the precocious child get on with it, sometimes produces elements of the most imaginative and appropriate constructions. This undirected play can also be remarkably productive in drawing attention to gaps, flaws and inconsistencies.

But for the research thinking to be fully effective, this undirected, or partially-directed, play has to be part of a total process that has strong elements of focus and management. The undirected play has to be interwoven with periods of rigorously directed thought. The imaginative playfulness has to be accompanied at some stage by critical and logical appraisal, and it has to have rigorous and repeated testing against the evidence. Overall, there has to be both freedom and control around the general line of advance; what Sidney Parnes, in a phrase that I particularly like, calls "self-disciplined squiggliness."[25] The spontaneity comes easily and naturally, the control involves considerable discipline and hard work.

Our minds, which are naturally disposed towards this playing and patterning, also tend to become used to (and at times get stuck in) familiar mental grooves. Creative play is at times a fight against the fascination and limitations which familiar associations and directions of thought exert upon us. It is a self-questioning and self-critical struggle to see and portray the world afresh. The challenge for the creative player is to develop systematically generative modes of play - ways of playing which are organised to disturb familiar connections and ease the development of new interpretations, explanations and configurations of ideas.

Together these different modes of play involve flying, so to speak, whilst not losing touch with the terrain. The play has to be liberated, unburdened, flexible, promiscuous, experimental and only lightly attached to particular ideas and relationships. But it also has to be grounded - disciplined by a range of constraining considerations. The focus of the research problem, the dialogue with the existing literature, the claims of evidence, the requirements of practicability, and also the rigour of personal and professional integrity, all act as proper and framing limitations.

Using Time

Both of these activities, the exploring and the playing, have once again brought us to a repeated theme - the use of time. I have had contrasting experience here which heighten my awareness of its significance. On the one hand, there have been many short-term tasks completed to set deadlines in the face of all obstacles. On the other, there have been long term projects which were finished years later than anticipated.

My primary method of research - fieldwork by participant observation - is often a lengthy process requiring a great deal of patience. In a sense also (to be explained in Chapters Three and Eight) you could see development of my research over thirty years as just one long intellectual journey in pursuit of better answers to key problems. This awareness of time is not just my personal sensitivity. It is something of a preoccupation for many of those who have made a special study of creativity. There is an intriguing contrast here between one of the strongest images that is held of creativity, and one of the strongest themes in the literature on the real process. It is the image of a sparkling, creative, inspirational moment contrasted with the theme of the longer-term, incremental, filtering and amending intellectual slog.

Creativity tends to be associated in the public mind with this inspirational moment - the "Eureka" moment - often seen as one complete leap forward to enlightenment and discovery. So, here is Pythagoras passing a brazier's shop, hearing the hammers beating, and perceiving the arithmetical relationship between harmonic intervals [James 1994 pp 32-33]. And Archimedes watches the water rise in his bath, and "Eureka!" - discovering the way to measure the volume of a solid object [Koestler 1969 pp 105-8] . All this may or may not have been true. But it does not surprise me that a forthcoming biography of Newton should suggest that Newton's falling apple was an invention covering up the real gestation of his work on gravity[26]. The Eureka moment is often a misrepresentation of the creative process.

This is not to deny that the stages of that process may well involve the sudden and spontaneous emergence of what Graham Wallas, (in his categorisation of stages of creativity as preparation, incubation, illumination and verification)[27] has described as illumination, and others have described as inspiration. Certainly it is a commonly described experience.[28] But, even when it has the ring of truth in conveying the feeling of the moment, it is probably failing to convey the full story. Generally, preceding the creative insight is a "long, gruelling, intense period of hard mental work"[29]. And the prevalence of metaphors relating to procreation also testify to the process various writers have described in terms of nurturing and developing ideas after the insight. There is often a long gestation period after the initial idea[30], and there can be an elaborate process of revision, amplification, refinement, and, sometimes, adjustment for practical application. Characteristic of the creative process as a whole is not one big leap forward in understanding, but a continuously associative, synthesising and adjustive development.

In their study of the processes accompanying significant inventions, Weber and Perkins conclude that it is almost always "a long haul" [Weber and Perkins 1992 p 319]. The striking feature of all the inventions reviewed, including some of the famous historical cases involving the Wright Brothers and Edison, was the duration of the process of the development of ideas and artefacts. Nearly every tale of invention unfolded over several years, sometimes decades.[31]

There were creative leaps of varying importance, but none so great as to constitute the entire story[32]. Thus it is that, surveying various eminent contributions to the study of creativity, Tardif and Sternberg point out that, "By far the greatest amount of agreement is with the statement that creativity takes time"[33]. For these reasons, the Eureka moment is better described and understood as a form of parable[34] rather than the accurate encapsulation of a creative process.

Now, it must be remembered that this emphasis on time in the literature is generally drawing from the evidence accumulated in relation to those creative products agreed to be work of special historic originality and importance. Here we need a broader perspective on the many different processes and outcomes of creative research noted in our previous discussion. In research, obviously much depends on the form, scale, methods and objectives of the project. Projects of varying sizes, kinds and complexity, in different disciplines, have varying constraints in relation to time. They also have their different obligations in terms of delivery and what will be judged to constitute an appropriate investigation. Research does not have to be creative to be of quality in relation to its purpose, and there can be investigations where the attempt to be particularly creative would be an indulgence. Nevertheless each project will generally involve some opportunity, at various stages of the process, for a creative approach which enlarges the possibility of generating a greater degree of appropriate originality.

Creative ideas can certainly be generated under pressure. Imagination may be brought to bear, new alternatives may be introduced, possibilities may be enlarged, and original products may well be the result. There is a considerable literature on creative strategies and problem-solving techniques which aim at assisting, and may well result in, the speedy development of novel ideas that can contribute towards, the solution.[35] "Brainstorming" (where as many ideas as possible are generated without immediate critical filtering) is one such technique [Osborn 1993 pp 151-196]. In my own work the creative processes explored in Chapter Seven have been productive in research projects both short and long-term.

Many of us have had the experience that in lectures, speeches, articles and conference papers produced to tight deadlines, as in other activities, urgency can produce a sudden quickening of mental and physical energy and an increased capacity for prolonged periods of concentration. It may be that, as Boden suggests [Boden 1990 p 257], anxiety stimulates a considerable boost to what she calls the breadth-first search for solutions and possibilities. With the development of the mature scholar's art, we also have the advantage of an expertise which finds various economical, efficient ways of dealing with familiar problem situations.

Nevertheless, having said all that, we have still to recognise that the highest quality creative outcomes may not be produced by sudden spurts and pressurised mental activity. They may only be generated slowly, incrementally and over an extended period. One distinguished specialist on the scientific process has put this in perspective, "imagine Einstein trying to brainstorm".[36]

Why does this produce a wry smile? I think that we see that some kinds of problems and projects require both more depth and a more prolonged attention. It can take time to take an in-depth measure of the problem. The problem may present itself differently the deeper the immersion in the field of investigation. As Dewey says in a more general appraisal of thinking, "The depth to which a sense of the problem, of the difficulty, sinks, determines the quality of the thinking that follows. Sometimes slowness and depth of response are intimately connected" in "getting to the roots of the matter".[37]

The critical factors in the length of search for a solution are likely to be the "toughness" of the problem, the complexity of the solution process that is required [38], and also, of course, what the researcher is prepared to settle for as the appropriate solution requirements [Nickerson, Perkins and Smith 1985 p 97]. In any field, what Boden terms depth-first search of a particular solution-path [Boden 1990 p 257], can take years. Doggedly pursuing problems as far as is necessary to their satisfactory solution, involves painstaking application and slow development. In these circumstances, the solution does not generally emerge complete as a whole. It develops slowly over time, "piece by piece"[39] in a process of repetitive adjustment.

It must also be appreciated that there are occasions when creative work simply can not be pushed quickly by determination, sheer force of will and intellect. [40] There are modes of focused creative thinking which require a leisurely approach [Entwistle 1988 pp 155-156]. Scholars of creativity, and creative people in different fields, have often described the helpful "pause" or "idle time" which has sometimes been described as the incubation of ideas. [41] The "pause" involves time which is not dominated by conscious problem-solving activity in relation to the project[42]. In a complex project there may well be a multitude of such enforced but productive pauses of varying durations.

In the light of all these points it is not surprising that creativity (meaning here the highest level of creativity) is described as "often ... a protracted affair"[43] and why it has been argued that the most creative solutions are the ones that are generated by people willing to wait [44].

SOLITUDE

Time is relevant in another respect. It is not just a question of the length of time taken. There is another dimension to be appreciated. Typically, in research as in most other forms of creative process, there is also a need for a particular quality in the time available. It involves having the opportunity for periods in solitude, without interruption[45] and with "the flow of life made easy and noiseless."[46] This, in my experience, requires that depth of concentration which is best achieved in blocks of time: the odd half-hour snatched between other activities has only limited use depending on the stage and type of work being attempted.

This solitude is ideally not simply a social solitude but, in a sense, a mental solitude, an opportunity for listening to the inner self. Experience suggests that it involves a state of mind which is at its most productive when not cluttered with urgent, distracting mental messages and other pressing problems and distractions which mean that we are not "all there".[47] These can arise from a variety of sources, some inescapable in life - grief for example, or deep anger. However it is often more mundane preoccupations which take up mental energy and become disturbingly intrusive; functional problems and obligations of home and work which interfere with the need for concentrated focus and reflection (a point often made about the value of Residential College learning). Women have found the clash of domestic and intellectual obligations particularly difficult in finding this inner as well as outer mental space.[48] University colleagues today are telling me of the increasing problems caused for their creative process by numerous mental reminders of other pressing bureaucratic obligations.

It is an old lament. Seventy years ago Graham Wallas pointed out the dangers to creative thought of administrative methods in the universities, "innumerable worrying details of filling up forms and sending in applications", destroying the possibility of fruitful incubation. "Their subconscious minds are set on the duty of striking like a clock when Mr Jones's fee must be paid to the Registrar"[49]. One can guess what he might have said today about the multiple and growing bureaucratic pressures on academic life and the time of the academic researcher.

"THE FLOW"

The exploring and playing processes, and the questioning which often accompanies them, provide the major generational forces feeding what I think of as "the flow" of the creative process. Here I must clarify what I mean by "the flow", as it differs from the way the concept is sometimes used in the literature on creativity, particularly in the work of Mihaly Csikszentmihalyi. In the literature, this notion of "flow" is of a peculiar state of experience in which deep enjoyment comes with a sense of complete absorption in the intrinsically motivated activity. There is a loss of ego and self-consciousness, and the disappearance of extrinsic concerns [50].

I know this feeling well. I experience it as a fulfilling and compulsive obsession, where I almost lose a sense of self and time. It is a state of mind where, if I am interrupted, I find it not only mentally disturbing but physically uncomfortable. However, the image that I have of "the flow" is of a broader experience with much less of a sense of personal control than in the Csikszentmihalyi concept. My own usage does however also have its resonance in the way that others have conveyed their experience of creativity [51]. Describing it will convey a much deeper sense of what is involved for me in the creative experience.

Let me put it this way. What I have presented so far gives a sense of the creative researcher as a purposive commanding actor determining the process; exploring, playing and so on. S/he is the strong subject creating the object. S/he is the lone innovating force. S/he is exercising control. That picture will emerge often in the chapters that follow. However, true as that is in many respects, it must be said that this is not quite my experience of the process, though this is how I expected it to be. In practice, I often have a sense of the process as one in which I am participating as much as controlling. At these times I have a strong sense that there is an "it" ("the flow") of which I am a part. In this flow I (the apparent subject) am being heavily accompanied and also subtly changed whilst the project (the supposed object) is to some extent transforming itself.

There are three interactive forces to be distinguished here. As I indicated, my mind seems to be in "play" in a way that is by no means under the full control of the conscious self. I can not switch it off - that is a crucial point. Nor can I always guarantee to switch its focus of attention. Just as the mental noise of other engagements can interfere with the creative process, so the creative process can distract other preferred activities, particularly sleeping.

I am also the object receiving ideas from others as much as I am the subject creating them. As I generate and develop my ideas, so they are also being fed from outside. Though I have a strong sense of my reflective autonomy, at times it is shadowed by a sense of fate. This is a general awareness that my life is a learning and socially influenced process, and the perspectives that I have on my project will, to some extent, reflect that experience - including what I am learning from a particular project. It is also an acute awareness of the way that the pains and benefits of outright chance influence the work and my approach to it. There is, furthermore, an awareness that my life-style and activities as a researcher are in various ways shaping me as a person. Over time as I gain more experience and more artistry, not only do my ideas change, so do I.

The sense of participating in a movement which is not fully under my control can be at its greatest in relation to the form and objectives of a project where a variety of forces (examined in Chapter Nine) give a feeling that the work has an inner dynamic of its own. I have a sense that it is pulling and moving me as I am pushing and shaping it.

So, overall, once my mind becomes seriously engaged with a project, a dynamic interactive process is engendered which is experienced as a regularly replenished current. This "it", which I call "the flow", is not entirely at my command as it constantly engenders change and transformation. Indeed, it is, to a degree, unpredictable in its courses, sometimes emerging in unexpected places with unanticipated consequences for the research project. With experience, I have learned to be at ease with the "the flow", even when it is at its most intrusive and anarchic.

And the fact remains that I do stimulate this "flow"; I monitor it, and can insert a feeding, guiding, managing and, ultimately, in the final form of the project, decisive control. Part of my artistic skill has been to make these initiatives and interventions blend into the current. Much of what follows in this study is about how this takes place.

CHAPTER END NOTES

[1] [Ford and Harris III 1992]. Calvin Taylor and associates have traced "some 50 or 60 definitions" of creativity, Taylor, C. 'Various approaches to and definitions of creativity' Appendix, in [Sternberg 1988 pp 118-119].

[2] [Boden 1990 p 32] distinguishes two senses of creativity - P (psychological) creativity from H (historical) creativity.

[3] Even amongst "optimists" there are also differences of emphasis in relation to the length of time, the degree of application and the specificity of the techniques in relation to the person or problem. Albert, R.S. and Runco, M.A. 'Observations, conclusions and gaps' in [Runco and Albert 1990 p264].

[4] In his work, A. H. Maslow was particularly struck by the many people who, in their daily lives, were original, ingenious and inventive but would have been judged to have had no noteworthy talent in areas conventionally associated with creativity. Maslow, A.H., 'Creativity in self-actualising people' in [Anderson 1959 pp 84-5].

[5] Roe, A ' Psychological approaches to creativity in science' in [Rothenberg and Hausman 1976 p 172].

[6] Perkins, D.N. cited in [Kirby and Kuykendall 1991 p 16].

[7] Guilford, J.P., 'Creativity: a quarter century of progress' in [Taylor and Getzels 1975, pp 38-46]. , Perkins, D.N. 'Creativity: beyond the Darwinian paradigm' in [Boden 1994 p 138] . Also [Welsh 1975 p 117].

[8] [Guilford 1968 pp 194-5]. S.J. Parnes 'Education and creativity' in [Vernon 1970 pp 341-9]. [Torrance 1965]. [Perkins 1981 p 206 and pp 214-9]. See also the examination of the literature in [Freeman, Butcher, and Christie 1968 p 71-2]. The analysis of [Rose and Hsin-tai Lin 1984 pp 279-290] indicated moderate improvements in verbal creativity and a strong impact on verbal originality. There were however great disparities in the effectiveness of different training programmes.

[9] Humour and laughter have often been linked with creativity. See for example [Koestler 1969, pp 27-86], on "The Jester". There is an excellent tabular summary of humour theories and their relationship to creativity in [Murdock and Ganim 1993].

[10]*ibid*

[11] A variety of studies have indicated that those who attain creative achievement generally have higher than average intelligence and that creativity tends to increase with intelligence up to around IQ 120. Ford C. M., 'Creativity is a mystery: clues from the investigator's notebook' in [Ford and Gioia p 30]. [Ochse 1991 pp 336-7]. But a high IQ does not itself guarantee creative achievement Eysenck, H.J., 'The measurement of creativity' in [Boden 1994 p 210]. Above that level of IQ 120 the creative performance will be more affected by other factors. It has been found that there can be various combinations of intelligence and creativity. Wallach, M.A. and Kogan, N., 'Creativity and intelligence in children', reprinted in [Rothenberg and Hausman 1976 pp 208-217]. [Welsh 1975 pp 88-107] differentiates "origence" and "intellectence" and produces a typology of combinations with variations from high to low. p 107.

[12]. Ford in [Ford and Gioia 1995 p 35] citing a variety of studies.

[13] MacKinnon, D.W. 'Creativity(1) Psychological Aspects' in [MacMillan/ Free Press, 1968, p 439].

[14] Perkins, D.N. in [Boden 1994 p 140].

[15] [Pesut 1990 pp 105 - 110]. Armbruster, B.B., 'Metacognition in creativity' in [Glover, Ronning and Reynolds 1989 pp 177-182]. There is evidence to suggest that metacognitive behaviour is modifiable and metacognitive skills are teachable. [Nickerson, Perkins and Smith 1995 pp 294-302].

[16] For the relationship between self-esteem and creativity see Hennessey, B.A. and. Amabile, T.M., 'The conditions of creativity' in [Sternberg 1988 pp 32-35]. Prince, G.M., 'Creativity, self and power' in [Taylor and Getzels 1975 pp 129-277].

[17] Barron, F. 'Putting creativity to work', in [Sternberg 1988 p 76].

[18] Runco, M.A., 'Cognitive and psychometric issues in creativity research' in [Isaksen et al 1993. p 350-1]

[19] The "personal style hypothesis " of W.T. Morris suggests that in creative decision-making there is more to be gained by attempting to enhance a

person's style than by efforts to reformulate that style in accordance with some other unfamiliar procedure. Morris, W.T., 'Matching decision aids with intuitive styles' in Brinkers H.S., ed, *Decisionmaking : Creativity, Judgement and Systems* Ohio State University Press, Columbus, 1972, cited by Craig C. Lundberg 'Creativity training and hemispheric function' in [Ford and Gioia 1995 p 153].

[20] Csikszentmihalyi, M. and Sawyer, K. 'Shifting the focus from individual to organisational creativity' in [Ford and Gioia 1995 p171].Farr, J.L.. 'Q. Does feedback enhance or inhibit creativity in organisations? A. Yes !' in [Ford and Gioia 1995 pp 139-140]. Amabile, T.M., 'Within you, without you : the social psychology of creativity and beyond' in [Runco and Albert 1990 p 76].

[21] Eysenck, H.J. in [Boden 1994 p 210].

[22] [Feldhusen 1995 pp 259-61]. Langley, P. and Jones, R. 'A computational model of scientific insight' in [Sternberg 1988 p199].

[23] [Lieberman 1977 Chaps 1V and V, pp 63-122]. [Storr 1976 Chap 9 'Creativity and play' pp 147-162].

[24] Freud, J.S. 'Creative writers and day-dreaming' in [Strachey 1969].

[25] Parnes, S.J., 'AHA!' in [Taylor and Getzels 1975 p 241-7].

[26] 'Newton's 'apple' hid a dark secret' John Harlow, *Sunday Times* 3/12/95 discussing a book by Michael White to be called *The Last Sorcerer*. Versions of the apple myth are recounted in [Roberts 1989 pp 11-15].

[27] [Wallas 1926 p 80]. Although there is research into creative performance which has confirmed the general diagnosis of stages of creative activity [Freeman, Butcher and Christie 1971 p 46] with particular reference to the work of Catherine Patrick, Wallas' stages have been criticised for rigidity in relation to the varieties of creative experience. Some have preferred to see the stages as aspects of the creative process which can occur in different mixes and orders. Others have seen the stages in different ways and with different terminologies.

[28] [Ghiselin 1954 p 5]. [Rothenberg and Hausman 1976 particularly Chapter Two pp 57-69] with extracts from Edgar Allan Poe, Samuel Taylor Coleridge and the scientist Walter Bradford Cannon. But see [Weisberg 1986 p 50] for the view that there is little reason to believe that solutions to novel problems come in leaps of insight independent of past experience. In this view people create solutions to problems by starting with what they know and later modifying it to deal with the problem in hand.

[29] Maddi, S.R., 'The strenuousness of the creative life' in [Taylor and Getzels 1975 p 179].

[30] Tardif, T.Z. and Sternberg, R.J., 'What do we know about creativity?' in [Sternberg 1988 p 430], citing the work of Perkins, D.N. and of Torrance, E.P. who emphasise the long gestation period. See also [Ghiselin 1954 p 5].

[31] *ibid*

[32] Perkins, D.N. in [Boden 1994 p 131].

[33] Tardif and Sterberg in [Sternberg 1988 p 430].

[34] Arieti cited by Schaffer in [Boden 1994 p 15].

[35] See for example [Osborn 1993 pp 86 - 290] and Parnes, S.J., 'Idea stimulation techniques' reprinted in [Parnes 1992 pp 154-7].

[36] Gruber, H.E., 'Darwin's tree of nature and other images of wide scope' in [Wechsler, 1978 p 137].

[37] All quotations are from [Dewey 1910 pp 37-38].

[38] Taylor in [Taylor and Getzels 1975 p 310].

[39] Sternberg, R.J.and Lubart, T.I., 'Ten tips towards creativity in the workplace' in [Ford and Gioia 1995 p 178.].

[40] Mantel, H 'Growing a tale' in [Boylan 1993 p41]. Tillie Olson gives various interesting examples from the diaries of Franz Kafka of his failed

attempts to force his creative writing. [Olson 1965 p 159]. Bertrand Russell also gives such an account in relation to his philosophical writing in [Russell 1956 p 195].

[41] [Wallas 1926 p 86]. [Osborn 1993 pp 314-5]. [Leytham 1990 Chapter Six pp 93 -109]. Frank. M. Andrews suggests that there are benefits of legitimised "incubation periods" in the creativity of scientists, Andrews, F.M., 'Social and psychological influences on the creative process' in [Taylor and Getzels 1975 p134]. [Perkins 1981 pp 50-55] and [Boden 1990 pp 244-5] emphasise that this beneficial time away from a specific problem may not involve some form of extended unconscious thinking: there may be alternative explanations of why conscious reasoning is effective after the pause. See also [Weisberg 1986 Chapter 2 'The myth of the unconscious' pp 15-34].

[42] Csikszentmihalyi, M and Sawyer, K. 'Shifting the focus from individual to organisational creativity' in [Ford and Gioia 1995 p 172]. Also [Boden 1990 pp 244-5].

[43] Mackinnon, D.W. 'IPAR's contribution to the study of creativity' in [Taylor and Getzels 1975 p 72].

[44] Sternberg and Lubart in [Ford and Gioia 1995 p 178].

[45] [Storr 1989 p 103]. [Ochse 1991 pp 338-9]. Fiona Williams 1993 p 20.

[46] Joseph Conrad quoted in [Olson 1965 p 160]. Interruptions to the process of getting into the right frame of mind and the appropriate degree of mental involvement can be particularly damaging. "Everything must be immobile around me so that my mind can take off and spin like a top.....When I'm in the process of turning slowly inward upon myself in order to take off, a little nothing, a word, a story, a newspaper, a visit stops me in my tracks and keeps me from becoming a gyroscope", Pierre Curie quoted in[Quinn 1995 p114]. But as Curie also indicates, there is a depth of mental engagement which can to some extent make the researcher impervious to some of the distractions of the ebb and flow of life.

[47] [Dilts, Epstein and Dilts, 1991 p 144]. [Maslow 1976 p 64].

[48] [Ochse 1991 p 340]. These problems are particularly vividly described in [Olson 1965 pp 153-161].

[49] [Wallas 1926 pp 90-91]. On the theme of the mind's requirements in terms of incubation and illumination see pp 86-93 and 147-9.

[50] [Csikszentmihalyi 1975 particularly pp 35-54]. Also, Amabile in [Runco and Albert 1990 p 64]. The experience occurs in a variety of activities and occupations where there is deep intrinsic involvement. In terms of the inspirational phase of creativity this has also been analysed in [Maslow 1976 pp 59-68].

[51] Some of what I am describing here is akin to a secular version of the experience conveyed by those who see creativity as a spiritually influenced process. A good example is [Cameron 1994] also [Metzger 1992]. [Leytham 1996 p 152-3] cites Kipling, Dickens, Flaubert and Thackeray amongst writers who felt that either they had spiritual assistance or the subjects and characters of their work were controlling them.

CHAPTER THREE

CREATIVITY AND PROBLEM-SEEKING

PROBLEMS AND DISTINCTIVENESS

At this point in the study, I am going to begin to link the analysis of creativity with a more detailed exploration of the substance of, and mental processes involved in, my own past research. This will set the scene for the remaining chapters by explaining the origins of the core problems of my long-term research interests. Before I do that, as an introduction, I want to examine some of the ways that I arrive at this focus of my research - the core problem or problems with which it is concerned.

Social science research can pursue a variety of goals - exploratory, descriptive, explanatory, predictive and policy oriented [Dane 1990 pp 5-9], and may be addressed by a variety of different kinds of question. My own research embraces elements of the exploratory and the descriptive, and some of my concluding prescriptions have been used as the basis for policy, but, fundamentally my purpose is explanatory.

This explanatory research can be understood as a process of solving problems. But the degree of distinctiveness and the quality of creativity in research may be as much a matter of the quality of the problem (or problems) that we choose to pursue as the solutions we then arrive at. Thus, problem seeking and problem discovery are also a vital part of the creative process; some have argued that problem-discovery may even be the most important part.[1]

The problems that we address in our research can come to us in a variety of ways and, of course, our contractual relations determine the degree of freedom that we have in establishing the project and its problems. Thus, some problems may be given to us, some may be suggested to us and some we may find for ourselves. I am in general a problem-finder, and as a curiosity-driven scholar, I attempt to pursue and develop the problems wherever they lead. Over the years my own problems have been generated from three separate but at times inter-related sources.

The existing academic literature - where others have written about what they found or did not find - has to be the reference point for our distinctiveness. It is often also our point of departure, the trigger for our research, as we respond to, and query, what has gone(or not gone) before. As with all scholars, I am in a constant dialogue with this literature which has yielded, or contributed towards, the definition of some key problems.

As immersion in the field of enquiry deepens, and as we explore and become familiar with the nuances and minutiae of the project, so our sense of wonder is aroused by what we see and what we fail to find. My values and social purposes, as well as my intellectual curiosity, often direct my attention towards particular developments, issues and incidents which lead to the pursuit of a query which can become the problem-focus of the work.

We all have some life experience of society, economy and politics which can provoke concern, curiosity and intellectual enquiry in the social sciences. My academic problems are also often activated from queries raised by a personal active involvement in the political process, and also by my reaction, as a concerned citizen, to how developments in my field of enquiry are portrayed in the mass media. Thus, I do think of myself as an *applied* political analyst, or political scientist in the sense that often I pick up not on abstract questions but on topics and problems in the real world, the clarification and solution of which I think could be of social benefit. My research projects, and "the flow" of the creative process when they are under way, have generally been stimulated by a combination of "real-world" problems, deep penetration of the field of study, and a dialogue with the literature which was available to explain it.

On the other hand, because in my work problem-seeking and curiosity-led enquiry has been a continuous process, my research has often had a *pure* trajectory. By the time the project is completed, the process of intellectual enquiry, and the creativity that accompanies it, may well have changed or enlarged the objectives from the original problem-focus. In any case, it is pure in the sense that, as the work progresses, I seek to enhance a theoretical understanding of the field that is under investigation. And although my work often leads to conclusions with immediate practical applications, or implications in the political field, this need not be the case for all that I have uncovered. (It must be said, of course, that we can never quite be certain as to what practical use others might put our research findings in the future).

That, then, has generally been my approach to research problems, and as a mature researcher I have rarely been short of important problems to investigate. However, this was not my understanding as a novice researcher. I did have a particular area of research interest as I will explain shortly, but I was not untypical of post-graduate students in being uncertain how to arrive at, and to formulate, a distinctive problem.

EXAMINATION, PECULIARITIES,AND PROBLEMS

Critical Examination

I have little recollection of what advice, if any, I received on this questioning and problem-exploration in the earliest days of my doctorate. What I do recall is that I floundered quite a lot in those initial stages, both in directing my investigations towards an appropriate and handleable problem and in terms of understanding the process that I was involved in. Unlike today,[2] there was not much guidance then from the literature in terms of problem-seeking.

Here, as I introduce the problems with which I became concerned, and the trajectory of my work, I want to emphasise three general features of the process of creative problem-seeking in my field of work.

The first feature is the most obvious, but also the most fundamental. It is the necessity for a period of critical, reflective immersion, not only in the literature but in the field of research itself. This is a rigorous and unremitting process of observation, interrogation and reflection, exploring as far and as deep as possible, following and playing with anything that looks particularly interesting and significant. The reflective perspective, from the first steps, must involve a flexible, multifaceted observation of what is encountered. The imperative is to question everything - including the questions that others have asked, even the questions that you yourself are asking.

This questioning can have a systematic form. My own approach evolved slowly over time as I became conscious of the way that any technique of creativity generation[3] could bring into visibility a new problem or problems. Sometimes, this was potentially a "core problem;" sometimes, it was subsidiary to a core problem, sometimes it was an application problem of how a particular area was affected by the researchers' proposed solution to the core problem; and sometimes it was an independent problem within the main problem area.

As I began, a novice researcher, to explore power relations in the British Labour Party, and particularly the processes at the party conference, an early influence on my questioning approach to exploration in research was a reference from Harold Lasswell.[4] In the study of political communication he suggested the usefulness of the question, "Who says what to whom in what channel with what effect?" To this I occasionally added the question, "Why?".

Some years later, I came to see this process as "Critical Examination" - a term borrowed from the field of creativity studies - and to appreciate its general usefulness. I adapted and modified P.R. Whitfield's very useful formulation of questions which formed the basis of his Critical Examination [Whitfield 1975 p 52]. The way that I have used it since has become so regular and automatic that I almost lost sight of what it was that I did. It involves focusing on any political phenomenon and asking six key questions - Who? What? How? When? Where? With what consequences? and then after each question, asking Why?.

This is a powerful inquisitorial tool and form of heuristic thinking throughout the research process, but it can also act as a systematic way of suggesting problems for investigation. In this way, such questions may well turn out to be "your..best friends", as George Polya described his mathematical version (What, Why, Where, When and How). You need "...ask nobody else when you need advice" [Polya 1957 p 225]. The tool becomes the more powerful and the more useful in problem-seeking if the "why" question is constantly repeated in response to every answer, attempting to dig deeper and deeper in questioning, and in constant reference to the evidence. Out of this questioning, a gap in knowledge may be revealed, an explanation may be missing or judged inadequate, or something surprising may emerge.

Peculiarities

This takes us into the second feature of creative problem-seeking that I want to emphasise. Eager minds find their own spontaneous questions, as they follow their curiosity, but one valuable focus of this curiosity is the response to the surprise of observing peculiarities.[5] What do I mean? In different ways, theorists of creativity have drawn attention to the fact that the creative mind is "cordial towards and curious about the new and the strange" [Prince 1968 pp 168-77]. The creative mind is frequently surprised or puzzled by what is observed.[6] I found my own way to this understanding a long time ago. Consequently, there is now a range of such possible surprises in research investigation which, to me, all come under the label of "peculiarities."[7]

The peculiarity may be diagnosed as a result of an anticipation of things that ought to be there (according to theories or past descriptions of the field) but are not. These are things that you expect to see happen, for varying reasons, but do not. And there are things that appear in a particular situation that you would not have expected. Of course, there are also things that are there as you expect, but strike you as odd for other reasons once you explore the context.

A sense of peculiarity may also be triggered by expectations related to values. One classic peculiarity is: why are so many people poor? Or it might be: why is this large group under-represented? Or: why is there democracy in this area but not in that one? Or again it might be: why is there so little deference to authority in this sphere?

There may also be peculiarities of repetitious or variable behaviour which are counter-intuitive. There can be anomalies, irregularities and paradoxes of behaviour, discrepant events or simply a "blip" in a line of figures which stimulates the curiosity and the need for further investigation. There can be unexpected and peculiar descriptions and identifications by the players involved. More vaguely, there may be things that just somehow "don't fit". Or there may simply be a sense of something missing or not quite right.

Developments of any kind in the field of study, but particularly sudden changes, often suggest peculiarities by highlighting the normal in surprising ways. Sometimes it is a question of why change takes this particular form and reflect these particular values in a situation where other reforms and values were on offer. Sometimes it is what does *not* change that is surprising. In that sense, creativity may involve refocusing on some very old problems. Sometimes it is simply that as a result of the change we are left with a new perspective on the old. John Dewey says of this phenomenon, "no object is so familiar, so obvious, so commonplace, that it may not unexpectedly present, in a novel situation, some problem and thus arouse reflection in order to understand it" [Dewey 1910 p 120].

A sensitivity to these and other peculiarities can lead the observer to see the larger implications of even very small events. For the creative researcher, such peculiarities provoke - in a sense, they demand - questioning, and they invite pursuit. Throughout the research process, puzzling over and following peculiarities can be a route to creative outcomes. As will be further illustrated in later chapters, as a form of heuristic thinking, it can enlarge the possibilities of the situation in that it can become a disturbance of old assumptions and understandings and it can open up new perspectives. But also, receptivity towards the peculiar feature can often generate key problems which are likely to lead to a particularly distinctive enquiry.

To the vigilant, curious and receptive, the research process itself tends to be a constant question-provoking process often drawn by peculiarities that puzzle, sometimes aroused by examination of minutiae and what at first glance might appear to be a triviality and thus pass unnoticed. The pursuit of the answer to one question often leads to findings which provoke other questions. Indeed, to the creative mind almost any surprising evidence that is part of an answer provokes a new questioning analysis and perhaps new lines of enquiry. Questions become exits to many new entrances. In this process there can be some rapid changes in judgement of what is significant and what is not.

Problem focus

Here I come to the third feature of creative problem-seeking that I want to emphasise - the shifting, repositioning, refocusing character of the process. What the problem is, and how it is defined and refined, may change as the researcher gets deeper into the immersion. So the project has to be allowed to "live", and the mind has to be allowed the time to play with various possibilities as information is being absorbed and a range of judgements are being made.

This period of free exploration, risk and experiment in defining the central problem or problems, is a normal, healthy and probably an essential feature of creative investigation. In this process it is not unusual for the ever-shifting project to appear, at times, almost to have a life of its own as the researcher makes and remakes the focus and shape of the project. This making and remaking involves not just an intellectual engagement. There has to be an openness of mind, a receptivity to the new, a sensitivity to time, and a willingness to tolerate ambiguity and uncertainty - not to mention resisting, for a while, a degree of pressure to "get on with it".

The fact is that what the "it" is, may reasonably be unclear for some time. Here let me point out the fact that I have referred several times to "problem (or problems)" even though both the literature on creativity and the literature on research methods tend to emphasise isolating and handling *the* problem. However, in interpretive social science such problems tend to arise in clusters. These could be (and often are) explored as separate projects, and this makes for handleability in research. But there are many circumstances where it would be limiting, and unsatisfactory, to deal with one problem in isolation. One such form of research deals with the combination of Who? How? Why? With what consequences? Another common format of problems asks: what were the characteristics, causes, and consequences? Or it might be: what is the phenomenon, why did this develop and why did it degenerate? Each could produce a separate research project, but in my field of work, depending upon the scale of the investigation involved, they are often dealt with together. It is also worth pointing out that in the research that I became involved in, the problems specific to a relationship in the short term had also to be accompanied by a problem relating to longer term variabilities. So the problems were not only: What is the distribution of power and why? But also: what have been the variations of that distribution over time and why?

In making all these points about problems, I am leading to an important observation that, particularly in research involving field studies, and where time permits, there are other reasons than the pursuit of peculiarities for attempting to preserve a degree of flexibility in formulating and reformulating the problems. The crucial point is that the choice of a problem, and certainly the emphasis placed upon a problem within a combination, may only usefully be clarified *during* the process.

Thus, for example, although the question "why" is generally the key problem, the "who" or "how" question, and the question of "with what consequences," may, upon immersion in the field of enquiry, come to appear far more significant. Even a subsidiary problem of one of these core problems can turn out to be almost as significant as the other core problems. That is one reason why a degree of flexibility can be so important, and why, especially in its early stages, the project "moves about". That very flexibility allows more room for different possibilities within the project and for spontaneous changes of direction in reaction to what is found. This is not uncommon in fieldwork [8].

A degree of openness in defining and framing the problem, keeping it from crystallizing too soon, has been seen by some creativity theorists as integral to the creative process [Getzels and Czikszentmihalyi 1976 p 247]. Deferment, in avoiding early definition of what the research is about, adds to the mental pressures on the researcher. It can be time-consuming to pursue the unusual at the expense of concentrating on the mainstream, the normal and the expected. If pursued without disciplined judgement, and a wary eye on the time factor, it can certainly add to the risks of non-completion. But it can also give more opportunity for creativity.

Problems, solutions and problems again

There is one final point about problems that I want to emphasise here. Problem discovery, problem pursuit, problem refocusing, problem solution and problem discovery again, are a flowing process in creative field-work research. As a result, it is sometimes the case that by the completion of one project, the mind is playing with another major problem (or problems) which has emerged. The regularity of this occurrence provides a wonderful vista of the endless generation of research investigations. It stimulates excitement and a constantly renewed motivation. However, on occasions, there may be the disconcerting discovery (as I experienced) that a reformulation and refocus of the original problems might have been more interesting and original in the project just completed.

Here I come to that focus and to the problems that have pre-occupied my thought and work over the years. This will further illuminate the process of seeking peculiarities and problems and also provide the essential context for what is to follow.

PURPOSE, PREOCCUPATIONS AND PECULIARITIES

Purpose

At the time that I became a postgraduate student and began research I had little grasp of the importance, let alone the subtleties, of identifying problems. What I did have, however, was the advantage of my experience before university which had already provoked important questions concerning democracy, representation and power. You could say that these problems had arisen, in a sense, before my eyes in the world of my political and trade union activities. Thus the trigger of my research had taken place long before I became immersed in the literature.

I placed, and still place, a high value on an active and participatory democracy, and I had become particularly interested in the degree to which there could be public control over those who exercise significant power in a democracy. When I began my PhD thesis in the mid 1960s, I saw key problems of democratic access and control in the political system located in the concentration of power within the political parties. I pondered over some not-very-original questions. Why did the membership not rule within democratic parties? Why was the distribution of power concentrated at leadership level? Under what conditions could such power be redistributed amongst the membership? I now see these questions as a limited and narrow perspective but at that time it passionately engaged my interest and it led to some very productive academic research.

In my university studies I found that the classic text in the literature was by Robert Michels [Michels 1962 edn], who had diagnosed at the turn of the century that for various socio-psychological reasons all large scale organisations were oligarchical, regardless of how democratic they professed to be. "Who says organisation says oligarchy." Implicitly, democracy is impossible. So that, apparently, was that.

The closure of the question seemed all the more complete in the light of the conclusions of Robert McKenzie's *British Political Parties* [McKenzie 1955], then a key work of reference on British party politics and power. His thesis was that for representational and Governmental reasons, in the British political system the Parliamentary Leadership dominated, and inevitably must dominate, the parties that they led. His conclusion was that the two major parties were basically alike in this respect, regardless of their rhetoric.

Though admiring the scholarship, I was never happy with the positions taken by either of these authorities. Ever since, although my work has taken various other turns, and been addressed to many other dimensions, I have been in critical dialogue with their texts in relation to the institutions of the British Labour Movement.

I began at that time a general quest for an understanding of the possibilities and limitations of intra-party democracy and for an intellectual framework which would hold my own critique of Michels and McKenzie. In relation to the Labour Party, I wanted to examine the twin problems: what was now the distribution of power and what were its variabilities over time? And, in each case, of course, why? In that quest I began a microscopic examination of the evidence in McKenzie in a way that proved very fruitful (as I shall explain later). I then started looking for the exceptions to the "is" and the "must be" in parties abroad, which were I thought usefully comparable to the British Labour Party. There were instances in Canada and Australia which did not seem to quite "fit" the Michels-McKenzie thesis.

My PhD thesis (and in a different form my first book) on the Labour Party Conference[9] was to be a very different, and in its complexity and detail a much larger enterprise from that which I had intended. It began as an international comparative study of party conferences and intra-party democracy, covering "Labour" parties (ie union-affiliated parties) in Canada, Australia, New Zealand and the UK. Initially, I aimed to compare and explore the different relationships between the Parliamentary Leadership of the parties and the extra-parliamentary parties, particularly the different party conferences. After a while this objective began to shift towards a focus mainly on a comparison of the conferences, their internal political arrangements, processes, and power relationships.

This comparison was to be handled within a model of conference power processes which I hoped to make into the basis of a universal "theory" of political conferences. Exactly what the immediate purpose of this model was, I was unclear. But, influenced by theorising that I had done on another project,[10] I thought that I saw a natural means of fitting all the emerging data into a model of "locations of dictatorial control" which might be exercised via a democratic conference.

Peculiarity: the agenda management

I soon began to realise that the project was hopelessly unhandleable geographically, and it was generating methodological doubts. Were any two conferences in different countries really the same institutions? Did they have similar composition and powers? Did they have the same functions? Did the actors give the same meanings to their activity? What might a detailed comparison tell us? At the same time I found myself extending and refining the theoretical model in the light of what I was learning. But, my attempt to make universal generalisations meant that it had to remain on a fairly high level of generality. I was beginning to enjoy the complexity, and growing refinement of the model, while worrying increasingly about its useful application.

Whilst I was worrying about those questions, the research took off in a new direction as a result of a surprising observation and a revealing remark. At the first Labour Party Conference I attended inside the hall, I watched with utter fascination an unexpected series of breathtakingly ruthless agenda manoeuvres which clearly advantaged the Party Leadership. I watched also what appeared to be extraordinary amenability on the part of many of the delegates in relation to this agenda management. I expected a much more powerful reaction from a conference denied the choices it might have had. Later I heard one delegate say to another, "How do they get away with it?".

That question reverberated round my head. Here was a puzzle based upon a peculiarity. The more I found out about the significance of the results of the agenda management, and the labyrinthine politics that went on around it, the more important the delegate's question appeared.

Slowly I shed the international comparative frame of reference and, very reluctantly and much more slowly, the theoretical model, which was mentally getting in the way of the build up of an appropriate framework for the single case (See Chapter 6). The delegate's plaintive query became the central, if unstated, puzzle, and trigger, of my research - the first extensive study of a British party conference.

"How did they get away with it" accepted in great measure *one element* of McKenzie's thesis, i.e. that power was being exercised in such a way as to favour the Party Leadership. At that time Harold Wilson's Labour Government was affirming its clear independence from the Party Conference and winning virtually all the votes there. So that part of the thesis was virtually indisputable.

I still had my eye on the other twin of the problem - the possible variabilities over time in the way that power was concentrated and might be redistributed. But, for the moment, that did not appear fruitful to pursue. What now faced me was the possibility of raising other questions - questions about the management of the agenda - which had not previously been asked by scholars of the Labour Party (or of other political parties as far as I knew).

What was the process of agenda management and what were the consequences for policymaking and the distribution of power?. One question was to lead to another in the process of Critical Examination. Who did it? What was done? How was it done? When was it done? Where was it done? With what consequences? It also became clear that these questions were more significant than the overall "why?" question which, once posed, had a rather obvious answer. These were therefore the problems to focus on.

They were problems not addressed at all in the literature. Indeed, at that time agenda politics seemed to fall outside the substance of any party political analysis. So much so, that the outline of my proposed book was, at one point, legitimately queried by the publishers. They initially asked me to "cut out the padding" on the agenda! I had patiently to explain the "peculiarity" of what went on and what they might be missing.

Eventually I was to amply illustrate the importance of agenda management in the distribution of power, and indicate how and why the agenda controls were often successful. I was also able to show that various features of Labour Party history - including its major ideological changes - could be reinterpreted via an examination of agenda management.

However, as I proceeded with that project it took on a second new dimension which allowed a re-evaluation and re-integration of my second original problem - what were the variabilities in the distribution of power over time?

It began to become clear to me in this period (in 1968) that a shift to the Left was taking place in the leadership of some key unions who held substantial votes at the Conference. As a result of the changes in union leadership, the old block of loyalist votes - allies of the Party leadership - was being broken. At the same time, there was a growing move in favour of intra-party democracy in the constituency parties.

I made the General Election of 1970 the end of the research period that I was examining and, as that date approached, my predictive judgement was that a revolt was waiting to happen over the neglect of the authority of the Party Conference.[Minken LPC 1978 pp 328-332 and LPC 1980 pp 364-5] That judgement, made against the view of much informed opinion at that time, turned out to be correct. This enabled me to connect the developing revolt with the one that had happened in the Labour Party after 1931 (which had also been followed by an attempt to recover and redefine intra-party democracy). Though it had been "on the back-burner" since I had shifted the focus onto agenda politics, I had never lost sight of the question of what were the variabilities in the distribution of power over time and particularly, what conditions might change this distribution. I could now see some of them beginning to appear as I judged that they appeared around 1931.

Hence, I was able to make a new interpretation of Labour Party history in terms of a pattern of waves of oligarchy and democracy, thus challenging McKenzie's version of the iron law of Labour oligarchy - the "must be" of his analysis. I explored some of the basic conditions for the re-assertion of intra-party democracy. These conditions, and the actions of the subsequent 1974-9 Labour Government, were to lead to a second and much more powerful Campaign for Labour Party Democracy "revolt" of 1979-81. Nevertheless, it was apparent that with the Labour Party back in Opposition after 1970, the Conference remained a highly managed and controlled event. The Parliamentary leadership was still the most powerful initiating and discretionary policymaking group in the party, albeit for the moment working under greater constraint.

Peculiarity : the union leaders

There was another peculiarity here - a big one, or rather a multiplicity of inter-related peculiarities - and my puzzling over it simmered away in the back of my mind for years. My later work, including my most important work on the trade union relationship with the Labour Party, gained a great deal from my own grumbling mental dissatisfaction with my earlier problem definition. I had focused, as did Michels and McKenzie, on the socio-psychological causes of the enhancement of the power of the Parliamentary Leadership, concentrating as they did, on the Parliamentary Leadership as the activating and controlling force. But I slowly came to see that the answers that I had given to the question, "how do they get away with it?", though very illuminating, were not fully satisfactory.

To an important degree, the success of the agenda management was reliant upon a particular approach to politics by the trade unions. Thus a more satisfactory and complete answer could only be focused not on the political leadership of the party but on the behaviour of the unions.

Here I could also see that there was a need to counter a new and dominant myth of the whole period of my research from its commencement in 1967. It was the unions, it was said, which, by finance and votes, controlled the Labour Party. They established its policy and supervised its organisational and political management. It was hard to get away from this myth. It was there in newspaper after newspaper and news broadcast after news broadcast. It was even there at the same time as the acknowledgement of the pre-eminence of the Parliamentary Leadership. Thus, even contradiction did not halt it. The unions were always portrayed as seeking to maximise their power and use it fully to their advantage. Yet something else was clearly going on under my eyes.

In spite of the movement for more democracy, and of a redistribution of power in the party which the new Left-wing unions appeared to support, in practice these leaders seemed unwilling or unable to play an active central role in pushing any procedural changes which would secure these objectives, or in challenging in any fundamental way the pre-eminent position in policymaking of the parliamentary leadership. All the time I kept coming back to, and stumbling over, the peculiarity that the new Left-wing union leaders of the 1970s, particularly Jack Jones of the Transport Workers and Hugh Scanlon of the Engineers, continued to allow many of the controls to function. Why, given their expressed political agenda? And why did they allow the Parliamentary Leadership to continue as the pre-eminent force in party policymaking?

More fundamental in appraising the distribution of power within the party, if so much formal power - particularly the bulk of party finance and the majority of Party Conference votes - was at the disposal of union leaders, why did they not use it to the full in controlling the party? So, though I continued the research on the conference with the original problem-focus, in my mind this frame of reference question was beginning to be superseded. The focus on the Parliamentary Leadership was becoming reoriented to a focus on the union leadership. The peculiarities of trade union behaviour were becoming the problem, and ultimately it commanded my pursuit. I became aware that, fifty years previously, an astute German observer of British politics, Egon Wertheimer, had come to the same problem by a different route but far from giving an explanation had simply redescribed it.

Over a long period my quest for a satisfactory answer in terms of trade union behaviour became the subject of many Conference and seminar papers, articles and chapters before and after the book on the Labour Party Conference was completed. In the end, it was to become the mainspring of *The Contentious Alliance: trade unions and the Labour Party*, which, like the earlier book on the Conference, was to be published, after a prolonged gestation, on the eve of a new movement of opinion within the Labour Party, and was to feed into the internal politics of the party in a way that raised interest in the research and legitimised its importance.

This was a comprehensive analysis of the complex relations between trade unions and the Labour Party. Its most important and original feature was the answer that I gave to the question that had provoked me for years. In it I illustrated the way that the relationship was patterned by inhibitions and unwritten rules underpinned by a cluster of fundamental values. The rules and the inhibitions arose out of an understanding of the differentiation of the spheres of the industrial and the political and what roles and behaviour were proper to each. Although there were mutual constraints, and inhibitions on both sides, the most significant effect was the limitation placed upon those who held the largest armoury of formal power - the trade unions.

This framework provided a new theory of power in the Labour Party. It enabled observers to see the party-union relationship in contrasting terms to those in which it was often viewed. It challenged the normal assumptions about the drive for power-maximisation of union leaders, and it gave a much more complete and plausible explanation of the pre-eminence of the Parliamentary

Leadership within a pattern of constraints. From this framework I was also able to offer new interpretations of a wide range of developments and to apply the theoretical framework to other features of Labour Party and trade union political activity.

I shall explain later how, and through what processes, this framework came about; how the many new perspectives and interpretations were creatively generated, and how, at one point, the central problem had to be reframed yet again. Over time, the pursuit of this explanatory framework has been the core of my research. Over time also, the pursuit has generated a much wider framework of research interests, projects and publications (Political Communication, Political Finance, Political Leadership, Labour Foreign Policy, Social-Democracy, British Communism and Eurocommunism, as it then was, and Second World War Radicalism) moving away from the central interest. But the peculiarity and the core problem described here have triggered much of my work.

I will now leave this for the moment (elements of the story will be taken up in Chapters Five, Six, Seven and particularly Eight) and explore another dimension of the mental process involved in research - the psychology of the creative mind.

CHAPTER END NOTES

[1] Jacob.W.Getzels and Mihaly Csikszentmihalyi argue that in creative thinking and performance in the visual arts and in general, problem discovery (finding a problem) may be more important than solving a problem, [Getzels and Csikszentmihalyi 1976 p 82].

[2] [Howard and Sharp 1985 pp 28-33] have a very interesting section on the application of three creativity generating techniques (analogy, relevance trees and morphological analysis) to the formulation of research topics.

[Blaxter, Hughes and Tight 1996 pp 30-42] offer a range of helpful suggestions. There are also two good chapters on the process, 'From topics to questions' and 'From questions to problems' in [Booth, Colomb and Williams 1995 pp 35-63]. For a feminist experience see Haggis, J., 'The feminist research process - defining a topic' in [Stanley 1990 pp 67-79].

[3] Thus the activities of the Detective and the Patternmaker in Chapters Five and Six, and the heuristic thinking explored in Chapter Six can all be helpful in this process of problem seeking.

[4] Lasswell, H.I. 'The structure and function of communication in society' in [Byson 1948].

[5] Only recently, some twenty years after I had developed my own systematic pursuit of the peculiar, did I read 'The serendipity pattern' in [Merton 1957 pp 103-108] on the way that the "fairly common experience of observing an unanticipated, anomalous and strategic datum" (p 104) stimulates the curiosity and become the occasion for a fresh direction of enquiry leading to a new hypothesis(p 108). Merton (p 104) also cites Charles Sanders Peirce on the strategic role of the surprising fact.

[6] Guilford in [Taylor and Getzels 1975 p 46].

[7] "Strangeness" and "peculiarity" here mean the same but as I work I tend to think of a sense of peculiarity arising out of particular and specific empirical observations and I think of strangeness as a characteristic of more general patterns. I generally see these as the different spheres of the Detective and the Patternmaker (examined in Chapter Six) but I am not fully consistent in this and in any case these characters are simply figments of one mind's imagination.

[8] [Baker 1994 pp 36-7] examining case studies of the work of Elijah Anderson [Anderson 1978] and Rosabeth M. Kanter [Kanter 1977].

[9] [Minkin 1978, 1980].

[10] This was a draft theoretical chapter that I had produced for a book on Dictatorship which had been commissioned by Penguin Books from one of

my tutors, Peter Nettl, who had asked me to become a joint author. He was killed shortly afterwards and I was left with my model and an unwillingness to lose it.

CHAPTER FOUR

THE PSYCHOLOGY OF CREATIVE RESEARCH

THE INTELLECTUAL AND THE PSYCHOLOGICAL

As has already been made apparent, there is much more to creative research than what is normally thought of as the engagement of intellectual skills. In the field of creativity studies there is a consensus that, over and above the basic minimum of intelligence required for mastery of the field, differences in creativity are related to non-cognitive [Freeman, Butcher and Christie 1968 p 15], "non-intellective" factors[1]. This insight from the literature on creativity adds an important dimension to our understanding of the research process, which is often discussed only in "intellective" terms.

The "non-intellective" factors to which attention has been drawn in the study of creativity are generally seen as expressions of the personality, and have been described in a variety of different ways: qualities and traits, dispositions and motivations, attitudes, expectations, beliefs, temperament, even style and values. Because it accords with how the word is commonly used in this context, I have brought these factors together here under the heading of "the psychological".

MacKinnon, author of the entry on creativity in the International Encyclopedia of the Social Sciences, tells us that although there is "no single mould into which all who are creative will fit"

[MacKinnon 1968 p 440] there is "an impressive congruence of findings" [MacKinnon 1968 p 438] concerning the psychological characteristics of the creative person. However, Perkins, another distinguished student of creativity, has noted that one encounters many variations in the different lists that are given, and that exceptions to the findings are easy to come across, as are differences related to gender, and field of work.[2] So, whilst noting the findings of this literature, I am going to stay close to my own experience, and occasionally to my observation of the performance of others. I shall also indicate exactly why I consider that these particular characteristics are important.

CREATIVITY AND PERSONALITY

Perceptions of the link between creativity and personality have origins which go back to the ancient Greeks who related genius to madness.[3] Since that time there have been two competing conceptions of genius, the one seeing creativity as the expression of a well balanced personality, the other seeing genius associated with mental instability[4]. I do not propose to dwell much on that particular linkage except to note the degree to which it has become apparent to me that certain individual differences facilitate the creative process whilst others inhibit or otherwise limit it.

Looking back over my research supervision and experience of the personality characteristics that get in the way of quality research, I can think of many such examples. There were cases of loss of confidence, fear of standing alone, unwillingness to risk failure, lack of persistence, eagerness for immediate rewards, not to mention examples of writer's block and procrastination, all of which militated against what would be measured as intellectual competence.

In the context of research there were even behaviour patterns which would normally be considered communally healthy, but which in extreme form could precipitate disaster -sociability is one example. Some of the recent texts on "How to Do Research" do now pay attention to some of the worst emotional problems of the researcher's life - coping with loneliness, anxiety, boredom, frustration, and the general ups-and-downs of the research experience.[5] There has also been a helpful shift recently in the role of the supervisor towards "the critical friend."[6]

However, academics operating in a milieu where the emphasis is on the intellectual assessment of a presentation, often find it difficult to accommodate (and share with each other, let alone with students) the fact that what they are involved in, and judging, is also a psychological performance. Also, because performance is all and assessment is perpetual, academics are more than normally reluctant to let the protective mask slip and allow the personal "weaknesses" and idiosyncrasies of their own work practice to be visible - or even, perhaps, to be fully acknowledged to themselves.

Yet, I would suggest that in terms of understanding and enhancing research creativity, that introspection, that openness and that discussion, ought periodically to take place. My experience suggests that new postgraduate research students are not made aware as often as they should be that the psychological "problems" are a task-oriented phenomenon intrinsic to the experience of research and common to many who are creatively fertile. In research as in other creative activities " ..feelings of confidence, conviction and commitment tempered by self-doubt; caution and humility mixed with bold originality are dynamically implicated in the psychological matrices within which creative endeavours evolve" [Bargar and Duncan 1990 p 61].

The study of creativity indicates that an awareness of the inner life, and an openness to feelings and emotions, are characteristics associated with creative people[7], and therefore to be encouraged. Individual students differ in the response that is required from supervisors at different stages of the research, and different personalities can respond to different styles of supervision. But, there are times when the greatest gift a teacher can give to others, in terms of encouragement, may well be simply to admit that Homer both feels and nods.

I emphasise this also because it is an area where some self-improvement that assists the creative process can unquestionably take place. Our development from novice to mature researcher can be a movement of self-discovery in which, to varying degrees, motivations, attitudes, and self images are modified or changed. In that sense, we can, to some extent, remake ourselves, inventing our own behaviour to make it more creative [Perkins 1981 p 218].

These characteristics of individual personality do matter in the conduct and management of research. As I will illustrate, their influence is pervasive in the creative research process.

MOTIVATION

There is little dispute in the literature on creativity with the view that one of the salient characteristics of a creative achiever is strong motivation[8]. Even the important initial decision on the form, scope and ambitions of the research project may be influenced by our motivations.

As the researcher then faces and overcomes a wide range of problems, the intensity of the motivation can be a crucial factor in research management and productivity. Certainly, no amount of domain mastery or creativity-relevant skills can compensate for the lack of it. Anthony Storr draws our attention to the relevance of the difference between two of Conan Doyles's characters, the Holmes bothers. Sherlock's brother Mycroft was superior in intellect but recoiled at the idea of having to rush around and do things [Storr 1992 p 49]. It is perhaps not so much the rushing around (although the energy of the researcher in the field is not to be underestimated), it is more often the quiet steely state of mind, prepared to engage in the longer term perspective, sustaining commitment, ploughing steadily through "the slings and arrows".

It has been found that motivation that is primarily intrinsic (work chosen and pursued out of interest, personal satisfaction or personal challenge) is more conducive to sustaining creative effort than extrinsic motivation (working on it because you "have to"). There is a strong connection between primarily intrinsic motivation and the highest levels of creativity[9]. It helps most, perhaps, if the project is a labour of love.

From the first, my own research motivation has been overwhelmingly intrinsic. The projects that I pursued involved problems that I was intensely curious about. In general I saw, and still see, the research as potentially a means of furthering a range of beneficial values. This motivation is constantly replenished by reactions to a variety of obvious public fallacies, and sometimes deliberately engendered misconceptions. I am driven both by a feeling that I have to seek to know "the truth" of it, and that I need to communicate that understanding.

In the process, as my expertise has grown, so the deep specialism has bred a passionate obsessiveness. This has carried with it a fascination with the minutiae of the field and a constantly aroused curiosity about how the field is changing. Both replenish commitment to the work. The fundamental rewards have been a sense of personal growth, self-worth and belonging. I have been relatively uninterested in formal positions, titles and promotions (making it much easier to step into a semi-early retirement). As for the financial gain, this was never much of a consideration in relation to being a scholar.

However, most people have to work to live, and are dependent upon the income from their working opportunities. "What came first", Ira Gershwin was asked, "the lyrics or the music?" He is said to have replied," What came first was the contract". To that extent, for most people, including myself, creativity is motivated both intrinsically and extrinsically [Adams 1988 p 7]. Nevertheless, money has not affected my choice of research, nor my attitude towards it.

Most researchers expect, and look forward to receiving, some form of social reward when their work is successful. This too can have its influence on the choice, management and presentation of research and the drive to complete it. When I research and write, I have a strong need for my peers to admire the quality and integrity of the work, and I have a strong sense of history waiting to judge me. My desire for this approval and respect has influenced my research aspirations and my research conduct since I started. It has not, however, produced a preoccupation with fame and publicity, although I have had a little of both at times. I can work the more effectively in the way that I do, as an academic researcher and as a political advisor, because I am rather uncomfortable under the public gaze and do not need to keep my name in the public eye.

For every individual the motivational mixture varies. In terms of creativity, much would appear to depend on how far the individual interprets and desires any extrinsic incentives. It is the judgement of one distinguished scholar of creativity, Arieti, that throughout history, external incentives and awards have had "a well known reinforcing effect" on motivation [Arieti 1976 p 324]. It is the judgement of another, Csikszentmihalyi, that "at different times, in different cultural settings, a concern for fame or money does not seem to have detracted from creative accomplishment"[10].

The need for creative achievement - and I certainly had that need - can itself be an intrinsic motivation regardless of whether the task is interesting in its own right.[11] This motivation to be creative, and the priority attached to it, can be influenced by external conditions. As might be expected, a working environment encouraging to creative experimentation is more likely to evoke it than an environment that is not[12]. And, as became painfully obvious to me, creative motivation can be adversely affected by external discouragement and by low expectations which may then become internalised, or may reinforce an internal lack of confidence.

DEFERMENT AND RISK-TAKING

The intensity of our motivation and our aspirations are also at work in what we regard as adequate solutions. At key points in the research process, some will settle for the use of available ideas or for the first ideas that appear suitable; others will seek a greater vision of what might be involved, pursue other alternatives, and the full flowering of the ideas that are generated. They are motivated to defer closure of the project if they judge closure to be premature - particularly if the immediately available solution would not be the best attainable.

In my case this motivation to deferment is additionally influenced by a need to be comprehensive in my coverage of the problem, or even the problem area. It arises from a nervous sense of academic vulnerability, as well as from a desire to illustrate total and thorough command of any and every possible dimension. This is not necessarily to be recommended - and it has been resisted in this present study.

Deferment may be uncomfortable. It involves the psychological willingness (and the values) to forgo "the glittering immediate in favour of the shadowy but possibly richer future"[13]. "Richer" here can mean both in terms of understanding and also social recognition.

There are moments in research when one experiences a yearning for an immediate recognition of what has been achieved. It is a feeling that is very powerful when you are a novice researcher. However, this yearning lives uneasily with the knowledge that the completion of the project is not yet satisfactory to the researcher's own standards. It takes an exercise of conscious determination to avoid the temptation to go for the immediate recognition.

It may also involve a moderate and calculated risk-taking in the pursuit of the novel. This is a motivational feature often seen as a characteristic of creative behaviour.[14] It has been said that "Great creators are great risk takers in their own fashion. We often do not fully appreciate this reality, owing to a widely circulated myth about the creative genius".[15]

In this risk-taking we are not here talking of capricious behaviour, nor of Damon Runyan's Nathan Detroit, praying for luck to be a lady. I have no sense of identification with that experience. It is more the readiness to experiment with ideas and to risk the possibility of making mistakes, and looking foolish [Cropley 1967 pp 42-3]. It has also been seen as a pitting of one's own efforts against the deeper uncertain circumstances [Taylor and Barron 1963 p 386], [Maslow 1976 p 65] - a calculation in the situation where we make the decision that we have a reasonable expectation of being able to handle what will develop.[16] Such judgements are always context-bound and are influenced by a range of considerations, including the exigencies of completion dates. In practice (as I shall illustrate in Chapter Eight about my own work) such may be the motivation and confidence of the research specialist that it may not look quite such a big risk to those taking it.[17] It may feel more like an act of faith; a kind of trust in the self that we can deal with any novel circumstances [Maslow 1976 p 65]. This trust, and the commitment that goes with it, can at times change the probabilities of success [Goleman, Kaufman and Ray 1993 p 42].

The motivation to risk, and the ability to live with the experience of such risk, is particularly tested at moments of acute adversity in the project. Not all creative people find their work a struggle, but metaphors for creative production are often heavy with psychological references which involve deep emotions.

EMOTIONS, MOODS AND SELF-MANAGEMENT

In these references metaphors of motherhood are not unusual. This is Balzac,

> To pass from conception to execution, to produce, to bring the idea to birth, to raise the child laboriously from infancy, to put it nightly to sleep surfeited, to kiss it in the mornings with the hungry heart of a mother, to clean it, to clothe it fifty times over in new garments which it tears and casts away....[18]

These images arouse in me a deep sense of familiarity. They are very close to some of the emotions that were generated in my own long-term projects. These could change rapidly as the project was experienced in its various phases and circumstances. In these changes other images and emotions could be evoked. They included a game, a disorientation (lost in the forest), a struggle, a heroic act, a carrier (of the creative flow), a love affair, an obsession, a revulsion, a beast to overcome and (on release) a peculiar mixture of liberation, estrangement and possessiveness. My creative momentum (even, at times, my ability to think clearly) was closely related to these changing moods.

Such moods may be complex and, at times, initially surprising enough to damage the will to go on. I had initially expected the sense of achievement and anticipation to rise as I approached completion. Indeed, it did as I imagined my book's publication. But this was accompanied by flashes of another mood - an unanticipated and sudden mixture of ennui and over-familiarity. It was a vaguely depressed condition in which the excitement of approaching completion was drowned by a sense of the stale and, it felt, unbearable ordinariness of what I was seeing in front of me. This mood made its terrible appearance despite the many discoveries or creative innovations that I had made. And it all seemed so damned obvious. Why had it taken me so long? These are undermining feelings which I have now learned, in the main, to take in my stride as a fleeting "false consciousness".

The mood swings go on till the last dot and comma (and beyond, if we have to deal with publishers). As a novice researcher, I had also assumed that the final stages would be a "tidying up" (as some people called it) with just a few minor difficulties to sort out. In practice I found that it was in the final stages that new and important creative movements took place, both within the presentation and even (as I shall show later) within the substantive project. It was also in this period that some of the most nerve racking problems occurred. Sod's Law had the tendency to make its appearance just at the point where one's resilience seemed to be weakened by fatigue.

It follows from all this, and I emphasise again, that managing a research project is not simply a formal technical, methodological or intellectual task. Success is related to our attitude towards the tasks and difficulties and our ability to manage the changing emotions and moods intelligently.[19] It is an essential, but often under-recognised, research ability.

I have couched this in individual and, perhaps, introverted terms, but it must be recognised that research does not take place in a social vacuum. It takes place within a set of work and domestic relationships which are worse for some than for others, and at times feel as though they were organised to cause the researcher maximum aggravation.

In the face of the inevitable personal and social conditions that arise, we attempt to develop our own techniques for protecting ourselves and for day after day, as it were, turning ourselves on in the face of a variety of moods and situations. We try to develop sensitivities which recognise warnings of when to stop, how to avoid distraction, and when to seek it. At the very least, we learn how to respect time and how we prioritise it for work and rest. If we are unskilful in this, we are unskilful at research.

PERSISTENCE AND EFFORT

Also we learn in practice the rewards of marrying committed work with dogged pursuit. Creativity has generally been linked with qualities of perseverance and persistence.[20] "High, but not the highest intelligence, combined with the greatest degree of persistence, will achieve greater eminence than the highest degree of intelligence with somewhat less persistence."[21]

This persistence is reflected in the willingness to undertake sustained effort. Francis Galton's view of great achievement in any field was that it was not just the product of ability but of zeal and the capacity for hard work [Storr 1989 p 251]. What is different between researchers is often focused motivation and mental energy as much as an intrinsic intellectual talent. It is in this sense that Edison is said to have described creativity as involving "ninety-nine per cent perspiration, one per cent inspiration" .

"What do we deserve credit for?" asked Francis Crick about the discovery of DNA? The answer that he gave was "persistence" and a willingness to discard untenable ideas. Despite being so early in their research careers, once he and Watson had selected the problem they stuck to it. "Practically nobody else was prepared to make such an intellectual investment" [Crick 1989 pp 74-5].

ANXIETY

Given these considerations it is not surprising that, for most of us, the research experience is accompanied by episodic bouts of deep anxiety and becomes a test of nerves. We would like our performance to be judged a success. We fantasise about rave reviews. We are, however, all too conscious of the difficulties that confront us in the project. We are at times unsure where it is going, and sometimes whether it is going anywhere at all.

As I became all too aware, the nervous tension is particularly acute for young academics. Bertrand Russell, no less, recalls:

> When I was young each fresh piece of serious work used to seem to me for a time -perhaps a long time, to be beyond my powers. I would fret myself into a nervous state for fear that it was never going to come right [Russell 1956 p 195].

Over the years Russell, having grown to understand better his own creative process, apparently developed ways of dealing with the anxiety. But for many people it is a persistent or episodic accompaniment.

I am reminded of when I was a postgraduate student on a trip down to Oxford for a funeral. I was travelling with another young academic and a very senior member of the profession. The latter had a list of publications a yard long, was on innumerable prestigious bodies and lectured and talked with a lovely ease and bonhomie. On the way, talking about research, I mentioned how unprepared I had been for the psychology of research, for its booms and slumps and stomach-turning misadventures. "I suppose", I said, "that with your level of achievement and experience you don't have any problem with that?" "Oh, no" he said (and at this point we both leaned forward to catch the reassurance and the secret, if any). "I have no problem. I just take two of these every morning." Thereupon, he produced from his bag a huge bottle of green and white tablets.

COMMUNITY, SHOWBUSINESS, MARKET AND "COURAGE OF THE MIND"

Some of this anxiety is connected with the fact that in academia we live within two value systems. We are in a community of scholars sharing our learning, gaining a deep pleasure and contagious excitement from our meeting of minds, and feeling a pride in our common achievement. But we are also sometimes competitors in a market place of intellectual property.

What results is an atmosphere that, in a way, resembles showbusiness. We are judged on the quality of our performance, but also in relation to others. Our reputation, our career futures, even our identity, are heavily involved in the success or otherwise of our performance in relation to these others. This comparative performance is, these days, ever more closely scrutinised, assessed and evaluated. We would not be human if we did not, to some degree, fear this scrutiny.[22] We try hard to build a co-operative relationship with others in the community of scholars and particularly with close academic friends. At times we try to negotiate areas of work which will not bring us into tricky confrontation. But nobody can (nor should) say where the creative process will lead. And at times we are in contention and competition.

In these circumstances, and accompanied by guilt feelings, the inner anxiety at times makes itself felt, particularly if we have been working hard on a project for some time. ("If I show them this and we start discussing it, how will we know to whom the idea belongs?" "If they are working in this area, will they publish it first?" And occasionally, "Will they steal it?") We try to dismiss all this as unworthy, to laugh at ourselves and wish it were different, but it is very difficult to become immune from the worst of these fears and psychologically very painful when worst fears are realised.

This endemic anxiety (and the tightness of the masks) has been accentuated greatly in recent years by the need to find financial support, and the need to fulfil quantitative as well as qualitative, targets in publications. And as market commercialism and performance indicators have come to dominate, so it has tended to undermine elements of community and collegiality, and to accentuate stress and anxiety. But, even without these new threatening pressures the anxieties are integral.

In general, the more creatively ambitious the research project, the greater the stress. The more problematic the enterprise, the messier, more hesitant, more fluid and more failure-ridden it is. The more ambitious the project, the longer the researcher has to live with and to tolerate the ambiguities involved. Tolerance of ambiguity - feeling comfortable when facing situations that are ill defined - is a quality considered "almost a *sine qua non* of creative performance".[23]

Under all these pressures, there has to be a strong sense of autonomy involving self-direction and independence of judgement[24] - what has been called a "courage of the mind"[25]. This independence of judgement manifests itself in many forms, including a willingness to challenge assumptions and orthodoxies, but also to deal with a variety of social pressures. In particular, the researcher has, at some stage, to live with pressures to publish. For some people such pressure may be the right thing, stimulating a new effort or calling a halt to an incessant "tidying up".[26] But for others the pressure may be both inappropriate and destructive. What is appropriate in pushing somebody to write or to finish the writing, may be inappropriate in terms of pushing them to think through a problem, or to refine a conceptual framework.

So much depends not only on the personality of the individual scholar but on the complexity of the problem under investigation, and where the project is in the researcher's creative time-frame. Inappropriate pressures can add heavily to the burdens of deferment. They can interfere (i.e make irrelevant mental noise) in the mind in ways which damage the creative process, and they can force decisions which are not the best for the circumstances of the project.

Social pressure to publish is part of the life of a researcher, even if it is only concerned curiosity, "Where is it?". However, much of the pressure is now built into the contemporary British academic culture as a result of new procedures of academic research assessment. The demands of the present form of assessment tend to reinforce inhibitions upon risk, and to discourage deferring closure of the project if it threatens to go over a deadline.

There comes a point where, in search of immediate publication, the novice researcher faces, in effect, the kind of advice James Thurber once received as a young journalist facing a deadline - "Don't get it right, get it written." The young researcher in today's climate might at times have to follow that advice. Certainly resisting it takes a degree of strength.

RESILIENCE, CONFIDENCE AND THE DESTRUCTIVE CRITIC

Developing this strength and the resilience necessary to live with the false trails and errors of judgement, with the distractions of other work and the pressures of time, as well as the sense of competition from others, seems to me to be a characteristic feature of the successful mature researcher. But, much more than is publicly acknowledged, there is often a struggle with a potential loss of confidence. Such confidence is crucial in creative activity.[27] As Samuel Smiles noted long ago, "it has been said that half the failures in life arise from pulling in one's horse whilst he is leaping"[Smiles 1996 edn p 198]. Loss of confidence can reduce energy levels, crush motivation and reduce aspirations. Of course, over-confidence, and a feeling of the lack of challenge, can also reduce motivation, [Adams 1987 p 48], [Entwistle 1988 pp 196-7] but it is not a problem that I have widely noticed in private discussions with those involved in academic research, in spite of the high level of accomplishment and in spite of the masks.

Self-awareness is an important asset in preserving confidence. In particular it is a necessary condition for gaining a degree of control over, or distancing from, the inner game, as played against a variety of destructive and obstructive internal opponents within the psyche that interfere with performance[28].

The primary enemy of creative confidence is that internal dialogue which takes the form of, what has been called, the Destructive Critic ("That's no good; it's a failure. It can't be done anyway; look at all the obstacles and problems. Anyway *you* can't do it. They will find you out. They will laugh at you. Hide it. Give up.") As Deena Metzger notes, "The external tyrannies are familiar to us, and we know their consequences and sometimes how to challenge or combat them. But the internal tyrannies are another matter. I have never met a writer who has not at one time or another been sabotaged by the critic within."[29]

The Destructive Critic gains enormous assistance from pathological perfectionism. This is not the rigorous drive to secure quality and distinctiveness, but the voice that tells us that nothing we ever do is good enough. It is reinforced by the fear of failure and encourages us to think that if we do not try to risk anything special, we can not be shown to have failed. It gains assistance also from useless and inappropriate comparisons (Compare your first draft with what X published, or compare your draft with your last polished publication.)

In most creative activities it is rare to get it right immediately, the first time something significant is attempted. To strive for immediate perfection in the process of writing may invite all manner of problems, including writer's block. Neil Simon points out that "some people misinterpret what writer's block is. They assume you can't think of a single thing. Not true. You can think of hundreds of things. You just don't like any of them"[Simon 1996 p 159].

THE DELICATE BALANCE

For many, an abundance of anxiety, worked upon by the Destructive Critic within, inhibits and undermines. On the other hand a degree of anxiety can be an asset, a necessary evil that provides the impetus to effort. It can lead to careful advance planning. It can also provide a reinforcement of energy. It can provide an adrenalin-pulsing spur to an examination of a wider range of possibilities.[30] But, the benefits depend upon us retaining an optimism that the task can be completed[31]. "The feeling that you can handle a task encourages intrinsic motivation, the feeling that the task is beyond you undermines it" [Perkins 1986 p 117].

There is a balance here which will differ from individual to individual. For me, it has been a delicate and, at times, very uncomfortable struggle - particularly difficult as a young researcher. Developing and retaining the confidence that I could do it has been vital. Increasingly, at crucial stages, it has enabled me to stay with a problem, move steadily into the unknown as far as might be necessary, in spite of the difficulties and the costs in time and postponed rewards, and to feel that wherever I emerge I will be able to handle the situation. The trick here maybe is, to adapt a line from the novelist Susan Hill, "don't look down"[32]. This means to me, don't focus on the immensity of it all, focus on the next problem or stage of work that you place in front of yourself.

Yet, at the same time, lurking around here, has also been the fear of failure. This has accompanied me since a childhood of what feels in retrospect to have been endless shortcomings and an epic lack of achievement. I am forever fighting with that past self-image and sometimes the fear of "going back". For some, this fear of failure could have fatally damaged their level of aspiration. For some also, the emotional kick of the various "failures" inherent in the creative research process can damage the will to go on. Thankfully, for reasons that I am still not fully clear about, it has not had that ultimate effect on me. The fear and the experience of "failing," in the main, tend to drive me forward.

It must be said, however, that it is sometimes a struggle. Indeed, there are crucial moments when it seems like my whole future is balanced on a knife-edge. It feels that a puff of wind, one way or the other, could make the difference between giving up or going on. As Fiona Williams expresses it, under these and other pressures, "you can be driven under, driven crazy or driven to write"[Williams 1993 p21]. In my own case the balance has generally tipped on the right side. The nearest to an explanation that I can give is to suggest that it involves a sentiment, an act of will and, at times, a sense of support.

There seems to be an aggressive and deeply resentful sentiment within me related to my past experiences; an "I'll show those bastards" motivation which so far has been just about strong enough to conquer the most adverse effects and detrimental working consequences of the anxiety and the fear. However, an understanding of this feature of my psyche has also led to this becoming a consciously engendered mood derived from a self-image of the strong and defiant - an act of will in the face of any landslide of difficulties which threatens to submerge me.

The strength and will to go on has often been bolstered by my working friendships. We gain all the time from those to whom we gravitate to give us companionship and, to a certain extent, reassurance and uplift in the solitary quest of the creative mind. Chance again is in play in whom we meet, but fundamentally we choose, and negotiate the closeness of, our working friendships in a world where we need each other to share our vulnerabilities and give intellectual and psychological nourishment to each other.[33]

Of course it is also true, as I have learned from experience, that whilst many of those that we relate to have the capacity for sensitive support and the sharing of criticisms, ideas and problems, others have the occasional urge to undermine and destroy. If you are not aware of this, careful in your relationships and robust in managing defences, the underminer and destroyer can forge a secret alliance with the Destructive Critic within. At the very least this can take a terrible toll of the mental time which should be more creatively engaged.

SELF-IMAGE

The cultivated self-image which bolsters the act of will has a more general significance. Self-belief and positive self-image -visualising the self as a person possessing creative talent - is recognised to be an important element in creative motivation.[34] MacKinnon, studying architects, makes the point at its strongest, "..we have found that self image and ego ideal are of crucial importance in determining the level of creativeness..".[35] Such images are often deeply rooted but they can be modified and added to. Others can assist us in this favourable reconstruction, but we can also consciously adopt ways of thinking about ourselves in action which reinforce the general encouragement - as I shall later illustrate.

In times of deepest adversity, there is for me a boot-straps process involved in the use of images. It has been a vital component of crisis situations that I have developed an image of myself as not only creatively skilled at dealing with problems, but also as an exceptionally determined person - a person who will never give up ("You did it once, you can do it again"). In this process, I try to frame prominently in my mind the examples of the adversity that I overcame in the past.

THE HELTER-SKELTER

In any research process, there are always the bad days to endure when the project appears to be moving into yet another crisis. Not surprisingly therefore, most researchers have problems of uncertainty and huge dips in confidence as predicament follows predicament, and obstacle follows obstacle. Part of the problem is that even the most consistent of researchers finds that their level of efficiency and creative performance varies from period to period, even from day to day. This appears to be generally true of creative production.[36] Also, in pursuit of their objectives even the most skilful researchers find that from time to time they have to move back as well as forward, acknowledge error or overwhelming obstacles along a projected path, and sometimes feel disheartened as a consequence. These variations, adjustments and changes of mood are intrinsic to the interaction between the researcher and the project, and emotional repercussions can be reflected back into the way we approach the work.

Certainly for me it's like that. Since I first set out, I have days when I feel that I am of very limited intelligence and my work is "crap".

For as long as I can remember I have had surges of feeling that either I'm "not up to it" or that I'm "past it". At such times I am always falling asleep ("I'm sure that there's something wrong with me, I'll have to go to the doctor - again"). On these days, I have some deeply averse reactions to the project, and at times appear to be caught in a downward spiral of confidence and competence. On these days, everything seems to go wrong at once. As Woody Allen might say, "Not only is there no God but you can't even find a printer that works."

One has to get used to the fact that there are always periods of,

the sleepless nights,
the daily fights,
the quick toboggan when you reach the heights[37]

However, the saving fact is that there are the heights. I have learned from experience the lesson that I will go up, as well as down, in confidence.

Patience is essential in living with this roller-coaster of moods. More often than not, I have a sense of purpose and quiet satisfaction in just being "on the job" and knowing the questions to ask. I also have many periods when I have a deep sense of professional competence, I think that I'm quite smart, I feel quite healthy and I would be nothing else but a researcher. There is also a mood (which accords with Csikszentmihalyi's description of "flow") in which I have such a sense of productive immersion that I feel at one with the creative experience and I forget the fatigue, ignore the pains in the hands, don't bother about the acid indigestion and I allow the music to play me.

The feeling of professional well-being is at its peak after a breakout from some (to me) outrageous problem. I have, I feel, reached a plateau after climbing a sheer cliff in the pouring rain holding on by my fingertips. Less often, but enough to make research the rewarding life activity that it is, it has involved for me a sense of excitement as I saw a very revealing connection, made a discovery, confirmed a novel interpretation, found a wonderful form appearing on the page, or seen the clearly emerging shape of a new conceptual pattern. On these very special days, I feel fulfilled and I have sometimes a sense of soaring upwards. We all respond in different ways to these moments, but I can easily imagine what others feel when they describe their elation at the sense of creative accomplishment. One eminent woman scientist even says, "I felt I was born for that moment....Let me tell you, there's not an 'I love you' in the world that can touch it. Nothing."[38]

Remembering all those good feelings, the fulfilling moods and that occasional sharp uplift is itself a source of retaining confidence. And an important motivating drive.

SUCCESS AND THE USE OF FAILURE

In developing our own mantra of confidence-building self-therapy, and in our dialogue with the Destructive Critic within, there is always something to build on in what we have achieved in the past. And in fighting the Destructive Critic, it is particularly vital that we are not undermined and misled by the comparison we make with others. Most of us carry in our heads images of the successful people - the others who are better than we are at something. There are always many of them, and it is all to the good if they are a source of education and inspiration, but destructive if we are constantly measuring ourselves by some idealised comparison.

We have of course to accord the greatest respect to, and can derive inspiration from, the legendary research figures and their activities.

Newton, Darwin and Einstein come up all the time in the literature and in educated popular consciousness. Valuable insight into the creative process has come from the study of these and other figures outstandingly successful in their various fields. But, creative ability tends to be over-associated in our minds with these specially gifted individuals and their impressive, even intimidating, Eureka moments. There are many forms of creative process and many levels of creative expression. And "genius", with abilities which appear to transcend the human, is rarely understood in context. Such people are normally building upon the work of countless others - if only to command the understanding of what it is that needs to be transcended. We rarely have a full appreciation of the circumstances in which their creative product emerged, nor a full understanding of the operational flaws of the creator in its production. The fact is that the process of creative invention (virtually everybody's process in any field of research) is characterised by an experimental trial, error and feedback. If the experiment is not on the apparatus or on the page it is in the mind.

It has even been indicated that there is a beneficial link between quantity and quality of output of ideas,[39] that "when it comes to creativity, if one takes more shots one scores more goals".[40] In this linkage, the erroneous or weak or non-productive ideas are many times as numerous as those that are well founded. The thing is that, as the distinguished economist Jevons confessed, "no record remains of more than the hundredth part".[41] In such creative experimentation and invention there are "many false starts and dead ends".[42] Indeed it could be put another way. In exceptional creativity, the highest and most acclaimed successes "are constructed on the low rubble of humiliating failure."[43]

FULFILMENT, THE PILGRIM AND FAUST

In the face of a variety of setbacks, obstacles, tests and temptations, the mental outlook of the creative researcher has to become, in effect, a kind of Pilgrim's Progress: facing a long journey and involved in a persistent struggle. There is therefore a sense in which the key questions for a creative researcher in mid-project may be more psychological than intellectual, and involve considerations that the researcher is in a position to do something about. It is not so much, "How talented are you?" but "How much are you prepared to risk?" "How strong are you in the face of failure and uncertainty?" and "How determined are you to overcome the problems and obstacles?"

There is another question too which should not be asked mid-project, but must certainly be asked prior to it. "How much are you prepared to give to it and for it?" It is an important question, and it has more than one reasonable answer. As Wright Mills pointed out, scholarship is a choice of how to live as well as a choice of career [Mills 1959 p 196]. It can be a process of self-discovery and self-development. Researchers can form their own self as they work to realise their potential, and to utilise and perfect their skills. That self may be both admirable and easy-to-live-with. But it can be otherwise.

There is, after all, more to life than an unremitting preoccupation with research. Work can be an escape from life, just as life can be an escape from the pains of work. Many satisfactions and sometimes great rewards accompany the creative process, perhaps even an ultimate sense of fulfilment. But there can be considerable personal costs, notably persistent stress and mind-bruising fatigue. There can also be relational costs involved in success when it comes: not everybody you know is happy for you all the time. And there can be social costs to the lifestyle that it demands and the kind of person that it can encourage you to be.

In dedicated focused activity you can lose a sense of the wholeness of human life. "I must confess", said Beethoven, "that I live a miserable life... I live entirely in my music."[44] At the very least, there may well be better things to do with your Sundays than to think about research problems. You can also damage your network of social relations by an obsessive focus on work and a mental preoccupation in playing with the project. Creativity can be the product of, but can also contribute towards, a psychopathology - the absence of close personal ties.[45]

There is something here in what Jung presumably meant when he said, "It is not Goethe who creates Faust but Faust which creates Goethe". "The work in process becomes the poet's fate and determines his psychic development".[46]

CHAPTER END NOTES

[1] MacKinnon,D.W 'The nature and nurture of creative talent' American Psychology 1962 Vol 17 p 493 quoted in L.Hudson 'The question of creativity' [Vernon 1970 p 226].

[2] [Perkins 1981 pp 268-9]. But Perkins agrees that there is such a thing as a creative personality and that certain traits do appear "again and again". A review of various studies in this area, by M. Dellas and E. L. Gaier, found that the evidence pointed to a common pattern of personality traits ... (which) ... may have some bearing on creativity in the abstract, regardless of field. They summarise the characteristics as (1) independence in attitude and social behaviour, (2) dominance, (3) introversion, (4) openness to stimuli, (5) wide interests (6) self acceptance, (7) intuitiveness, (8) flexibility, (9) social presence and poise, (10) an asocial attitude, (11) unconcern for social norms, (12) radicalism, and (13) rejection of external constraints.

Dellas, M. and Gaier E.L. 'Identification of creativity: the individual' Psychological Bulletin 1970, 73, 55-73 quoted in [Welsh 1975 p 8].

[3] Eysenck, H.J. in [Boden 1994 p 211].

[4] For contrasting perceptions see [Barron 1963], Gedo, J.E. 'More on creativity and its vicissitudes' in [Runco and Albert 1990 pp 37-8]. Lombroso, C. 'Genius and insanity' in [Rothenberg and Houseman 1976 pp 79-86.] [Maslow 1976 Part II 'Creativeness' pp 55-97], [Prensky 1980], [Sandblom 1992], [Storr 1989 p 250], [Storr 1976 pp 72-146 and pp 252-267].

[5] See for example [Blaxter,Hughes and Tight 1996 pp 135-8, 166-7 and 227-8] and [Phillips and Pugh 1987 pp 72 - 81].

[6] Burgess, R.G., Pole, C.J. and Hockey, J. 'Strategies for managing and supervising the social science PhD' in [Burgess 1994 pp 28-9].

[7] [MacKinnon 1968 p 439]. MacKinnon, D.W. 'The study of creative persons: a method and some results' in [Kagan 1967 p28].

[8] Ableson in [Kagan 1967 p 193], [Feldhusen 1995 p 262], Guildford in [Taylor and Getzels 1975 p 45]. Maddi in [Taylor and Getzels 1975 pp 185-187], [Ochse 1991 p 334], Roe in [Rothenberg and Houseman 1976 p 171].

[9] [Amabile 1983]' Amabile in [Runco and Albert 1990 p 78], Csikszentmihalyi in [Runco and Albert 1990 p 196].

[10] Csikszentmihalyi in [Albert and Runco 1990 p 197].

[11] Wilson, J. cited in [Entwistle 1988 p 193].

[12] Ford in [Ford and Gioia 1995 pp 28 and 35]. Also in the same volume contributions and references on p 118, pp 140-1, pp 174-5 and pp 358-360.

[13] Gordon, W.J.J. quoted by Parnes in [Vernon 1970 p 349].

[14] This emphasis on calculated risk-taking can be found in many writers on creativity including [Adams 1987 pp 43-4], Barron in [Sternberg 1988 p 78],

Cropley, A.J. 'S-R psychology and cognitive psychology' in [Vernon 1970 p 123], [Feldhusen 1995 p 262], McClelland, D.C. 'The calculated risk: an aspect of scientific performance' in [Taylor and Barron 1963, pp 184-192], Roe in [Rothenberg and Houseman 1976 p 170]. Simonton, D.K. 'Creativity as heroic: risk, success, failure and acclaim' in [Ford and Gioia 1995 p89], Sternberg, R.J. 'A three facet model of creativity' in [Sternberg 1988 p 144].

[15] Simonton in [Ford and Gioia 1995 p 89].

[16] Sternberg in [Sternberg 1988 p 144].

[17] Kaplan, N. 'The relation of creativity to sociological variables in research organisations' in [Taylor and Barron 1963 p 201].

[18] Honore Balzac quoted in [Olson 1965p 156].

[19] The analysis here is consistent with some of the characteristics of what Daniel Goleman terms "emotional intelligence" - "abilities such as being able to motivate oneself and persist in the face of frustrations; to control impulse and delay gratification; to regulate one's moods and keep distress from swamping the ability to think" [Goleman 1996 p 34].

[20] Gruber in [Wechsler 1978 p 137], Maddi, S.R. 'The strenuousness of the creative life' in [Taylor and Getzels 1975 pp 173-187], Roe in [Rothenberg and Hausman 1976 p 171], Sternberg in [Sternberg 1988 p 144].

[21] [Cox 1926 Vol II The early mental traits of three hundred geniuses p 187] quoted in [Welsh 1975 p 15].

[22] There is a beautifully honest and informative expression of this in relation to writing up research - Pamela Richards 'Risk' in [Becker with Richards 1986 pp 108-120].

[23] Sternberg in [Sternberg 1988 p143], also [Adams 1987 p45], Barron quoted by MacKinnon in [Taylor and Getzels 1975 p 62], Ford in [Ford and Gioia 1995 p 24], Roe in [Rothenburg and Hausman 1976 p170].

[24] Guilford, J.P. 'Creativity: a quarter century of progress' in [Taylor and Getzels 1975 p46], Roe in [Rothenberg and Houseman 1976 p 170], Maddi in [Taylor and Getzels 1975 p 182], [Perkins 1981 p 269].

[25] MacKinnon in [Kagan 1967 p 27].

[26] Howard Becker [Becker 1986 p 130] points out there is collective value for the various activities involved in a scholarly discipline in scholars having different psychological dispositions towards "Getting in out of the door".

[27] Ford in [Ford and Gioia 1995 p 24] cites thirteen different sources that associate self-confidence in skills and ability with the motives that facilitate creative acts.

[28] There is a very interesting discussion of this "self-interference" and suggestions for dealing with it in [Green and Gallway 1986]. There is also a useful series of books produced within the framework of neuro-linguistic programming including [Bandler 1985]. Methods of modifying internal dialogue that undermines creativity are referred to in [Nickerson Perkins and Smith 1985 pp 265-8]. Various exercises for this purpose are also given in [Goleman, Kaufman and Ray 1993].

[29] [Metzger 1992 pp 33-4]. Writers on these matters give this psychological character different names. See for example [Cameron 1974 pp 11-13], on the "Censor" (and how to handle it). [Goleman,Kaufman, and Ray 1993 p 65] refer to it as the "Voice of Judgement". In his autobiography, the playwright Neil Simon refers to it simply as "Panic" and gives us some wonderfully honest examples "You're not good enough. The first one was a fluke" etc etc. On one occasion he fears his sarcastic typewriter saying to him "Got yourself in it *this* time, didn't you, big shot? Well, I'm waiting for you to be brilliant. Anytime you're ready" [Simon 1996 p158].

[30] On the relationship between anxiety and confidence see the very interesting discussion in [Boden 1990 p257].

[31] Ford in [Ford and Gioia 1995 p 345].

[32] Hill 'Heady stuff' in [Boylan 1993 p122].

[33] Over the years at various times I have had an important dialogue about my research with Jim Jupp, David Coates, Arthur Lipow, Leo Panitch, Eric Shaw, Patrick Seyd, and particularly with Bob Fryer and David Howell. In this present study I have broadened the circle of this dialogue in a way which has been heartening and promising.

[34] Albert in [Runco and Albert 1990 p 21], Ford in [Ford and Gioia 1995 p 24], [Perkins 1981 p 272]. Helson, R 'Creativity in women: outer and inner views over time' in [Runco and Albert 1990 p 47] points to the special problems women have in developing this perception.

[35] MacKinnon in [Kagan 1967 p 34].

[36] The creative career may be slow, irregular and intermittent [Arieti 1976 p 474]. Periods of great creativity may be followed by periods of much less direct productivity [ibid p 382]. [Guilford 1968 p 79] notes that "some writers on the subject even speak of rhythms of creativity". There may also be life cycles of production. Creative production appears to peak around the age of 35. Ford in [Ford and Gioia 1995 p 31]. Amongst academics it has often been recognised that there has been a general pattern in which the "big" book or paper has been done early in the career.

[37] Richard Rodgers and Lorenz Hart "I Wish I Was in Love Again" (song).

[38] [Gornick 1984] quoted in [Charlesworth, Farrall, Stokes and Turnbull 1989 p126].

[39] Simonton in [Sternberg 1988 p 404-5]. In terms of the generation of ideas, the principle sometimes evoked is that bombarding the mind with the greatest variety of random input increases the likelihood of a chance connection that is fruitful. Parnes, S.J. 'AHA' in [Taylor and Getzels 1975 p 225].

[40] Ford in [Ford and Gioia 1995 p 3.].

[41] Jevons, W.S. quoted by Simonton in [Sternberg 1988 p 404].

[42] Perkins in [Boden 1994 p 131].

[43] Simonton, D.K. 'Creativity as heroic: risk, success, failure and acclaim' in [Ford and Gioia 1995 p 89].

[44] Ludwig van Beethoven letter to F.G.Wegeler 1801 quoted in [Watson 1994 p 113].

[45] "It is an ... interesting fact that most of the world's great thinkers since the time of the Greeks have not married or formed close personal ties" [Storr 1989 p 266].

[46] Jung, C.G. *Modern Man in Search of a Soul* Routledge, paperback edition 1984 p 197, derived from a reference in [Ghiselin 1954 p 4]. Howard Gardner develops this point further in a study which indicated that a range of creative people "became embedded in some kind of...Faustian arrangement" such that they sacrificed all, in the conviction that if the bargain were relaxed their creativity might suffer, [Gardner 1993 p 44].

CHAPTER FIVE

ROLE PLAYING AND CREATIVE RESEARCH: THE DETECTIVE

THE SECRET LIFE OF WALTER MITTY

Now I want to turn back towards the intellectual activity of the researcher, and to the process by which the creative researcher investigates and explains the political world. My approach in this chapter and the chapter that follows, signalled by frequent literary shifts from first person to third person, starts from the perspective that what a creative researcher tries to do "will grow out of his or her conception of personal actualities and potentialities" [Perkins, 1981 p 272]. It has been observed that "many people define themselves as uncreative, tell themselves that they are being uninventive while performing creative tasks, and in general talk themselves out of their own potential" [Nickerson, Perkins and Smith 1985 p 266]. Conversely it has been found that people can be got to behave in creative ways "by inviting them to pretend that they are artists or bohemians".[1]

All this (and the evidence presented in Chapter Four) indicates the importance of the image that we have of ourselves in our work. It is vital that it contributes to, rather than hinders, the creative process. Much of what the rigorous scholar does is mundane, involving the dedicated accuracy and methodical routines of the clerk. Nevertheless, it may still be helpful for the creative researcher to be like Thurber's Walter Mitty, readily changing mentally from one extravagantly heroicly creative role into another, and forever in action and combat in what I think of as "the theatre of the mind".[2]

It is in this spirit that contrived self-images play a significant part in my own creative art. The way that I visualise myself "on the job," and the way that I utilise these images, make a significant contribution to my mental approach to the work.

There are a variety of roles that I play in the creative research process. I visualise myself as the Detective, linked to a Watcher in the wings, as a Juggler, linked to a Patternmaker (Chapter Six). The Patternmaker whose role it is to theorise - preparing the conceptual and presentational framework - is a schizophrenic: he is the Patternmaker-artist and the Patternmaker-realist - as we shall see.

Other important characters will later make their appearance in Chapter Seven, including the Chattering Monkey and the Awkward Sod. The reader of Chapter Two will have already met an Explorer as well as a Player - characters who are often emphasised in my role-playing visualisations. In Chapter Four they will have encountered a Pilgrim and his Progress, and in Chapter Eight will be made aware of the important role of the Navigator. This is a very active cast in my theatre of the mind. In carrying out research, as I engage in many mental activities - some of them simultaneous - I am moving between a variety of roles, often adopting the appropriate self-image. Between the various characters there is a constant dialogue, but it is the role of, and the dialogue between, the investigating Detective and the theorising Patternmaker which are central to the creativity of my research.

These, and other roles, act as a series of confidence-raising self-images, shaping and reinforcing my view of myself as an effective, creative researcher. They are sustaining symbols of professional pride in my artistry. They also assist the process of sustaining, modifying and developing different elements of the personality, thus, to some extent, re-inventing myself in ways conducive to the creative process.

Together with the "villain" of political creativity - the Destructive Critic (encountered in Chapter Four), and the Vicious Circle of critics (to be introduced in Chapter Seven) - they can also provide illumination in the process of generating and maintaining self-awareness in thinking about thinking. Certainly, they help me to monitor, differentiate and refine my mental activity and research behaviour.[3] In these various ways, and particularly in the dialogue of this theatre, they facilitate my ability to act creatively.

In this and the following chapters the roles also provide a useful illustration of my mental process. In my descriptions I move periodically between first and third person as I describe my behaviour. It is a literary form intended to keep the reader aware of the different characters, and aware of this other dimension of my approach to creativity. It also helps to prevent a degree of literary indigestion in the repetition of the first person singular.

THE DETECTIVE

Image and reality

When I think of my research exploration and the mental activities around it, I think of it as the conjunction of persistent, unremitting curiosity and determined, obsessional, pursuit. Questions - including self-interrogation - are so much a part of my work that I am often, in my imagination, *a Detective*. This image itself is no novelty. It is to be found in many places in the literature of research into history, science and creativity.[4]

There are clear similarities in the two occupational activities. A key characteristic of my research is that I believe in going out on the beat, making my own contacts, looking for, and at, the evidence myself rather than relying on the observations of others. In this work I am involved in assessing evidence, picking up clues, drawing inferences and making connections in the attempt to describe and explain what happened. I am often following a speculative hunch, or pursuing a hypothesis, and seeking confirmation of the behaviour that I am tentatively expecting. And in trying to prepare a "case" which will "stick," I am seeking to offer a convincing explanation based on rigorously confirmed evidence.

In some key respects which, in terms of creativity, may well be crucial, my Detective is more like a literary counterpart than a real policeman. It is not enough for him to solve cases. He consciously seeks a quality of originality in the problem-cases he chooses, and in the way that he solves them[5]. His view is that the more creative the quality of the process, the greater the chance of solving hard cases, and also the better the interpretations and explanations that may emerge. Thus he is addicted to the flair of the style of his investigations, a delight in the unusual, and the satisfaction of the novel or unexpected twist.

However, there can also be some important differences between my Detective and the literary variety (apart from the obvious ones). In particular, once a crime has been committed the problem is clearly focused on the detection. "Who dun it?". But the creative "pure" researcher is often as much concerned to find and define the crime (or crimes) as to solve them. In effect, the researcher becomes a criminal detective, much like the Agatha Christie play in which the policeman "did it".

From the past, to the present as past

I began my own research career with a critical review of secondary sources - the relevant literature - attempting to clarify and understand more about the problems with which the project would be concerned. I then moved into an analysis of primary sources, of memos and minutes, of conference reports and official publications, of correspondence and agreements, of diaries and autobiography. I also moved into field observation and investigation of the present political relationships which then, as I analysed it, became of course the present as past.

The Detective is always flitting between these three frames. One moment he is seeking to gain a better understanding of the history of that which he is investigating, the next, he is back into seeking to understand the contemporary world. One moment he is preoccupied with uncovering these contemporary events, the next he is seeking to explain them in the light of his historical knowledge. His contempary observations and the reports given to him of contemporary developments become part of his records and the meat upon which his reflections feed. As he gains in understanding of the contemporary field of enquiry, so he returns to the primary sources and to his notes from the distant past, interrogating that past from a new perspective.

Watching, questioning, listening, sensing

The creative Detective of contemporary political analysis is always probing, constructing and reconstructing a problem, or problems, which might (or will) be "the crime." As understanding of, and access to, the field of enquiry grows, so the Detective is, in a sense, actually watching for the crime or repeats of the crime - watching the build up and watching the execution. He is a watching

Detective - a participant-observer, observing from the wings and occasionally from the stage itself.

Increasingly in my form of research, as I have come to understand the field of enquiry, and be an accepted academic part of it, this has involved questioning the participants before and after various anticipated major developments. In this role, I am often involved not only in focused questioning but also at times in more general appraisals. I am asking, "What's happening? What's new? What's changing? and What's different?" testing these against my prior assumptions, expectations and theories, and assessing them against past history.

I am also involved in watching from the distance - my observations mediated by a range of sources. These include the television, radio, press and journals. I am an assiduous cuttings collector and records-keeper, to the despair of my family and the amusement of my friends. But, I have learned to distrust the cuttings (and any academic articles that I discern are written mainly from the cuttings in this time-pressured research culture). I am very sensitive to the question of which journalist has written the cutting, and I am always judging it in the light of my knowledge of their track record of understanding and accuracy. I read the newspapers and journals not only for what the story is, but for who fed it there, in that form and with that angle. Back to the questioning again to seek the answers.

To fill in the details, to get close to "the real picture," to substantiate information and also to dig that bit deeper, I interview a lot of people and talk informally to them, often on repeated occasions. I have got used to the idea that a degree of resourcefulness and persistence is necessary for this deeper excavation. An access may open up suddenly, or close just as quickly, depending upon the changing political circumstances. Intermediaries, who can effect introductions and assure integrity, play some part in the expanding process of information-gathering. Reputation is the biggest asset of all.

Face to face, and on the telephone, I share in, and listen avidly to, the gossip of politics and not just for its enjoyment. It is often a crucial source of information and multiple perspectives, and occasionally (to adapt some of the terminology used in the prologues of Henry James[6]) the "germs" and "seeds" from which the story, characters and themes begin to emerge. I use hearsay as a potential signpost for my speculations, but I try not to rely on it. Somewhere in the back of my mind I have my own scale of suspended belief (affected by my experienced nose about the source) and I am constantly freeze-framing and exploring the picture in the light of new evidence.

Occasionally, as I watch and listen, I get "hunches" which sometimes come to me as if they were from a sixth sense. (This official has changed her political alignment, or this person has an important link to X.) Sometimes there is a clear sense that this does not "feel right", or "something new has happened here". On one occasion, in the late 1980s, when there was an effusive public greeting and affectionate embrace between two politicians who were known to be close allies, my antenna vibrated. "There is something wrong here. This doesn't ring true. Is this hiding a new crisis in their relationship?" Indeed it was, as I later confirmed.

What is probably happening in these situations is that my observations of the minutiae, and my increasing command over the nuances of the actors and their context, allow me to make a confident and very speeded-up evaluation of what would be appropriate behaviour, and to sense a peculiarity.

Responsibilities of observational vigilance

In shaping the interpretations that come with, or will emerge from, the observations and enquiries, the Detective tries to give a plausible meaning to what has been said and done. To do this job, he has to have a command over the verbal, body and sign language of politics and the politician[7]. He also has to be a ferocious worker, going through rigorous routines of enquiry.

Playing the Detective, I have four responsibilities of observational vigilance which become essential elements in developing an understanding of the context, and an appreciation of the subtleties and wholeness of the picture.

(i) I have to locate the actors historically and socially. This involves commanding the maximum possible detail about the person whom I am watching. Who are they? Where did they come from? What do they do? How do they relate to others? Where might they be going, and, especially, where do they hope to go? In this position what would they know, with what degree of reliability?

(ii) I have to look behind the rhetoric and the self-idealisation and match them with the behaviour. Why is this being said here? Why am I being told this? How honest is this politician behind the facade? Does s/he mean what s/he says and say what s/he means?. Are they telling themselves the truth? Is s/he normally consistent, or better characterised by what is described as a "ducker and a weaver"? If so, what is the intention? What is the agenda? What is the angle?

(iii) I have to dig deep "into the basement" to see whether what happens there belies the surface appearances. Although sometimes a lack of access or detailed information forces me to move up a level of generality, more often I am trying to push the analysis down from the normally accepted level of generality.

This involves a sensitivity to underlying variations of subtext. Political dialogue and action has many such subtexts. I am constantly asking what else is going on here? Even the simplest observation of who is there and who isn't, who speaks on what, who sits with whom, can mark a significant development and begin an important line of thought. But also there is a judgement to be made about how the message is being received by different listeners.

There is also an awareness that behind every political initiative or interaction there is normally a sub-politics involving assistants, advisers and officials. It is at this micro level that I now expect to find surprising features and hidden activities which belie appearances. I am constantly asking, what, or who, is behind the person who is behind the person who is .. etc.

(iv) As I try to "build the picture" and weigh the evidence, I have to make a whole out of the partial views offered to me from the various sources, and sometimes out of the views offered to differing audiences about the same events.

The testimony and the various written sources often do not cohere. With the purest of intentions, memory can be imperfect. But also, as is well-known amongst researchers in this field, politicians are not always the most reliable sources of accurate information.[8] So, I have not only to mentally challenge each source - matching words with past actions and with whatever other evidence I possess or can obtain - I have to assess the different audiences and contexts. What is the best interpretive sense that I can make of all this evidence? What does the whole picture look like? Is the interpretation coherent? Is it plausible? Is it the most plausible that is available?

Discovery

Discovery is one of the peaks of this detection process. By a "discovery" I mean here significant evidence which contradicts established understandings and/or establishes new understandings. Some of these discoveries are apparent almost the moment you look at the data, if only because of the contrast between what is there and what has been said to be there. I am constantly amazed by how many times this happens.

Thus, the Detective assumed that it was correct, as was often asserted, that the battle between the Labour Government and the unions over industrial relations reform and the retreat over the White Paper *In Place of Strife* damaged Labour's chances at the 1970 General Election. It had been authoritatively argued that by making the strike question the test of Labour's competence to govern, the Prime Minister Wilson had succeeded in demonstrating the opposite of what he intended [Jenkins 1970 p 164]. The Detective took a look at the poll data. By October 1969 (after the battle was over), Labour was back ahead of the Conservatives in terms of "best able to handle strikes and disputes" and at a higher figure than before the dropping of *In Place of Strife*. Why was this not noticed? Weird. [Minkin 1991/92 p 117].

On the other hand, much of what is discovered is not a matter of immediate observational vigilance. It takes time, effort, a lot of patience, sometimes simple but numerous quantitative assessments, and regularly, a mountain of clerical work. Such findings emerge from classic procedures of scholarship - conscious, rigorous, systematic examination of the data. The researcher is differentiating, selecting, focusing: case after case, speech after speech, manifesto after manifesto, item after item, conference decision after conference decision, resolution after resolution.

Did the unions take the initiative in 1979 in producing the constitutional revolt which caused a crisis in the Labour Party? This was the general view, but the Detective was not so sure. What could be an appropriate test? Submissions to the agenda of the Party Conference in 1979 would give a strong indication. Obvious when you thought about it, but it had not been done. The resolutions were examined. The clear discovery was that not a single resolution or amendment was submitted by the unions relating to the three constitutional issues under discussion. [Minkin 1991/92 p 196].

In this process the Detective has to make sensitive judgements as to what is worth this kind of examination in the field under investigation. Sometimes this is obvious, sometimes it is an informed guess, sometimes it is a sudden stumbling awareness quite late in the development of the project, sometimes it is triggered by other re-interpretations. Did the policy of the Transport Workers change overnight when it changed leadership in 1956, as many a knowledgable commentator said? At first the Detective simply accepted it and had no intention of investigating it further. Then much later, something in the evidence caused second thoughts and a more thorough investigation. Decision after decision was examined, and behaviour in one forum after another was checked. Eventually the evidence was overwhelming. There was a *continuity* of policy, not an abrupt change.[Minkin 1978/80 p 117-8].

For reasons which will be explained in Chapter Seven, very late in the investigation of the agenda politics of the Labour Party Conference, the Detective had cause to query the extent of support within the trade unions for the shift of Labour Party policy on public ownership between 1956 and 1961. A painstaking analysis showed that, contrary to the accepted view, and measured in terms of the conference decisions of the affiliated trade unions over these years, there was never a clear mandate for the revisionism which shed the commitment to extending public ownership.[Minkin 1978/80 p 126].

This is a dedicated but grindingly routine procedure, familiar to experienced research workers in every field - what I think of as the "coal face" of scholarship. It is lightened only by the wonderful sense of rapt involvement as the analysis proceeds and significant discoveries are made, or new interpretations and explanations begin to suggest themselves. This can be one of those experiences which keep the momentum of the research moving, producing the feeling that you want to sing at the richness of it.

ENLARGING THE POSSIBILITIES

Discoveries highlight the master task of the historian as Detective, which is "to keep the human record straight" - as Wright Mills puts it [Mills 1959 p 144]. However, this is seldom a straightforward operation, and the evidence in relation to important discoveries is rarely as clear and convincing as the cases described above. Establishing what the record is, is a selective and an interpretive exercise - an exercise which may well be influenced by a variety of preconceptions.

In his observations and reflections, the Detective will probably have had indications from others as to what he will observe in that situation, and he will also have his own expectations of what he is likely to see. Working in territory which is familiar may give him an edge in understanding its subtleties, but it can also make him vulnerable to a variety of unquestioned assumptions that are weak, and to a bias that is so ingrained as to be invisible. All this makes his earnest self-questioning an imperative. He has constantly to ask himself, "Are those indications I have been given and those expectations I had, borne out by the evidence?" He also has to ask himself, "What else might be here?" and "What other meanings could be given to this situation?". Thus, in his attempts to make better sense of the world that is under investigation, he is often asking, implicitly or explicitly, "In this situation how can I mentally enlarge the possibility of new and better interpretations and explanations emerging?"

For the Detective using these general methods of field enquiry,[9] the enlargement can take place in two ways: through the kind of observational vigilance already noted (seeing what others have missed, seeing the wider significance of routines or "trivia", or seeing the opportunities available from chance findings and meetings) or through a mental experimentation - a heuristic thinking - which assists in the generation of original features in the research.

The Detective has slowly developed these heuristic thinking skills over the years. They take various forms. The mental play has, at times, much in common with the notion of lateral (as opposed to vertical) thinking.[10] He sets out "to explore and develop new perceptions,"[de Bono 1993b p 53] using at times "unorthodox or apparently illogical methods"[de Bono 1993a p 52]. In this process the player tries different provocations, concepts, and points of entry, to see if something new and useful is yielded. At times it also involves switching "the mind's eye to its wide-angled lens"[11] in order to expand the field of view, and extend the possibilities for seeing a problem in a different perspective.

It can take the form of a rigorous Critical Examination where the repetition of the seven questions, and the constant repetition of the "why?" leads him to dig deeply into every facet and interconnection of the phenomenon under investigation. As he plays with questions and answers, his inquisitorial and provocative probing is here a search for unnoticed elements of possible explanation which can form the basis of a new or enriched understanding.

He also plays with different descriptions of what he is seeing in order to clarify and finesse his perceptions. He adopts the most startlingly different or heretical interpretations, to see if they might fit, or where they might fall short. He changes or subtracts elements in the situation to see if this adds a new dimension to his understanding. He analogises, asking himself what else this event or situation reminds him of, and then he explores similarities and differences, causes and consequences to see what might be learned. Persistently, he attempts to deny the most fundamental shared "truth" of what he is observing, just in case it does not stand up to questioning, or in case some other more plausible "truth" gives hints of emerging. (On these activities see Chapter Seven).

Following the peculiar

The enlargement of possibilities is also fed regularly by a combination of observational vigilance and a key heuristic precept we have already encountered: watch out for the peculiarity. The Detective is very sensitive to peculiarities and in Chapter Eight we will see how this affected the Patternmaker's development of the theoretical framework based on observation of the inhibitions of trade union leaders, and their restraint within the relationship with the Labour Party. Here let us note two particular peculiarities which had an important effect on his thinking.

In an examination of 70 years of Conference resolutions and amendments, the Detective (a relative novice in the field at this stage) was surprised by an omission - something he expected to see that was not there. Why did affiliated unions so rarely submit resolutions about the administration of the Party, even in years of heavy criticism? He investigated the matter and questioned various people in the unions. What he came across was, in effect, a self-denying ordinance. They accepted that the government of the party was a matter for the elected party leadership. It also became clear that they wanted to reinforce the autonomy of their own organisations from political intervention. So there was an important discovery here of institutionalised restraint, and also an indication of an overall reciprocity which was not immediately obvious to anybody examining the relationship. Later, this finding would have its effect on the development of a key conceptual framework of unwritten rules.

Another peculiarity. Why was there sometimes a marked difference between the political composition of the National Executive Committee, as elected by the Conference, and the Conference decisions on policy - in some periods to the Left and in other periods the Right?

A detailed investigation followed which did come across some contingent and fortuitous factors, but mainly focused on the unwritten rules which regulated union involvement in these elections. So powerful were these rules that they dwarfed considerations relating to factional political alignment, and to any attempt to maximise the power of individual unions. This created a time-lag effect on major changes in the political composition of the conference. This explanation was important in its own right, but it too was later to affect the construction of the conceptual framework based upon the idea of unwritten rules.

Peculiarities and the politics of the block vote

Peculiarities can also be a potential Godsend in uncovering much more than was searched for.

I remember looking through periodicals for the 1950s and finding an obviously well-informed article in the *New Statesman* on the first offers from the BBC to televise a Party Conference. In it there was a reference which said that the Labour Party General Secretary, Morgan Phillips, was unhappy that television would show union leaders standing up to cast their block votes. My immediate reaction to this article was that its assumptions were just wrong. True, union leaders did stand up to show the union card with their vote on it at the Trades Union Congress; but at the Party Conference they cast cards from a book of cards (card vote one, card vote two, card vote three etc..) into a ballot box, in a much more discreet process.

Some time later I found myself thinking. Could they get something like this as wrong as this in this particular story? Peculiar. I wondered whether union leaders did actually stand up to cast their votes in that period. If so, when did they stop doing that? When were multiple voting cards and boxes first issued? From this point I started to dig. It was a longer dig than I had anticipated, and it took me a long way away from my original quest. In fact I had to leave it for some time and only returned to it for an article, 'The politics of the block vote', commissioned for the launch of a new journal.[12]

In the end, what emerged was far more important than the voting card procedure. True, I did make the discovery that the present voting system was actually created in 1954, and was not as old as had been thought. But, I also came across the more surprising and important discovery that before 1954 some unions actually split their block votes with several cards issued to the members of a union delegation. It was a myth that union votes had always been cast as indivisible blocks.

Of course, not every pursuit of peculiarity is particularly fruitful. A lot of effort may not reveal much at all. Some peculiarities are just that - peculiarities. They prove after investigation to be simply mistakes, personal quirks, and particularly, exceptional behaviour - explicable purely in terms of the particular context or the distinctive values, beliefs and objectives of those involved in the activity. The behaviour of the left-wing Miners' leader Arthur Scargill, and the right-wing Electricians' leader Frank Chapple, often came into this category. However it could, and did, highlight the force of a pattern of behaviour involving the other unions' leaders.

CONTEXT AND PERSPECTIVES

Both Detection and Patternmaking (of which more later) have to be carried out in ways that are alert to a wider context and broader influences than those immediately in view in the field. The Detective is the "nitty gritty" man, with a keen eye for the local and the specific in his investigations, but throughout the investigations the Detective's questions and his perspectives are being fed to an increasing degree by the Patternmaker's theorising which is producing a new conceptual framework. So he is investigating new areas with an eye on the emerging patterns, and revisiting old investigations in the light of the framework.

Explanations may not be adequate without reference to the broader context. In this sense the researcher, whilst growing in expertise within the immediate field of investigation, has also to be a cosmopolitan in his or her awareness. Thus, in puzzling over the peculiarities, in questioning old assumptions and associations, and in reaching towards new interpretations, I am often attempting to expand the field of view in order to gain a broader perspective. This is all the more necessary because I am viewing a consistency and variability of patterns within one institutional complex in one national sphere, and (broadly speaking) one cultural tradition. From this frame of reference it is necessary to flit back and forth in comparison between different institutions within the national sphere, and sometimes between the national and international perspectives.

Simply moving the focus upwards, and seeing the project from high above a wide range of such cases can radically affect how the project is viewed. It is an obvious point, but deep into exploration it is often a lesson that has to be learned. There was a time in the research on the Party Conference when fascination with the volume, complexity and detail of the material was preventing the novice Detective from seeing the wood for the trees.

A timely international conference and an early published contribution to a special journal edition on the relationship between trade unions and political parties took the novice Detective away from his preoccupation with the entrails of the Party Conference, and in doing so, recast his perception of the pattern of forces engendering change within and around the Conference [Minkin 1974]. (It also gave the Patternmaker the bones of a new outline of the Party's history, and allowed him more clearly to appreciate the distinctive features of a functional differentiation of institutional roles - trade unions and party -taking place in the British case.)

To generate alternative perspectives, as either the Detective or the Patternmaker, I occasionally go though a routine of different relocation games, sometimes as a glancing movement, sometimes as an in-depth analysis. I try a prism of perceptions, viewing the evidence though the eyes of people with a variety of methodological and disciplinary perspectives and with a variety of political commitments. I try to view a specific situation as though it was foreign. Or occasionally, I even play with the present from the speculative perspective of the future, or, more often, the past.

In these assessments I remember and delve into past "cases" in the history of the relationship which might be the clue to who or what "dun" it today. In comparison, I also reach for examples from abroad - cases which associate and disassociate particular variables that are involved here[13] - and try to see if they are consistent with what the grounded investigation is apparently showing. These changes of focus can, in principle, give an understanding of a broader pattern of causation, and act as a counter-evidence to "accepted" associations and causes.

The imaginative process can, of course, work both ways. A broad knowledge of history can raise the level of understanding of the present, but the present can also illuminate the past in new ways. From behaviour within the Labour Party since 1979, I gained a much deeper understanding of the behaviour of the party and the unions in the 1920s - particularly the shift of the TUC towards new forms of accommodation with the employers after the General Strike, and the ascendancy of Ramsay MacDonald as Leader of the Labour Party.

The particular experience can deepen understanding of similar occurrences elsewhere; even outside the immediate field of study. Recently, a member of the Shadow Cabinet was reported as playing, in effect, the same mental exercise in relation to "new Labour" - seeing the behaviour of its Leadership cadres in pursuit of internal party revolution as illuminating his or her understanding of party transformation in Stalin's Russia! [Bevins 1996] The same point might be made about any observation based on close acquaintance. They can each illuminate another experience or enhance a much broader understanding.

EMPATHY

In this imaginative shifting of perspectives the Detective has to have the ability to understand the motivations and actions of the participants as they interpret them, and also to give them a meaning from the position of the detached observer. He has thus both to empathise with, and to stand apart from, the participants. Over time he has developed his own mental variant of the tender and tough routine - a sequence of empathy (how does it look to them ?) and objective detachment (what meaning do I give to this, given all the other knowledge available to me?)

From time to time, in attempting to reconstruct a particular event or development, he adapts a game - empathic inference - used by dramatists and novelists through the ages. (This can also be an enjoyable social game, played often over a dinner and a bottle of wine at the Party Conference). It is a technique in which, knowing the nature of the characters well, and understanding something of their motivations, you give them a context, lay down the general outlines of the plot, fit in some bits of known evidence, and imagine them acting and speaking. You ask questions like this:-

> What would they have wanted?
> What would they have said?
> How would they have responded to each other?
> What would they have done or not have done?
> Crucially, what consequences would this have had, and what might have been the outcome?

Often, as a result of these exercises and games - rigorously pursued - you clarify what their perspectives and intentions are, you see more of the subtleties of their relationship, and you work out where their thoughts and conversation might have led in particularly intriguing cases. As a result, a suspicion can become reinforced or rejected, and a hypothesis or a plausible interpretation is sometimes generated.

PITFALLS AND PRATFALLS OF DETECTION

Although this is a creatively fertile process - building from what is explored, and what is noticed, what is connected and what is generated - by no means all of this is successful. Or rather, there are degrees of success and, regularly, there is outright failure. The hypotheses may prove unsupportable, the hunches can be wrong, the inspiration faulty, the games lead to nowhere. The mind can conjure up a misrepresentation, the strangeness can turn out to be trivial. The evidence may be too flimsy to stand the test of rigorous questioning, the interpretation may be weak compared with others on offer.

There is also the fact that, for the Detective operating at the margins of the participants' memory, the limited primary sources, and the availability of live testimony, evidence can sometimes be both compelling and tantalisingly incomplete. More than one such important case has been gathering dust in my files for years. Further, wrong turnings, faulty assumptions, searches in wrong places, interviews where the responses are a waste of breath, time spent in mind-numbingly boring meetings observing nothing of any significance, are endemic pitfalls of the detection process, and I have had my share of them.

In particular, personal competition amongst politicians, factional antipathy from groups on Right and Left, the diagnosis of conspiracy theorists, and the misleading "spin" by the growing army of doctors, are a constant source of misdirection as well as sometimes of valuable information.

It must also be admitted that there are pratfalls - interviews badly handled, problems which might have been foreseen, notes taken later to the wrong depth with the wrong focus, notes incomplete because tiredness got in the way. A bored, deaf ear to what later was suddenly (oh God!) perceived as a vital conversation. We all have days when we play Inspector Lestraude as well as Holmes.

Of course, we can learn from our mistakes. I can even remember one day when, as a novice post-graduate researcher, I was foolish enough to accept a sociable drink from each of the MPs I was interviewing. By the time I was talking to the last one, I was in a state of such benevolence as to make all my judgements questionable and my notes virtually useless. I did not do that again.

INTERVIEWS, CONVERSATIONS, JOINT ENQUIRIES AND THE CREATIVE DIALOGUE

Interviewing and recording

I can also remember the way in which my "recording" process changed in interviews as I learned the disadvantages of a rigidity of method. And here let me turn to the important process of interviewing, the Detective's role and the creativity that can be involved in it.

Close analysis of the exercise of power at national level in political parties gets the researcher into sensitive territory. Over the past thirty years, I have interviewed countless people at various levels in the Labour and trade union movement - many of them senior politicians, Labour Leaders and Ministers. Given the sensitivities involved in this area, the aware researcher has to receive everything with a degree of scepticism and suspended judgement. Although politicians are very different as personalities, and different too in the integrity that they bring to bear on their relationships, it has to be said again that collectively they are not noted for their scrupulous regard for truth. They have often a deep sense of the importance of a beneficial "spin" on their personal activities. They are also very sensitive about how they are viewed by history and historians, and are apt to complain loudly at being misrepresented.

So, in some recognition of these behaviour patterns, as well as because I thought it was the only way to do "proper" interviewing, I began my research by carefully planning all my questions and all my tactics. I went through them systematically, and sought to get down what was said as immediately, as accurately and as comprehensively as possible. As I thought was expected from researchers at that time,[14] I took detailed notes during all interviews. I remember a fellow-novice telling me that he even used to send his meticulous notes back to the interviewer for confirmation. I did think of adopting that procedure, but in the end decided against it: it seemed too time-consuming but also a formalist's recipe for inviting the witness to have second thoughts. But I do remember wondering whether I was "doing it right".

But doing it right means doing it effectively, and this sensitive area of investigation had to be handled with a degree of flexibility and experimentation.[15] I soon became aware that those being interviewed would occasionally be following the movements of my pen as they slowly and thoughtfully considered what they might say. In one early interview, when we began with a friendly informal chat, just at the point at which I knew that I was about to be told something important I flashed out my efficient-looking pen and notebook, only to have the informant slowly clam-up - eyes rivetted to what I was falteringly writing. After that, I ignored all the advice I had received about note-taking and decided that the form and timing of taking notes was itself a delicate "political" judgement, which was sometimes decided in advance by the Detective, and sometimes played by ear when the interview began.

The interview as conversation

I also changed my approach to the interviews which became more variable in form. As an inveterate planner, I still attempted to anticipate the interview and to foresee all eventualities. But in general, my interviews became more loosely structured around a few key themes and questions whilst allowing flexibility within the line of enquiry.

Crucially, over time I also changed my mode of questioning, making the exchange much more a dialogue than an interrogation. Or rather, this was how interviews developed as those being interviewed often sought my views and, over time, my "expert" opinions. Although I did not know it at that time, many field researchers have made this transition in interviews to what the Webbs called "conversations with a purpose".[16]

In some interviews, I did make the judgement that taking detailed notes was probably the appropriate thing. Certainly this was the norm when I was interviewing rank and file members of the Labour Party or the unions. I adjusted back to taking notes on the spot here because I found that not doing this was often taken as a signal of lack of respect - indicative of my regarding what they said as unimportant. Note-taking was also the norm when officials were prepared and keen to give me a full account of some development simply to get the record straight or to be very helpful.

I have to admit that I did not always get right the style of my approach or the judgement of what and when to record. On one occasion an MP who had a deep contempt for "intellectuals" suddenly demanded to know why I was *not* taking notes. Thrown off balance, I said truthfully that I was memorising what he said. He just glared. Our relationship (and the value of the dialogue) was not improved one bit by the exchange.

Sometimes the form would change mid-interview, where life history details were being given, or where there were intricate but non-contentious details to uncover, or where procedural arrangements were being described, or where I was being asked to take note of something held by those who were being interviewed to be particularly worthy of note. But most of the time, after the initial phase of my work, interviews were normally conducted with nothing to distract those being interviewed from the flow of the dialogue.

For a Detective who is always on the job, every political encounter, however brief and episodic, is potentially a conversational way of "making enquiries". Snatched conversations in conference corridors, a leisurely and gossipy meal, a few minutes on the phone, even a row or an exchange of intimacies with an old political friend, can all be part of the process of acquiring new knowledge and developing new understanding. Many were worthy of record, but more often than not, the recording was done outside of the interaction.

In most such conversations - important interviews as well as all the *ad-hoc* discussions - I did my best to memorise as much as I could of the conversation. To do this, initially I operated with an image of a house with key questions and topics in the rooms which I went through as systematically as the relaxed conversation allowed, and then in a cafe immediately afterwards, working round the house, I tried to recall word for word what was said. Later I tended to prepare a priority list of things that I needed to know, memorise them, and then later to work backwards from memory over the list.

I am sure that some things did get lost, but in this process I did seem to develop a remarkable memory for dialogue and phrasing. The activity and the effort involved did seem to encourage me to listen intently. After a time, the key bits, remembered later, seemed to have a particular luminance. Any doubts about the information reinforced my routine of seeking confirmation from alternative sources and sometimes returning to the original informant. I seldom used a particular phrasing as the only source for an interpretation unless it was clearly etched and very strongly in accord with my feel for the terrain. In any case, I generally worried myself into a multitude of cross-checks and confirmations of various forms.

Subsequently, I grew to be reasonably skilful in how I interviewed people. The movements of people's eyes and bodies in response to questions fed my discernment. I became increasingly adept at picking up and feeding from clues, particularly the last minute throw-away remark after I have said, "Thank you", that initially I had found puzzling or even irrelevant. I watched for the revealing aside, the slight rise in temper, and the suggestive reaction when caught unawares. Some of these were obvious in their significance, some were mentally noted for later consideration.

I picked up on cues which indicated a degree of ambivalence and then sought to explore it. (If, as the party official sensed, "the union leaders seemed very uncomfortable and ill at ease on the Party's Commission of Enquiry" why was this?). I tried to be alert to the way that the wind was blowing. (When the man in the Communication Department said quietly to me, " The next move is to get rid of the unions," who was he speaking for/about ?) I developed a sensitivity to, and a good memory for, inconsistencies. (If there was no politically motivated management of the agenda why, in his account to me, did the Chairman of the Conference Arrangements Committee say to Gaitskell, "That's the best that I can do"?).

The more experienced I became in interviewing, the more I tried always to expect the unexpected and to take advantage of it. Above all, as the reader might now anticipate, I watched out for peculiarities - to be questioned either then or later, or both. In interviews there are often verbal clues which have an element of the peculiar that can alert the vigilant Detective to something worth following. Why did the Secretary of the Trade Union Group of Labour MPs say to me that Neil Kinnock was "not a real trade unionist"? It was a very peculiar thing to say about a man who had been a prominent member of the Transport and General Workers Union and its Parliamentary grouping for some years. What did it mean?

Questions were asked, but were not very satisfactorily answered except that Kinnock was simply not a manual worker. Later, as I mulled over various hypotheses, the more intriguing it all became and I resolved to dig deeper. Eventually, after an investigation, it became clear that there was more at stake than simply prejudice. This definition of who was, or was not, a "real trade unionist" was being used to filter entry to the leadership of the group and in effect to keep control of it [Minkin 1991/92 p 259].

The interview as joint enquiry

There were times when, depending upon who was being interviewed, these discussions were virtually unstructured. Sometimes they were just exploratory, seeking to find out, "what's happening?" and "why?". At other times, I had in the back of my mind the important questions which still needed answering, and from time to time I attempted to steer in their general direction. But I always tried to preserve a sense of "just discussing" or "just chatting".

And the "just chatting" role could only be fully sustained if those I interviewed had the reassurance that, if that was how they wanted it, I would never reveal the source. If they said that some particular information was absolutely private between us they meant just that - it could not be revealed, stop. Over time, my success in interviewing also grew out of their confidence that I was not likely to go to the press with a revelation, or to involve myself in the role of the media pundit - these had to be part of the self-denying ordinance of the Detective. In a political world where information is gold, there were some personal disadvantages to all this restraint, but there was also an enormous bonus in trust and the conveying of a sense of integrity to the role.

Given where I was coming from politically, and the political commitments that I retained throughout, it is important to register that I did not play this research role with the classic neutrality of the Detective. The view that "the interviewer must maintain a neutral stance"[17] can be over-restrictive, and in certain circumstances positively unhelpful. Even "sympathetic neutrality"[18] does not quite fit the diversity of forms of conversation that I have had to be involved in as a participant-observer.

I interviewed people who, over time, were fairly clear on my political positioning which was sometimes close to theirs and sometimes very different. Over the years, many to whom I talked became my friends, some of them very close friends indeed. The development of this closeness, which began fairly early in my research, is not unique to my mode of operation as a researcher.[19]

My *persona* in this interviewing varied considerably. It could range from the polite neutrality associated with the conventional academic, through various degrees of sympathy and empathy, to the complete political identification of the partisan. Even when there were known political disagreements, there was often a friendly, mutual respect.

This, I acknowledge, was a problematic mode of engagement for a research scholar (as I will discuss later) and not one which is to be recommended for the inexperienced or the unaware. I was always aware that, in an atmosphere of closeness, it was vital to retain (or, if lost, recapture) a sense of distance, professionalism and the avoidance of bias. I prided myself on my ability to see the weaknesses of any position that I shared and to take account of its shaping of perceptions. This was even more urgent where those being interviewed had a different perspective from my own. Their feeling of talking to somebody who, though possibly critical, also had a sense of appropriate empathy and detachment, was vital in generating the trust of those being interviewed. I sought mentally to stand in their shoes to see the world as they might see it. I also saw it as test of my professionalism that I could (and did) put their case as strongly as they would have done, in anything that I wrote.

But I also found that the skill of productive interviewing involved less a sense of showing neutrality than the sense of indicating at times that "we" were involved in a joint enquiry to find out things and to explain them. This "we-ness" was vital in overcoming the barriers of role, suspicion, anxiety and sometimes acute political difference. It was an opening to the perception on the part of those being interviewed that, far from me being neutral, we were, in pursuit of the enquiry, in some sense on the same side.[20] Consequently, in many interviews there was a periodic movement of varying duration into a mood where the two of us were seeking answers to problems and puzzles that were, or could be, "shared." ("It's funny how this often happens isn't it? It's strange that this should happen isn't it? It always seems to be like this doesn't it? This seems to be a regular pattern doesn't it? Do you understand that? I don't.")

Over the years, with a wide range of people, the interviews often became genuinely sharing engagements; they became more and more communicative and less simply elicitative, more and more joint investigations. This was true even when we both knew we had areas of major disagreement. To some extent, it was at first a tactic of interviewing, but as my identity as a scholar-observer-participant became more widely accepted so there seemed to be a deepening of authentic mutual responses across the board. Thus the lone scholar found it natural as well as beneficial to develop a "collective" style. As I became more experienced I would, if necessary, sacrifice the advantages of the more obvious tactics of questioning or rigorous probing, for the benefits of preserving the sense of genuine exchange and the "we-ness" that went with it.

On occasion, the probing did become harder and more adversarial, particularly in pursuit of inconsistencies, conflicts of evidence, and the verification of an important but controversial interpretation. I was probably most like that in some of the important interviews where I knew that the meeting was a one-off event, or at least an appointment which was unlikely to be repeatable in the near future.

But in many cases, I found the mutuality involved in the style of the shared enquiry too valuable to risk.

The interview as creative dialogue

In this context of mutuality - and this was a much later discovery - detailed note-taking could be as distracting to the interviewer as it was to those being interviewed. Indeed, it could be a series of breaks in the focus of concentration, not only limiting the powers of observation but impeding the mental space for a creative response.

The important point here is that over time I came to appreciate that interviews, conversational or otherwise, were not simply tools for drawing information but exchanges which could stimulate creativity in a variety of ways. In planning and managing the form of the interview, this creative dimension of the communication could not to be disregarded without potential loss.

In some interviews, however calm the atmosphere, the intensity of the mental engagement and the excitement of the subject under discussion could cause the adrenalin to pump and the mind to race, enhancing the mental energy and the creative process. As a result, various unexpected and useful thoughts could be released by the exchange.

Even when this heightened state was absent, new information and new cases which might mentally be linked with other examples, could break old assumptions and associations and trigger new lines of thought during the interview. Sometimes it paid to think through and probe the new line of thought there and then, or even, where a connection or pattern had been suggested, to return the discussion to an earlier comment in the interview rather than focus on noting exactly what had been said.

Further, in interviews conducted at national "insider" level in politics, I was often in conversation with people who were themselves acute professional observers and interpreters, and knowledgable amateur historians. They were generally fascinated by the pattern of the political terrain on which they were working and particularly ready to welcome a broad overview. In the dialogue that ensued, it helped (so they told me) not to be part of the "London common sense" about what was going on. There could be a freshness about the difference in the perspectives which was welcome and creatively useful to both sides.

Such dialogues might offer new insights and interpretations, perspectives which changed the angle of my perception and questioned some of my fundamental assumptions. As mutual trust developed, so these discussions could, on occasions, become broadly diagnostic and reflective. They could become dissections of the body politic, stimulating a nuanced differentiation of concepts and descriptions of behaviour. Occasionally they could even become sites for the Detective to act as Devil's Advocate or Awkward Sod (See Chapter Seven) and testing grounds for the creative process as those being interviewed responded to some of the unusual patterns that I was beginning to see.

As a result, there were often developments in theorising which partly took place in the creative dialogue of the interview. Or there were creative reverberations which followed a brief unplanned digression in the interview as I responded to what was being said. Various analytical distinctions and conceptual developments in my work arose out of probing the broader significance of a penetrating observation, a subtle distinction, revealing self-confession, or even a novel diagnosis on the part of those being interviewed. Certainly there were changes in the developing analytical framework which owed their origins to, or were finessed as a result of, these joint explorations. Indeed, one whole chapter in one book [Minkin

1991/92 ch 6] was stimulated by a discussion on one aside, "We are schizophrenic but anybody who thinks we do not take our responsibilities seriously doesn't understand," made to me by a left-wing union leader in reply to my questioning of his political identity.

Of course, in these circumstances there were times when I thought it necessary to jot the odd word, phrase or idea on any old sheet of paper in order to give myself a note of what we had said or a reminder to think the thing through. But, in general, as I monitored my mental process, I took the view that detailed note-taking on what was said could constrain my immediate thinking process as well as inhibit those involved on the other side of the conversation.

Flexibility in response to the conversation facilitated this creative process. It allowed me to make the solid information-seeking enquiries on which the creative scholar depends, but also, on occasions to make detours down interesting byways where I saw a connection or a revealing insight. It enabled me to probe the detail of the bits of the jig-saw that might make the picture clear, and also to query those that did not quite fit. It permitted me to explore an emerging pattern of cases, and to react, there and then, to the sudden appearance of the peculiarities that my nose told me could fruitfully be followed. Thus, I was happy to allow the conversation to take unexpected courses and, at times, to meander along, risking that it would have its creative benefits, providing that I could, periodically and gently, return it towards the priority areas of enquiry.

This style of my work is now a technical and intellectual routine, although from time to time I have tried various adjustments. These days, such is the level of trust that there are many who I talk to who seem unconcerned over whether I am writing something down or not. There are some participants who give me a routine debriefing session, in person or on the phone, after important political meetings. Others routinely exchange observations and insight about the week's events, trusting me in how and when I use the information.

Changes in routines can be unsettling to both sides. A few years ago, a party official who had for years supplied me with information, and engaged in discreet discussions in conditions of absolute trust, suddenly got it into his head that I ought to use a tape recorder. "These days, others do it a lot". He had, he said, always been fascinated by the singularity of my working methods. "Why go through the burdensome delayed note taking process? We trust each other." "Use a tape." So on the next visit that is what we did.

Unfortunately in the session that followed, with the tape going, he then began to reply to my questions as though I was an audience in Trafalgar Square! Occasionally, as I asked him the usual kind of questions he eyed me carefully as he addressed me. So we laughed, gave it up and we went back to chatting freely.

I can see how the tape-recorder might liberate the mind. I can also see that, with some people and in some intense discussions, an invisibility could begin to affect any recording instrument. But there are, I am sure, losses as well as gains. In the deeply sensitive political areas I have been working in, there are many situations where I cannot imagine opening up by pulling out a recorder, saying, " You don't mind if I switch this on?" and getting the depth of honest information and opinion that I have become accustomed to.

PROBLEMS AND DANGERS

This unusual style of the Detective, with its pragmatism of chosen personae, its variation of participant and observer, its mix of lone investigation and collective style, its projection of neutrality with mutuality, and its welcoming of a creative partnership in the interview, was not without problems, dangers and ethical dilemmas.[21] Indeed in this situation, in one way or another, the researcher as Detective was making difficult ethical choices all the time, some of which caused considerable *angst*.

In the style of interviewing, where information was given and opinions were expressed on both sides with varying degrees of confidentiality, there were many delicate moments. In all this exchange of knowledge and perspectives in a friendly atmosphere, it was sometimes difficult to keep appropriate levels of confidentiality and secrecy between interviews. Generally, over the years I must have done this reasonably well, but, as I write, I can bring vividly to mind various stomach-sinking, undiplomatic comments and also some botched attempts to recover the situation.

There was also the constant danger that the Detective, with his friendly "we" inclusiveness when operating deep in the "underworld," could become prey to a variety of temptations. The more extreme of these ("You write me up well and I'll tell you whatever you want to know"[22]) I have had little difficulty with. My work did not normally involve pointed attributions of personal praise or blame, and I always attempted to portray all political activities with as much respect as I could muster - however deep the skulduggery or questionable the motives. So, some of the most sensitive difficulties could be avoided. But that being said, "deals" were out. I never made that kind of accommodation. I never gave any guarantees about the form of publication, other than it would be academic. I rarely showed any sections of my drafts to participants, and when I did I made it absolutely clear that the drafts were never altered to suit any individual.

I also had a strict rule that I never asked for patronage and therefore did not incur any specific obligation. But it also helped that, for myself, I had absolutely no political ambitions, and when the occasional prestigious carrot was dangled under my nose I was not much interested in it.

I did recognise an element of reciprocity in accepting the anonymous, and occasionally deeply confidential, terms in which I received some information. If I agreed not to disclose something, but to regard it as for "background" understanding, I kept to that. Occasionally to get round a tricky area when I wrote it up, I moved the whole section up a level of generality.[23]

Sanctions became less of a problem for me as my reputation grew. In the search for information the cold shoulder that seeks to manipulate the novice researcher can be a difficulty, threatening access and seeking to pull the researcher into line. But, where this is clearly a tactic, there comes a point where this just has to be ignored and other means of access found. If this could not be done, I changed the focus of research, returning when either the mood or the personnel had changed. As Harold Wilson said "A week is a long time in politics." If the exclusion was permanent, and, from a very few, occasionally it was, then that was how it had to be. They too lost something - the opportunity to have their views and perspectives directly represented.

Much more difficult have been the contrary problems. Time - accursed time - makes it impossible to interview everybody about everything that takes place. However comprehensive the investigation, there has to be some selectivity in sources.

Unfortunately, who you talk to in politics can be interpreted as a comment on status. As a result, there have been, at times, expressions of prickly resentment if it was known I had talked to one official but not another.

More significant, closeness, shared political values and the developing role of benevolent "expert," tend to draw the Detective into a warm embrace and into a deep concern for the success of the organisation and for those who keep it going. In the literature of sociology and anthropology, this is sometimes referred to as "going native". None of us is completely immune to these influences - especially if we already have a commitment to the organisation and were always part of the tribe. I have no doubt that I made various unconscious compromises, as well as the occasional conscious one, involving omissions in what I wrote. It would require a much larger canvas and perhaps more passage of time to deal with those in detail.

Nevertheless, what can be said is that my work did focus to an unusual extent on the flaws of national political processes, on modes of political management and on political manipulation at the highest levels. Over the years I have wrestled regularly with a variety of ethical considerations and with different criteria of the greater good, as I attempted to explore and portray honestly a variety of power relations. There is no easy formula for dealing with every situation, but I always attempted to live up to the self-image of the scholarly seeker-after, and communicator-of, truth.

Through a process of self-questioning, one seeks an awareness of the influences that are at work. Through a process of self-criticism and a regular post-mortem over errors of judgement, one tries to stay on the straight and narrow, at least when, in this kaleidoscope of changing roles and personae, one is clear exactly what that path is.

SERENDIPITY AND THE PREPARED MIND

Over time, the mature research scholar learns to reduce the pratfalls and to respond positively to the pitfalls. Indeed, to some extent to see both in positive terms, as the price to be paid for the trial-and-error process of creative enquiry, as a developing education in what is comfortable to the mind and to the art of the researcher, and as a part of the mental preparation and awareness which increases the general level of competence and the chance of serendipity.

Here I turn to this element of the research experience. There was one very surprising feature of all this detective work which took a long time to understand. As a novice Detective who was by nature rather pessimistic, I never expected chance to be on my side. I operated more on the neurotic assumption that as the proverb goes, "where there is ointment there will be a fly". In particular, if there were two important events to attend they would be on the same day at the same time but 200 miles apart, and I would be in the wrong place at the wrong time!

Therefore, it came as a very welcome surprise to me that I seemed to be very lucky in the findings of my research. And the more I learned about the domain of my work, the more some helpful things seemed to fall into my hands. A journal picked up with vague interest in a waiting room, a programme caught by chance on a car radio, a casual conversation on a train, a report given to me by a next-door neighbour - all could hold a relevant gem. It was not quite what it seemed. There undoubtedly are lucky findings or even gifts[24] which are of benefit to the research. When they happen they carry you forward with a sense of good fortune and a feeling of the beneficial power of "the flow". But there are also occasions when more than the fortuitous is involved. There is also a form of "sagacity" (as Walpole put it [Roberts 1981 p ix]) that facilitates the beneficial conjunction. In this sense, chance, as Pasteur said, favours the prepared mind.

This sagacity of the prepared mind can take different forms. If we take the word "prepared" to include the kind of qualities referred to earlier - observational vigilance, open-mindedness, sensitivity to connections and patterning, and independence of judgement - then probably the prepared mind does not need to have been focused on the particular problem, or even to be expert in the particular field, for the discovery to occur.

However, more typical, in research, is that we help to make our good luck by our focus on particular problems, our dedicated pursuit and our specialised domain professionalism. There is likely to be a high incidence of systematised chance in our encounters[25]. It is persistence which often allows us more opportunity to be in the right place at the right time [Weber and Perkins 1992 p 320]. It is our active mental engagement which encourages us to question the unexpected - the surprises and the peculiarities. And it is our competence as we become more confident and more knowledgeable, building upon accumulated observation in our field [Foster, Scudder, Colson and Kemper 1979 p 330], which often enables us to give meaning and connectedness to the "accidents," the fortuitous archive findings and the beneficial encounters. It also enables us to know what would be the fruitful questions to ask. (See Chapter Eight and the Case of the Missing Tanks.)

The case of the missing link

My favourite example - a fortuitous encounter and a discovery - the most memorable and perhaps the most important, happened to me on a bus going towards Labour Party headquarters.

As a novice researcher I had been puzzling for some time over how the agenda management at the Party Conference might be systematically organised to favour an agenda which would help the Parliamentary Leadership, given that the Conference Arrangements Committee was elected by the Conference, and worked to customary rules which seemed to guarantee fairness. Direct questioning of officials tended to bring the same response as that put out by successive Labour Party Leaders. They denied that the Conference agenda was or could be fixed by them. The Conference Arrangements Committee had nothing to do with the Leader. It was an independent body. Occasionally, as when talking with one young and more open member of the Conference Arrangements Committee and one long-retired official, I had glimpses of another covert process which put me on the alert and caused me to seek to dig deeper.

One day, on the bus, I stood by chance next to the new Assistant General Secretary of the Labour Party. He had been talking to the holidaying Prime Minister (Harold Wilson) on the phone (about Rhodesia I think). In the odd time-filling remarks that he made to me, he obviously thought that he was impressing me with the importance of the conversation that he had just been involved in, whilst telling me something utterly trivial about that conversation with Wilson. And from the perspective of Government policy he was. But he was also, by his tone and assumptions, alerting me to the primary covert political channel of agenda control at the Party Conference. What he said implied, at least to my mind, that authoritative signals came from the Prime Minister to the General

Secretary and were thence relayed to the Assistant National Organiser. This official also acted as the Secretary of the Conference Arrangements Committee, and in theory was responsible only to the Committee in supplying it with a draft agenda in accordance with guidelines laid down by that Committee.

In fact, the official listened to two authoritative voices, and chronologically the first voice to which a response was made was that of the Party Leader. I could suddenly see it because I was alert to the problem, I was in the right place, and I commanded the mental context to understand the relevance of even oblique references.

I confirmed this later with retired Party officials - including a Chairman of the Standing Orders Committee from the 1930s, who I pursued to the garden of his retirement bungalow. I found that in practice, the draft was the P.M.'s draft and there could be as many as eight drafts before it was ever put to the Committee.

The Committee members were busy union officials who were not much prone to arguing unnecessary technicalities with the Committee Secretary, and in any case shared some common assumptions about what would make for "a good conference". When put to the Conference there was every reason why the union delegates would, most of the time, think twice about rejecting careful agenda arrangements done, apparently, by their hardworking colleagues.

Once it was accepted that I was "in the know," and a genuine long-term academic researcher who was not about to betray a trust or misuse material, the serving officials began to regard me as an acceptable part of the political environment and to open up, even welcome me, as they warmed to the exposition of their hitherto hidden or unrecognised professionals skills. This became a two-way acceptance of professionalism and quality. It was a pattern of behaviour which I grew accustomed to evoking across the whole of my field of research.

ENQUIRIES AND SIGNPOSTS

This opening-up was, by no means, a complete process. Secrecy surrounded much of this realm of Labour Party politics, and the Detective had to do most of the foraging and inquiring for himself. He had to be particularly careful to remain vigilant in his observations. The theory of cognitive dissonance indicates to us that observers tend to see what they expect to see, or what their attention is drawn to. This is a general research problem, but in my field it takes on a special dimension. Skilled political managers and spin doctors play upon this with cynical realism. The vigilant Detective can see though it (although not necessarily immediately and not necessarily all the time).

For sheer *chutzpa*, take one very illuminating example that happened in 1969. There was a printer's error in the National Executive Committee Report to the party relating to the controversial White Paper, *In Place of Strife*. This paper had proposed unprecedented legislative initiatives on industrial relations by the then Labour Government. The NEC had refused to accept all its provisions but (by one of those misfortunes that give party officials heart attacks) the word "not" (before the word "accept") had been missed out of the report. It was an error which, if taken literally could have plunged the Party into a new row after the dropping of the proposals. The obvious course might have been simply to openly acknowledge it as an error. However, knowing the psychology of conferences, it was agreed at senior levels in Head Office that rather than draw attention to the error (and thereby to the whole issue) nothing would be said about it. It seemed to me to be a risky tactic but, lo and behold, it did appear that not one of the thousand delegates in the hall noticed it as the Conference quietly accepted the NEC Report.[26]

There were less innocent purposes involved in the activities of the managers. For years I assumed that the annual report of the Labour Party Conference was an accurate representation of the proceedings - and in the main it was. Reports to me by aggrieved delegates of various cases of managerial skulduggery and of procedural arguments between them and the Chair of the Conference Arrangements Committee seemed to involve failures of memory warped by grievance and suspicion. Then, at the 1968 Conference I distinctly heard the Chair talk about the retiring Sara Barker the Party's National Agent and the "dirty jobs" she had been required to do for the party, only to discover later that the reference had been doctored in the report. Hello, hello, what's all this?

It could have been a one-off alteration. But, suspicions alerted that maybe the delegates' testimony had to be re-evaluated, I started to dig. I managed to wangle myself access to an old Granada TV film of a debate on the report of the Chair of the Conference Arrangements Committee during a particularly contentious year (1965). It fully confirmed my suspicions that the report was not the verbatim account that I had been led to believe. Subsequently, I expanded the area of search of issues of agenda management, in line with delegates' accounts.

As I realised the full significance of the agenda controls at the Party Conference - the dog not allowed to bark - and the scope of their operations, I began to redefine the questions in my problem-seeking. Crucially, I learned to ask the question, "What was the Conference *not* allowed to decide?". Digging out a full range of past agendas from a variety of sources, I set to work. The more that I explored the more I noticed. As there was little in the way of written records of the background discussions covering this political activity, I pursued any union or party official who was prepared to talk about the past form and political purpose of these controls. By this process I slowly uncovered many examples which shed new light on the formal history.

It was not just over the agenda that, time after time, observers of the Labour Party followed the signposts and missed things which were labelled "insignificant". For years the press discussed developments over the union block vote at the Labour Party Conference without noticing the pathbreaking relevance of voting reforms at the Labour Women's Conference, because that Conference was considered unimportant. Yet when reform came, it was heavily influenced by that precedent.

Of course, even the vigilant detective can be fooled by the "politically insignificant" label. Walworth Road, the Labour Party's national headquarters, had for years in the late 1970s and early 1980s, very troubled industrial relations. There were many minor industrial actions, even occasionally a strike. Yet I (and others) failed to see the political linkage and political significance of these internal industrial relations between the unions and the Labour Party -particularly their effect on election preparation.

In fact, I did not see its significance and connect it with my project until after it had been pointed out to me several times by a militant member of the staff union. Only after I saw how the themes might be connected with the pattern of the framework that I was constructing to understand the relationship as a whole, did I see the now blindingly obvious relevance. I began gathering and analysing the data and built it up into what I think is a very illuminating chapter [Minkin 1991/92 ch 19]. Of course it was written in the usual style of the academic - purposeful, discerning and omniscient.

THE OBSERVER-INSIDER AND CREATIVE RESEARCH

In principle, though I came to research after years of active involvement in the field, I always attempted to play the role of Detective with some sense of detachment from the field of enquiry and from my own values and prejudgments. Indeed, I saw it as a test of my professionalism. As a novice researcher, I reduced my partisan political activity to a minimum and kept it well away from the areas of investigation. Though sometimes torn between the research role and the political work I was involved in, I attempted in those days not to intervene in, or otherwise disturb, what was being observed. Occasionally I wavered in my definition of what was right and what was acceptable, particularly in sharing my growing understanding and offering persuasive interpretations, which were different from those conventionally on offer. But the line that I did consistently keep involved fidelity to sources, a conscious effort at appropriate empathy and objectivity, and a reluctance to use for partisan purposes anything given to me in confidence as a researcher.[27]

However, as I realised after a while, in practice, in one form or another, intervention is almost inevitable - particularly for the established "expert." Any researcher who writes about the field, and is read by those in the field is, in a sense, intervening because an interpretation is being offered which is likely to affect behaviour in the field. Also, the longer the researcher is in the field, the more personal relationships develop, as indicated, involving varying degrees of closeness, confidentiality and trust. These bring with them, at the least, a sharing of perspectives. This interaction with participants goes wider and deeper. As we have seen, once an expertise is developed, many participants invite responses from the observer and conversational interviews become the mutual exchange, and sometimes the creative dialogue, that I have already described.

Crucially, over time, as in my case, the observer can become "the adviser" who is consulted and expected, informally, to express an expert view upon developments in the field. Sometimes "the adviser" is formally invited to offer prescriptions and assistance, including speechwriting.[28] In recent years, I have gone even further than that, becoming an insider in another sense - not just a participant but an expert/adviser/player, at national level with a mixture of roles which involve, on occasions, a formal role in organisational decision-making[29] and some discreet high level consultations and interventions.

For me this was an unexpected development with both new possibilities and new constraints. I have had to become even more self-aware and self-critical in the attempt to preserve a degree of scholarly detachment and define appropriate codes of conduct. In the field of politics, this research scholar/advisor/player combination is not always a comfortable fusion of roles. Even if you work discreetly, you take on a higher political profile. At times of deep controversy, your politico-academic perspective can become subject to the war of intra-party faction. It can meet fierce disapproval. There is a disturbance of normal expectations of your behaviour as an academic. Some of the lines of communication can become more politicised and uncertain. To an extent, relationships change and have to be renegotiated. I am, in some ways, still working on what the new "rules" of engagement entail in the attempt to reconcile the various ethical obligations and responsibilities that are involved.

For a dedicated researcher, one happy result of this new form of involvement was that there has been a steady supply of inside information and fresh opportunities to make direct observations. But to retain trust and a sense of integrity, I had to ensure that others involved could feel confident that what they said and did would not be misused or transferred from situation to situation as I wore the different hats. In particular, there was the problem of how I treated information which came to me from privileged access or from being in a position to observe things that would otherwise not have been open to me. I came to the view that it meant that there were key meetings that I became involved in where, diplomatically, I could not publish anything about what transpired for some time. Even my own submissions within that context became subject to a degree of self-imposed public restraint.

However, there is another point that I want to make here, apart from noting once again the complexities and delicate lines of propriety between the academic scholar and the adviser-participant-observer. It is that an observationally vigilant and "playful" researcher who intervenes, or is drawn into intervention in any of these ways, can, with some imagination, turn it also into the creative Detective's role.

This is not just a matter of sensitive observation; it involves mentally raising conjectures about the impact of the intervention. Even routine activities can be productive in this respect if vigilantly followed though and thought about. Reactions to just my presence in a location may vary in an illuminating way (alarmed/ suspicious/ welcoming). The reactions can be probed. Why are they responding in this way? Reactions to more active initiatives give opportunities to assess the responses and follow the reverberations. The speculation, "What if there had been no 'intervention' on my part?" leads on to other questions. Did this development actually come from me or from some other source? How precisely was the intervention interpreted? How did the intervention ripple along the lines of communication? What does this suggest about the recipients? What does this indicate about who talks to whom? What was the outcome? Why?

THE STYLE OF THE DETECTIVE

The development of my expertise over time was paralleled by the growth of this quasi-advisory status, and yet, in a sense, also by my legitimate "invisibility." People get very used to you being there[30] - a process which reduces any initial sense of awkwardness.

The awkwardness was often there in the early years. When I first went out on the beat at national level, as a new Detective I felt self-conscious, uncomfortable and unconvincing in the role. I was a stranger in a strange place where I felt that I did not belong. Slowly, over time, I became more assured and more at ease. To some extent, my persona seemed to blend more easily into the different cultures - the intellectual Morse to one group, the white collar proletarian Sergeant Cuff to another. The personal style became more relaxed and unintrusive - a bit like the innocuous Colombo.

Later, the acceptability of my regular presence "on the job," and the advisory role that often accompanied the role of detective, became much more reminiscent of Miss Marple -knowledgeable, one of us, from the local village. In style the Detective also came to resemble Inspector Jack Frost in his reliance on experience, his lack of deference, his distaste for pomposity and snobbery, and his irreverance for over-rigid professional conventions in "getting at the truth". He did his own thing, to his own judgements, by his own values, and without asking favours.

HEURISTICS OF THE ROLE OF THE DETECTIVE

Long experience in making these judgements in a wide variety of watching, listening, and questioning situations has now taught me to establish certain professional rules or heuristics. They are the summation of my understanding of the role of the Detective. I think of them along these lines:-

> Creative detectives always do their homework on the context and the suspects,
>
> Are always making enquiries, and are never completely satisfied with the answers,
>
> Prepare a line of enquiry and anticipate alternatives of where it might lead,
>
> Always make their own judgement, and never follow other people's signposts (however illustrious or official the signposter),
>
> Are fascinated by peculiarities and are persistent in seeking to explore and explain them,
>
> Are freeze-framing the evidence within a plurality of possible perceptions,
>
> Are proud of the professionalism that enables them to sideline their own emotions and prejudices and, if necessary, to shed their preconceptions,

Always try to tell themselves "the truth" about themselves and about the world that they investigate, even if they have to face the uncomfortable and to admit error.

CHAPTER END NOTES

[1] [Hudson 1966] quoted by [Cropley 1967 p 49].

[2] The importance of role-playing in the head, as part of the creative process, was elaborated by the author in a Professorial Inaugural Lecture at Sheffield Hallam University on 26th June 1996 in a Lecture entitled *Political Research as a Creative Art* and sub-titled *the theatre of the mind and the creativity-generating society*.

[3] The roles as images are distinct: the roles in practice are by no means mutually exclusive. To find an adequate explanation, the Detective has to be aware of patterns. To reveal new and useful patterns the Patternmaker must be able to detect them.

[4] [Winks 1968], [Cannon 1945]. The major chapter by Ford in [Ford and Gioia 1995] takes the form of investigating a mystery. See also the novel by Josephine Tey [Tey 1951] on the policeman as historian.

[5] Note on this the obvious but sage advice of D.N. Perkins, "If you want to be original try to build into any outcomes the quality of originality" [Perkins 1981 p 215].

[6] Henry James 'Prefaces to The Spoils of Poynton; A London Life; The Chaperon.' in *The Critical Muse : selected literary criticism*, Harmondsworth, Penguin, 1987, pp 529-532.

[7] As a political adviser, in 1975-6, I listened and watched whilst the playwright Trevor Griffiths, who had created a realistic but imaginary world around the life of the Labour MP 'Bill Brand', gave confident directions to the actors with nuances derived from a dazzlingly rich control

over the English language. It heightened my awareness that language structures the perceptual vigilance of the creative detective.

[8] "...the least satisfactory group are (ex) politicians who often encounter pathological difficulties in distinguishing the truth, so set have their minds become by long experience of partisan thought" [Seldon 1988] quoted by David Richards [Richards 1968 p 201].

[9] Fieldwork researchers have much more freedom and creative scope than either experimenters or survey interviewers but methodological dexterity can take a variety of creative forms. For a brief summary with some examples in relations to other methods see on this [Baker 1994 particularly pp 25, 36 and 37].

[10] Edward de Bono [de Bono 1993a, p 53]. Vertical thinking is thinking that is directly built up from, or logically related to, a given position or base.

[11] This is Whitfield's metaphorical interpretation of Guilford's notion of "divergent thinking" (as opposed to "convergent thinking" which brings selected areas into close detail) [Whitfield 1975 p 16].

[12] *New Socialist*, launch edition Vol I No I September/ October 1981.

[13] Hugh Stretton is very useful in clarifying the fruitfulness of such comparisons (and other imaginative historical exercises) [Stretton 1969, pp 245-252].

[14] I was not well advised on any of this. My knowledge of interviewing and its techniques came mainly from trial and error and from word of mouth from other researchers. I have only recently read William Foote Whyte 'Interviewing in field research' in [Burgess 1982 pp 111-122], which is a very useful summation of the options and is reprinted from a 1960 publication. It did not teach me much that I did not know but had I read it thirty years ago it might have saved me some anxiety and a lot of misunderstanding.

[15] [Lee 1993 p 207] argues that sensitive topics encourage the researcher to be imaginative and innovative.

[16] [Webb and Webb 1932 p 130] quoted by [Burgess 1982 p 102].

[17] Brenner, M. 'Intensive interviewing' in [Brenner, Brown and Cantor, 1985 p 151].

[18] L.A. Dexter quoted by Moyser, G. 'Non-standardised interviewing in elite research' in [Burgess 1988 p 125].

[19] "..often the researcher... is involved in an intense and non hierarchical set of relationships with his or her informants and has no intention of deliberately manipulating them or maintaining a social distance from them" Burgess, R.G. 'Conversations with a purpose: the ethnographic interview in educational research" in [Burgess 1988 pp 138-9]. See on this also the important article by A. Oakley 'Interviewing women : a contradiction in terms' in [Roberts 1981 pp 30-61] also Janet Finch 'It's great to have someone to talk to: the ethics and politics of interviewing women' in [Bell and Roberts 1984].

[20] In a very suggestive passage, Jane Jorgenson points out that "The ways in which interviewees make sense of and respond to the interviewer's questions depend in large measure on how those being interviewed represent the interviewer and her objectives to themselves - whether as a friend, a detached scientist, a 'generalised other' or perhaps all of these". 'Co-constructing the interviewer /co-constructing "Family"' in [Steier 1991 p 223].

[21] There is now a considerable literature on the ethical and political dilemmas involved in fieldwork although much of it to came to my attention much too late to be either illuminating or consoling in dealing with basic problems. See for example [Barnes 1977], [Barnes 1979], or not open [Beauchamp, Fadden, Wallace, and Waters 1982], [Bulmer 1982], [Emerson 1983 particularly Part 1V 'Ethical and political issues in field research' pp 253-311] also Thorne, B. 'Political Activist as Participant Observer: Conflicts of Commitment in a Study of the Draft Resistance Movement of the 1960s.' pp 216-234. Punch, M. 'Politics and ethics in qualitative research' in [Denzin and Lincoln 1994 pp 83-97].

[22] As a young researcher, I met the bluntest expression of this proposed deal from an official who had been central to agenda politics during some of the most crucial Conference decisions in Labour Party history. I turned it down flat but from time to time since then I have wondered what it was that I might have missed.

[23] There was one particularly tricky area where I developed my own rule of balance, which was never to write up bits of evidence about involvements with the foreign embassies or security services, from whatever side, Left or Right. My view on this was that I was in an area where my knowledge could at best be sketchy and I could not give an account that I would be reasonably sure about.

[24] An archivist once handed me a folder marked "Trade Unions", saying that he had "just found this". "Is it any use?". Wading through it, I found that it contained important and confidential minutes of a very low profile war-time party-union committee which had met towards the end of the war with a view to preparing Labour's peacetime organisation. [Minkin 1991/92 pp 62-65].

[25] Perkins in [Boden 1994 p 132].

[26] This was one of those occasions when, having noticed it myself and privately raised the matter with an embarrassed and ashen-faced Research Director, although I would loved to have told somebody and watched the delegates' reactions, I felt bound by the confidence.

[27] There is a golden rule, nicely expressed in another context by H.Russell Bernard, "Do nothing that you cannot live with professionally and personally", [Bernard 1994 p 156].

[28] Over the years I have drafted a variety of speeches for senior members of the Labour Party of which perhaps the most important was the speech for Neil Kinnock at Stoke on September 12th 1983 just before he became Leader of the Labour Party which I entitled, "Rebuilding the people's party". It outlined a programme for what was to become the long-term reform of Party organisation following Labour's defeat at the 1983 General Election.

[29] After the 1992 General Election I became academic adviser to, and a full member of, the Labour Party National Executive Committee "Review Group on Party-Union Relations". I provided its *Framework of Working Principles, Themes and Values* and a range of other advisory material. The report of this group and the consequent constitutional amendments were accepted by the Party Conference in 1993. In 1996 I became co-adviser to the NEC's "Party into Power Project", preparing the organisation and working procedures for relations between the Labour Party and a future Labour Government.

[30] There was a time when I would have raised doubts about this concept but I have learned otherwise. In the late 1970s I worked as an adviser on a television series on the Communist Party with Roger Graef - a highly skilled specialist in "fly on the wall" observation - and was astonished at the extent to which two men with a camera could apparently become virtually invisible to people involved in the most sensitive of political manoeuvres and some sharp political rows.

CHAPTER SIX

ROLE PLAYING AND CREATIVE RESEARCH: JUGGLER, PATTERNMAKER AND COMPANY

THE JUGGLER

The process of production

Logically, we think of the production of the outcome of a research project as involving a clear sequence of two processes -a process of doing the research and a process of writing up the findings, a process of investigation and reflection followed by a process of presentation. One still finds studies of research where the would-be researcher is advised," When all the hard work of gathering and analysing evidence is complete, you will need to write a final report" [Bell 1987 p 151].

Sometimes that may be a reasonable account of the sequence of how it happens in practice - particularly for the inexperienced researcher [Torrance and Thomas 1994 p 113]. However, in my fluid, adjustive style of work, the process of production is very different. Even though I always have some kind of plan of campaign in relation to the project, and I systematically prepare for sequential stages, mentally at least, the two processes tend to develop in an unpredictable interaction with each other until the project ends with the submission of the paper or publication.

It is certainly true that there is a period at the end of the work when it is mainly writing-up and checking, but normally, from the very earliest days of the project, I am beginning to write, assembling on paper (however crudely and with little regard for syntax and verbal refinement) the outline patterns of the architecture of the whole structure. This has been the way that I have approached the production of my research since I first started. It just seemed to grow that way. In this sense I have an extreme "holistic" style[1] - seeking an outline of the totality then moving back and forth between the parts and the whole.

Both the whole and the parts will go through countless reconstructions and drafts before they approximate to something that is acceptable and presentable. This is not unusual in the productions of an academic researcher [Becker with Richards 1986 p 14]. For various reasons which I will explain later, the projects develop their own dynamism and the writing has to accommodate to the various shifts of form and changes of objective. At any one time the sections can be in different stages of completion, regardless of any chronological, logical or planned order. Movements back and forth will often depend on the way that the mind engages with and connects the data, as well as the way that the data is accumulated.

In this repetitive process of writing, editing and rewriting, the quality of the different passages slowly improves until eventually I have a sense of the whole thing getting leaner and tighter, with the good bits joining together, the weaker sections becoming stronger, and the worst bits becoming more acceptable. As draft succeeds draft, the entrances become more inviting, the transitions become clearer, the linkages more secure, and the exits become more satisfactory. As Howard Becker points out [Becker with Richards 1986 p 14], each stage must have its own criteria of excellence: an insistence on polished precision and clarity appropriate to a late stage can undermine the creativity involved at the stage of generating ideas.

Frameworks

From the first, I am mentally juggling with the construction and reconstruction of two frameworks, covering the substantive and the presentational. I think of these frameworks as being composed of patterns of various kinds and I think of myself as a Patternmaker who is also a Juggler.

(i) Primarily, I aim to construct a coherent and adequate conceptual framework grounded in the repeated occurrences found in my empirical investigations. This framework is always analytical in the attempt to establish a pattern which makes sense in describing and categorising relationships and developments across time, but it also aspires to be explanatory, organising the material in such a way as to indicate solutions to the core problem (or problems) and related questions under investigation, seeking to account for all cases within a particular historical and cultural setting.

(ii) But I aim also to present the material within a coherently structured textual framework. This arrangement involves judgments of the most appropriate mode of presentation, the most useful organisation of chapters, sections and paragraphs, the best clustering of topics and issues, and the most satisfactory continuities and juxtaposition of themes. The textual arrangement has to be accessible, appropriate, and linked by patterns which are characterised by clarity and (hopefully) a degree of elegance.

In the light of the Detectives' fieldwork, I juggle evidence, interpretations, concepts and explanations within one framework, and I juggle topics, sections, paragraphs and other textual arrangements within another. There is no preordained blueprint, but I do have the advantage that my mind has the capacity to stop the frame at any time, when the form and pattern appears satisfactory - even though I know that it may be only a temporary satisfaction.

The "juggle" - working mentally with and within these two complexes of patterns - is a fundamental part of the creative process. Although over time the indispensable scissors and staples have been replaced by a tidier business of using the keys of a word processor, the process is inherently problematic, hesitant and messy as different criteria collide. It is a juggle marked by numerous failures.

As the Juggler of the presentation, I have some tricky but now predictable difficulties to deal with. These are problems of what is said and what is not said, what goes where and particularly what goes first, what is clustered or linked together and what is kept apart, what is expanded and what is reduced. (The sections that I am writing here have been a classic example of the delicate decisions involved.)

To help with these kinds of decision, and the often complicated constructions and reconstructions that are involved, I developed the practice of using a "Summaries" file. This file contains chapter headings, sub-headings, sectional précis, main themes and threads, and key examples, which change as the work progresses. It is the paring down of the material to its most basic elements. It is a particularly useful tool for dealing with choices in complicated rearrangements. But it can also be a valuable aid to creative play. As the research progresses, I try as much as possible to hold this file in my head and keep playing with it, changing patterns, mentally editing, breaking it up and clustering it into different forms and sequences in the light of the developing conceptual framework and the changing evidence. Sometimes, as with my other files, simply mentally flicking through it and juxtaposing items introduces a heuristic element. Chance can produce new associations and new productive connections.

Juggling, writing and the creative process

Juggling involves playing - experimenting and toying in the head with numerous elements which are changing as the investigation proceeds and the patterning of the frameworks develop. It is a very fluid process and the fluidity is enhanced by the activity of writing. Research writing (as I slowly learned to appreciate) was not simply the end product of a creative activity - not simply a technical registration of where I was, what I had done, what I had found and what I had constructed. Even in the representation of a scholarly exercise where there had to be a scrupulous respect for evidence, the compositing process could be an agency of discovery and creative innovation.

In this and in other respects, my writing process was not as I thought it might be when I started out in academic research. Nor was it how, for a long time, I thought that it ought to be. For years, the idealised model that I had in mind of the academic researcher as a writer was of an intellectual who ruminated, reflected, decided what s/he wanted to say and then wrote it all down. Sometimes indeed it happened roughly like that. But, much of the time my own process of writing involved, in practice, a variable and almost indescribable, interactive mixture of different activities in which there was no clear break in process between the composing of thinking and the composing of writing.

Though much of the writing did follow a period of thinking and planning in which the overall content of what I was aiming at in that session had taken a clearish shape, rarely did that shape on paper follow exactly the outline of what had been in my mind. At other times difficult sections might begin as disparate comments, bits of evidence and underdeveloped thoughts, which were written down before I began a design process of giving a coherent meaning to the whole. Often, in a complex and (in conscious terms) undifferentiated process, I planned, wrote, re-thought, planned again, juggled, amended and thought again as I wrote. Often also, in the attempt to pull the whole intellectual edifice into an acceptable shape, I found myself juggling and amending different sections from different parts of the text, seeking an overall coherence and changing meanings and interpretations as I went along.

This activity of writing, as I discovered, could assist the creative process in a number of ways.[2] In writing, there was often the discovery of a degree of ambiguity, confusion, inconsistency and, consequently, a conscious pull towards clarification that could cause me to look afresh at, and reinterpret, what I "knew". In this process there was an interdependence of language and thought [Berthoff 1988 pp 21-3]. Fresh interpretations could suggest themselves as my vocabulary was brought to bear on the process of clarifying and amending what I had written. The process of groping for the language to convey a precise and appropriate meaning, sometimes caused me to re-examine the logic of an argument and its implications, and to change what it was that I was arguing.

Transitions - linkages from chapter to chapter or section to section - are vitally important in a coherent presentation, and had to be managed for their capacity to convey both continuities and departures. In the process of their construction and clarification, the entrances and exits could develop a logic and momentum of their own, with new lines of thought emerging, covert knowledge being brought into play and new connections made. Even small changes in transitions could take the argument in unanticipated and significantly new directions.

This writing process involved, of course, reading what I had written, and critically reflecting on it. In this critical reading it also involved a constant repositioning from the perspective of the author to the receptivity of the reader - or rather a variety of different kinds of reader. In this reflective activity and change of positioning, perspectives on the content could change, and lead to a variety of creative adjustments. Many things become clearer, or stand revealed anew, in this writing process. The major and minor bones of the argument became much more obvious when written down, making the mental creative play that much easier. Also, the laying out of the total picture of my thoughts, on the screen but particularly on paper, enabled me to scan them more easily from different angles and starting points - sometimes noting new connections, juggling different features and suggestive potential lines of enquiry. Adjustments to achieve a satisfactory aesthetic form, and even the arrangement of footnotes, could break old associations and suggest new connections (Some of the heuristic possibilities here are explored in more detail in the next chapter).

This creative process can also be encouraged by a deliberate exercise in free expression alternating with a more rigorous analytical mode.[3] This is not something that I have sought to do as a conscious exercise in my own writing, but occasionally something like it seemed to happen, particularly when I was attempting a very speedy assembly of the skeleton of a chapter, or part of a chapter, and just letting my rough plan and top-of-the-head knowledge drive it forward. The writing, even sentences, occasionally took on new content, involved new arguments and moved in unplanned directions. This seemed at times to involve an element of spontaneous creativity in which new ideas were generated in ways which are not the product of prior or of conscious thought. Perhaps the crucial word here is "conscious". In the writing process we are carrying out a variety of thinking processes, but often not recalling them. [Flowers 1989 p 31], [Bereiter and Scardamalia 1987 p 88].

In all these various ways, and on many occasions, writing involved not the recording of a creative outcome but participation in a further creative process. In this creative composition, I found myself raising new questions, generating new ideas, and in general discovering and adopting new positions in relation to the material. Writers in various literary fields have drawn attention to this phenomenon. Putting it at its most extreme case there is the poet W.J.Auden who asked, "How can I know what I think until I see what I say?"[Berthoff 1988 p 22]. Or perhaps, as the novelist Fay Weldon says, "...you begin to discover what went on in your head by reading what you have written"[4].

Now of course this might seem, at first sight, an inappropriate, unacceptable, even non-rational way in which to approach scholarly research presentation. At times, indeed, I have wondered who might employ a researcher who emphasised Auden's or Weldon's approach to his or her work. However, the attention paid to recent studies of the writing process indicates that this may become more recognised and accepted as a productive element in the work of academic research scholars.

In particular, the work of Bereiter and Scardamalia has suggested that a "knowledge transforming" (as opposed to a knowledge-telling) process is common amongst experienced researchers. There is a two-way interaction between continuously developed knowledge and continuously developed text. [Bereiter and Scardamalia 1987 p 12]. In the process of writing, experienced writers not only often considers changes in text, but also in what they want to say [Bereiter and Scardamalia 1987 p 11]. The composing process affects the ideational content of what is written. [Bereiter and Scardamalia 1987 pp xv-xvi].

Overall then, the process of writing involves an interpenetration of two processes often conceived as different categories of academic activity - the technical shaping of the presentation, and the interpretation of the substance of the inquiry. The interaction can generate a range of developments which were unplanned, and can give the content of the research unexpected features and dimensions. In this composing and juggling activity, the role of the researcher as writer can be as creative as it is in other aspects of research. And in this activity also, the role of the researcher has something in common with that of the sculptor "finding it in the wood".

To this extent the injunction "Don't get it right, get it written", when applied at draft stage, may be misleading. The reality is that you certainly don't have to get it right before you begin to write, and you don't have to get it right the first time that you write. And you have more chance of getting it right if you do write.

THE PATTERNMAKER

Reorientation

The failure of my attempt as a novice researcher to construct a theory which could be applied to all political conferences, contrasted with the exciting new possibilities which opened up from deep immersion in one important segment of British political life, and led me to a pragmatic adjustment in my approach to theorising. I lost the aspiration to generate and apply a grand theoretical schema to different international settings, and turned instead towards patternmaking grounded in particular evidence of variations in one national institutional complex over time. This was not an abandonment of theorising (although from this point I began to use the word less and less frequently) but it was the acceptance in my own work of a narrower scope of the theory.

I continued to feed in to this process an assessment of the utility of a variety of interpretations, concepts and major theories already on offer in relation to the particular area of research. These were considered, evaluated and returned to in the light of the information and explanations produced by the Detective. They were judged both in terms of their general usefulness and their particular insights. But the Patternmaker increasingly operated on the assumption that the top-down application of theory was not likely to be as fruitful for him, in his kind of work, as a bottom-up assembly of a framework grounded in the evidence. He became more comfortable in generating his own concepts and theories focused on significant political problems, than in testing or refining the theoretical work of other scholars. With time precious, he grew to believe that he was likely to gain far more by his deep immersion in the intricacies and subtleties of his field than by his deep penetration of a variety of theories provided by others.

Accompanying these developments came also the slow growth of an understanding that, though ambitious attempts at producing new theory could continue, they were likely to involve long periods of patient intellectual adjustment, attaining their highest quality in constructions that were built up over time rather than in one period of systematic activity.

This move towards patient, self-reliant groundedness, focused on significant political problems, was not an abandonment of the imaginative-creative process either, although, for a while, the novice researcher found himself focusing heavily on an exploration of the terrain and the accumulating of empirical evidence. What it did involve was a greater appreciation that, though there might be repeated imaginative forays, many sudden, surprising and heart-lifting insights, and innumerable small, creative leaps forward, these would arise out of a mental play with evidence derived from, and tested by, the investigative field work.

In short, though imaginative play was essential it was not enough. There had to be a concerned and rigorous search for relevance and plausibility in relation to a body of evidence, and a concern also with crafting the practicable in the way that the ideas were applied. The conceptual framework had to be constructed not only in terms of its novelty but also in terms of its capacity to order the data. Typically, in my work, the framework involved a large amount of such data, illuminating new facets of the relationship under examination and covering dimensions not normally given close attention.

Theorising involved the assembly of analytical categories and concepts derived primarily from empirical analysis of the immediate period in which the problem occurred, but the categories and concepts were so constructed as to make them explanatory in relation to this problem for other periods of the relationship. In terms of the Labour Party - trade union relationship, the aspiration was to establish a framework which was explanatory for the whole history of the Labour Party. Some of the frameworks that I produced over the years remained relatively static in their development. Others were reconstructed and refined many times as new understanding developed about the problem area.

Patterning: divergence and convergence

As an example, throughout the 1970s I was puzzling over the causes and consequences of a crisis which followed the publication in 1969 of the White Paper *In Place of Strife*. Some of those involved in this conflict had spoken to me later of this as the worst crisis in the party since 1931. Forecasts proliferated about the likelihood of a split in the relationship between the party and the unions. Yet, by the mid-1970s, the relationship with the unions was closer and, it appeared, more firmly based than ever. There were two intriguing problems here. What had caused the crisis to be as severe as it was, and what had produced the new accommodation? In my first approach to this, for an international conference in 1973 on trade union relations with political parties, I developed an explanatory framework which focused not on the immediate and particular causes of the rift in 1969, but on a pattern of recurring conflicts and long term trends, and the reinforcing tensions that they had produced by the end of the decade [Minkin 1974]. The events around *In Place of Strife* became simply the focal point of the crisis.

My ideas on this developed over the years. For a later conference I attempted a more comprehensive framework focussing upon both the patterning of forces which pulled the relationship apart and also those which held it together[Minkin 1978a]. In the construction of this more developed framework, I expanded elements of the first analysis in the light of new experiences in the relationship itself, and a new appreciation of some common patterns in previous recoveries from crisis. With this new understanding I sought for the elements of a framework which would be strong in its explanatory value of the immediate period of the problem but also consistent with and illuminating about the whole historical pattern of the relationship.

The framework at this second conference was held by two overarching themes - "dynamics of divergence" in the relationship and "dynamics of convergence". Within these, I attempted to focus both on factors which would be agreed to be of major importance, and also on causes and features which were much less noticed by other observers. Subsequently, over time, the explanatory concepts covering these factors changed definition and became refined in different ways, but by 1979 when I left this problem for some time, they had become "electoral orientation", "functional differentiation", "social empathy", "ideological cleavage", and "industrial conflict".

Images and the drama of politics

Looking back on that framework and others that I have produced, I can now also see a representational feature which was fairly common in my work but not obvious at the time. There was often a dramatic pivot around which the framework was ordered - a predicament, sometimes a state of crisis or a series of crises - with the presentation patterned around explanations of how the actors arrived at the crisis or contrived to get out of it.

This focus on crisis, and a dramatic pivot was, in part, a response to the political realities. For almost forty years the Labour Party had moved from one crisis situation to another. Repetitive crisis was virtually the norm of party experience. But, the presentation in terms of a dramatic pivot was also shaped by my own approach to the work - particularly my strong sense of politics as theatre. This was reinforced in the 1970s by work on various plays and drama documentaries. Long before and after that experience there were enduring influential images of the Labour Party Conference. It was a deeply serious decision-making body, but it could also be a great dramatic event, covering issues of great moment, with people moving from audience to stage to make their contributions, leading up to what could be the pivotal point of a crucial vote. This dramatic pattern was often playing in my mind as I viewed and wrote about other developments in the Labour Party.

Creative patternmaking and symbolic representation

The transference of patterns - in this case of crisis around a dramatic pivot - from one domain to another was not unusual in the work of the Patternmaker. As he became more sophisticated and self-aware in his work, observing patterns, and playing mentally with them, became a permanent feature of his research process. In his creative construction and reconstruction, in his patterning to create an appropriate understanding of the field of enquiry, the Patternmaker was (like the Detective) always on the job. And virtually everything he encountered began to be experienced as relevant to the project and a stimulant to his imagination about it.

He became increasingly aware that he lived in a world of multiple symbolic representations of the patterns he visualised in the substance and presentation of his research project. In the creative constructions and reconstructions of this patterning, he played constantly with analogies and metaphors, using every example as a means of galvanising repeated attacks on the task in hand, and also as a possible source of ideas which could expand the possibilties in managing it. In a constant process of comparison and reflection, his ideas about the project were fed and fed again by the similarities and differences he saw in the structure, shapes, textures, shades and inter-relationships of a variety of social phenomena, including those seen in the pastimes and activities he turned to for escape.

If he went to an orchestral concert, his mind drifted off to ponder the pattern whereby the themes in the exposition were introduced, fragmented and then combined. He flitted back and forth between what he was hearing and what he was doing in his own project. Could his presentation be structured as variations on a major theme? Were the themes of his own overture explored satisfactorily in the text? Were they all pulled together in his conclusions? Could the themes of his overture be somehow blended together anew in the finale? Could it work with two finales, each focused on a different set of themes?

If he saw a new building, so in the patternmaking around his own project, he saw himself playing the various roles involved in the construction of the building. As he studied the architecture and design, so his mind played with different foundations and superstructure in his own work. Combinations of the horizontal and vertical in the architectural structure often became chronological and analytical arrangements of his own project. Time and again his mind played with the way that the functions were integrated into the structure - particularly the location of pathways, entrances, steps, windows and avenues of vision.

When the Patternmaker read a book, he was now always on the look-out for the varieties of arrangement that might be adapted to fit his own designs. In a novel, he explored the structure as much as he enjoyed the plot, developing a deep appreciation of the skilfully woven theme that reappeared in an appropriate location. He took deep satisfaction from the profundity of the exploration of a conflict or a crisis, and from the excitement generated by the overcoming of obstacles. But he also admired the integration of the parts with the whole; the flashbacks into history that blended easily with, and illuminated well, the contemporary story; the commentary on the human condition that accompanied and captured the essence of a specific predicament.

Even the movements in a Rugby League game kept distracting him towards the effect of the game on his mind, and towards the universality of relevant patterning. Whereas the skilful innovations in play excited his senses and involved his emotions, it was the flowing repetitions and the pauses that somehow freed the imagination to float above the experience. The Patternmaker dwelt on the combinations of power and inhibition, violence and authority, rules and culture that made up the game. He pondered on the role of crisis and adversity as a necessary prerequisite for the drama of triumph. He saw both the cohesion and the conflict, the force and the fraud. He appreciated the distinctive contributions of skilled individuals, and the unified might and teamwork of the collective. All these fed back into the mental play with the content and shape, history and analysis, of his own political projects.

He became fascinated by the interplay of innovation and repetition across all the various fields of human activity, as well as in the substance and presentation of his own work. In the search for aesthetically satisfying repetition, he toyed with alliteration, rhythm and symmetry. In the search for appropriate novelty he played with the introduction of contrast, counterpoint and discord. In monitoring and formulating patterns of change, he was fascinated by forms of movement over time - forward and back, in and out, rising and falling. And he was constantly searching for the way that disparate and changing elements, variations and continuities, could all be combined to produce a satisfying pattern out of the whole.

The dialogue with the detective

In playing with and building the new patterns, the Patternmaker was constantly in discussions with the Detective. There was a two-way sensitivity in this internal dialogue. The Patternmaker was repeatedly attempting to enlarge the scope of the Detective's perception by developing the broader patterns. He shared with the Detective an overall concern for seeing the bigger picture, taking into account evidence from outside the national field of reference. But he also fed from the Detective's reports - evidence, peculiarities, interpretations - hoping to be able to see broader connections. If it was not necessarily practicable for the Detective to provide information on every nook and cranny of the field, the Patternmaker sometimes sent him on "tester" probes of various kinds, just to be sure that there was nothing surprising hiding there, and to be clear of the scope of the pattern and the extent of any novelty.

Though the Detective's observations will have been "theory laden" in the variety of assumptions he has brought to bear on the investigations (if only in the judgement of what was important) this will not necessarily have dictated the outcome. The processes often involved, or led to, reflections by the Detective or the Patternmaker that broke away from past perspectives.

The Patternmaker fed off the Detective's findings to keep on top of the overall picture of developments in each segment of his specialist area, noting the differences and similarities of the various changes - watching particularly for that consistency and completeness which heralded a major development across the whole of the project area; watching also for the regularity of unusual and peculiar features, locating, if possible, the consistency of inconsistencies, and seeking to make sense of and highlight the significantly unusual.

Working with the Detective he tried to follow not only the patterns of public activities but the patterns of subterranean life across the field. Were the significant subtexts all moving and developing in the same direction? Was there a significant counterflow? Were the developments consequential or complementary? Intimations of new developments were picked up and linked together. Were these signs of a significant break with the past? Was it breaking down overall? Was this relationship being undermined in this particular area? Was there a political realignment of factions taking place? Was a new axis of conflict emerging? Was a new distribution of power taking place?

To broaden his understanding of the weight to be given to various explanatory factors, the Patternmaker attempted to keep abreast of developments in similar political systems and in parties with similar goals, social base and organisational structure. The effect of wider forces was played with in the light of what the Detective was revealing. Changes in the party, or parties, were related to the changing cultural, social, economic and political context, and to a variety of international developments. In particular, the Patternmaker attempted to trace the patterns of transference between parties. At various times in history, the German Social Democratic Party, the Swedish Social Democratic Party and the U.S Democratic Party had been held up as desirable models of organisation, aims, values and strategy. The Patternmaker mentally played with the influence of these developments. He did the same with the interaction between British parties, assessing in particular their impact upon the evidence that was being produced and the patterns that he was making of developments within the Labour Party.

The patternmaker's tasks

The Patternmaker produced many patterns of description, narrative and argument as, with the Detective, he sought to give meaning and coherence to the investigations. However, his primary objective was an analytical patterning which provided an arrangement of repeated occurrences. At his most ambitious, he sought from this patterning a comprehensive explanatory framework.

In this patterning, he played and juggled with the evidence in terms of whatever design was immediately to hand, but particularly what design he could himself construct. Just as he attempted to make himself aware of the major patterns that had structured previous perceptions and interpretations of his area of research, so he tried to clarify his own perceptions, and to make himself aware of his own hidden assumptions. Looking outwards and looking inwards, he was always on the challenge so that he could fulfil his primary task; to seek the best possible understanding and representation of the significant patterns of his field of enquiry.

His skill lay in analysis and synthesis. He broke down relationships into different dimensions, segments, properties and facets - different historical phases also. In the light of the empirical evidence, he played with the fractionated elements, searching for repeated occurrences and asking "How might this pattern be related to that?" "Why?" and "With what consequences?". Where he thought it relevant, he took features of a relationship and combined, clustered and categorised them. He assessed consistencies and variations, and sought explanations.

In the pursuit of clarity in this patterning and these explanations, he sought to clarify a range of uncertainties and ambiguities in the subject under investigation. This was no easy task. In this field in particular, there were always special problems of ambiguity in understanding multidimensional relationships, which were often in a state of flux. On one occasion (in a study with Patrick Seyd) [Minken and Seyd 1977], when competing forces were in various states of precarious balance, it was possible to make the ambiguities themselves the central focus. The "search for an identity" became the conceptual ordering device which enabled us to present Labour's dilemmas in terms of the heritage of Labour's past. Justified, but not repeatable too often.

The search for " appropriate strangeness"

Over time, the Patternmaker's ambitions to be a creative artist became enriched within a national focus. In that process the patternmaker attempted to build novel frameworks in what might at first sight appear to the observer to be a strange representation of reality, but could be shown to be an "appropriate strangeness."[5]

This search for appropriate strangeness in novel arrangements led him into his own form of heuristic thinking. He drew from the Detective's investigations in searching for patterns based on features which were unusual, hitherto un-noticed or unexplored, or in this context, unexpected. He then aimed to create an unusual conceptualisation, central theme, or typology of explanatory factors involving this strangeness. Above all, the Patternmaker aspired to create a comprehensive framework based on a pattern of peculiarities.

But "appropriate" here meant that the "strangeness" must also have an intrinsic value in heightening understanding. It must facilitate a useful new perspective on the field of investigation, allowing him to order the material for a maximum illumination of the problems and/or the maximum possibility of explanation.

In the presentation of his work the Patternmaker has also learned to heighten this sense of strangeness by enhancing the significance of the unusual feature. The more that this was brought to the fore in the rhetoric, the sectionalisation and titling of the presentation, the more this essentially persuasive magnification took place.[6]

In Chapter Eight, taking up the story left in Chapter Three, I shall be examining the long-term generation of a theory based on a framework of unwritten rules. The strangeness of the framework lay in its integration of patterns of peculiarities. In this construction I slowly pulled together the research of over a quarter of a century on these peculiarities. But here, following a research problem noted earlier, let me give one example of the Patternmaker's utilisation of the unusual in the Detective's observations.

After the 1987 General Election I prepared a chapter for a book on Political Communications at that election to be edited by Ivor Crewe and Martin Harrop. At this time, my interest had become focused once again upon divergence and convergence in the trade union-Labour Party relationship. In particular there appeared to be a new pattern in which the Labour Party and the Trades Union Congress re-asserted their functional differentiation from each other.

The Patternmaker saw resemblences with developments seen before in Labour Party history. The Detective probed questions concerning the source of this new differentiation, and speculated about its possible consequences. Exploring the field, the Detective heard a very acute set of comments and noted a distinctive use of language by the (then) TUC Assistant General Secretary, John Monks.

I could see that this language of "space" (to pursue an independent strategy) and particularly "distance" (in public identification of the two sets of institutions) was shaping the management of, as well as describing, the relationship of the unions with the Labour Party in the pre-election period. I then played with the idea of utilising the verbal clues to turn that language into an unusual academic conceptualisation of electoral strategy - a conceptualisation which might be used of Labour history as a whole.

So, after much experimentation, I made these concepts of space and distance the central organising themes of my analysis of communicational strategy [Minkin 1989]. This was not what would have been expected in an analysis of the communicational role of the unions at that election, but it did portray something very significant in the patterns of behaviour of politicians and union leaders. It did so in a language which, though then unusual in that context, now seems fairly commonplace in the examination of Labour's relations with the unions. The conceptualisation was used in my later work to link these developments to the pattern of previous Labour Party experience.

Analysis and chronology: problems of presentational patterning

Over the years of playing the Patternmaker, I have had both general and particular problems in the process of presentational patterning. Through trial and error, and then with the help of lessons learned from approximate precedents, I struggled (sometimes unsuccessfully) to deal with them.

Like everybody else who is involved in this kind of work, I have had general problems in every project with the marrying of an analytical approach (actually a combination of analysis and synthesis) with a chronological narrative of developments, and I am constantly aware of the dilemmas that are involved. Crudely speaking, the fundamental choice is between historical phases introduced within an analytical structure, and an analysis integrated within a historical structure. However, there is also often a more complicated mixture, including a historical introduction, or historical sections, which are followed by analytical sections.

The analytical approach involves breaking something down into component parts and re-assembling the components in a new pattern, often out of background context and historical sequence. It can illuminate, but it can also be cumbersome. The chronological historical format is more easily constructed and accessible, but it is limited in what it can reveal.

The chronological format also limits discretion, but it gives a guiding line; the analytical approach leaves more room for creativity and for problems of design and theory. The chronological can highlight context, texture and uniqueness; the analytical can illuminate a larger design across a broader canvas. Historian and Political Scientist struggle with the fusion of their two favoured approaches; choices, difficult choices.

The choices are there all the time, but specifically studying the Party Conference, I had a particular insight into the importance of the agenda. I visualised policymaking as a confluence of two rivers. There was one, the obvious one, which everybody analysed - mobilising, persuading, mandating and casting votes. There was the other, initiating, producing and managing the agenda. Could the book be patterned mainly in terms of these two rivers? If it could, then could historical developments and patterns of power be built into each analytical section? The answer to these questions proved to be yes. It worked, but only after much juggling experimentation and re-adjustment [Minkin 1978/80 chs 3-7 pp 65-206].

I had another insight that different periods of history saw developments of the different parts of the jigsaw of the framework of unwritten rules covering the relationship between trade unions and the Labour Party. Could the study have four historical introductory chapters, each of which would have an analytical element which illuminated a development of the rules as well as building up the history? Difficult. Very difficult. I just about managed it [Minkin 1991/92 chs 1-4 pp 3-101].

In making those choices the Patternmaker has to play and juggle, and play again, designing and redesigning in the head. He has the Summaries file which can assist the process. Sometimes alternative outlines are tried on paper, or reconstructions are tried with a piece of chalk on a board. But in the end it is all settled by trial and error, with nothing fully satisfactory, just "this works better than that".

The deferred-judgement principle, and the battle of the patternmakers

Behind every form of patterning and every finished product, there are a hundred flawed, adjusted and at times wasted efforts. Behind many a mundane arrangement, there is a failed attempt at something more ambitious. It can be a frustrating process as the Patternmaker's flights of imagination and startling creative configurations are brought down to earth. Over the years, this tussle between the imaginative and the down to earth, the artistic and the realistic, has come to take on a form embodied in different characters and their dialogue.

At times, in all this creative playing, designing and construction, assisted by elements of heuristic thinking, the Patternmaker feels himself to be a frustrated artist whose dreams and visions of what he would like to represent are held back by the real world. He is an adventurer who yearns not simply to highlight obvious and well accepted features, but to create a patterning which will be seen as strikingly novel.

In this mood the Patternmaker-artist is constantly striking out, chancing his vision in seeing how far any pattern can be pushed in terms of originality, completeness and inclusivity. He sees it as part of his job to exaggerate, to caricature and to "strangeify" the world, regardless of how far this is at odds with common sense. The strangeness may just be found to represent a new and better understanding. In this role he particularly admires Copernicus, who was prepared to say publicly that the earth moved, in spite of the reactions of those who judged him mad.

The Patternmaker, as an artist, regards himself as a free spirit who does not allow censors or critics the premature access that will inhibit these flights of imagination and extensions of possibility. However - and this is the first crucial point about the process - he enjoys this freedom and this egocentricity because he is reassuringly aware that he is working in alliance with a gritty Patternmaker-realist who is cautious, strict, practical, rigorous, reasonable and self-righteous, and who will, in the end, keep a sharp check on any excesses.

At times the Artist is so outrageous in his posturing that the Realist strikes to obliterate the idea immediately. But generally, and this is the second crucial point, a thinking space and what has been called "the deferred judgement principle"[7] (which suggests that judgement and attempts to verify are best withheld during the generation of ideas) is respected. The Realist is generally tolerant, allowing time and space for the flights of imagination. However, at some stage, inevitably, there is a psychological and intellectual struggle - a dialogue sometimes cool and rational, sometimes emotional and panicky - where the Realist will regularly draw attention to four imperatives.

First, the Realist will always emphasise the messy particularities, complexity, and at times incoherence, of the real world, and will constantly challenge the Artist for the justifying evidence. The Artist is regularly reminded that he does not have the freedom of the canvas or the novel. Though there is "no knowledge without a knowing subject,"[8] though knowledge is produced by a combination of the researcher and the researched, and though it is the patternmaking which is giving meaning to the world, it is a real not an imaginary world. Creative patternmaking can extend the possibilities of how we can view the world, and enlarge our understanding of it, but only if it is grounded in, and respectful of, the evidence. The patterns can only usefully be constructed out of the empirical investigation, and the patternmaker is, in that sense, pattern-*finding* as he is patternmaking.[9] The pattern has to fit the evidence and it has to be so plausible as to be convincing. The Realist challenges the Artist to meet these criteria.

Second, the Realist points out that the Artist's presentational patterns must be accessible, must involve meaningful narrative and must be in a form acceptable to the publishers and to the Patternmaker's academic peers. All right, the Patternmaker-artist always wants to make it like a novel or a drama with a plot, a crisis and a denouement, but does this get in the way of conveying the substance of the analysis? If the answer is "yes," then the demand is "change it". O.K. so he wants to paint pictures with the material, but will the audience be able to understand them? If the answer is "no," then the demand is "do something about it".

Third, the Realist will generally raise awkward questions when there is a value conflict with participants or competitors in the field of enquiry. Has the Artist been pandering to his prejudices? Does he do their position justice? Has the Artist put their case at least as strongly as they would?

Fourth, the Realist will remind him of his moral obligations. He is there to assist his students, his colleagues and the people at large, in understanding the political world. This must override the desire to show artistic "genius." He must not do this at the expense of advancing understanding. He must not do this by distorting evidence. He must not do it by creating a misrepresentation of the world. He can only do it by living up to his self-image of scholarly truth-seeking.

What results from this dialogue is a repetitive mental struggle of competing arguments and personae in the attempt to make sense of the terrain of the problem area, and to create original but plausible and defensible patterns that cover the presentation as well as the substance of the enquiry.

In this dialogue there is a filtering process at work - seeking the precious metal, the workable innovation. It involves the survival of the fittest idea. A key feature of this struggle which generally sustains the creative momentum is that it often results in a movement by the Artist from his most far-out interpretation and expression to a more defensible position, but one which may keep important features of his first vision. After appropriate modifications, artistic wildness became "appropriate strangeness."

It is a problematic and messy struggle characterised by what Herman Melville in Moby Dick calls "careful disorderliness."[10] This characteristic is inherent in the conflict of personae that I have described, but also in the attempt to order the parts when it is not quite clear what the whole will be. It is present also in the attempt to create the whole where the meaning of the parts may be unknown or uncertain, and shapes the decision about which parts are necessary and which are potentially available[11].

Methodical and disorderly, as the Patternmaker changes personality in this dialogue so he moves constantly from the particular to the general, from micro to mezzo to macro levels and back again. Does he have enough evidence? He can visualise this other evidence. He can in his imagination temporarily introduce it into the juggle, providing that the material is in principle available. Time after time the Patternmaker has to hold the overall provisional pattern in his head as he changes back to being the Detective and, sighing deeply, goes back out on the beat, re-questioning the usual suspects and looking for more evidence.

POTENCY AND FALLIBILITY

These roles have been described mainly in rational purposeful terms, with deliberately self-sustaining and semi-heroic images of a solitary, creative, vigorous but also controlled and rational thinker. Sometimes I do seem to approach this, typing away at my desk. I am, I believe, also at my best setting out on a train journey with a nice looking pen and a clean new pad in front of me, my thoughts eased along by the rhythmic movement. I am, I know, at my happiest and most rigorous with (thank God!) a draft which I can attack, correct, and reshape. I feel at my most potent at around 11.30 a.m. when I am letting the caffeine send me bounding on with "the flow".

But, if I described my work *only* in terms of control and rationality it would be very misleading, mainly because my activity is, I have to say again, flawed. I am prey to many of the problems outlined earlier, of bad days and good days, pratfalls and misadventures - as well as all the uncertainties (even in the most rational activities and on the very good days) that affect anybody whose mind is engaged in a creative enterprise.

Further, self-observation has drawn my attention to the fact that the Detective and the Patternmaker both have a pathology at the extremity of their virtues. The Detective is highly motivated and a ferocious and persistent worker but at times he pushes himself so hard that he gets "talk-fatigue", when he is listening but no longer hearing. He afterwards realises he has only half-understood what was being said. Something a bit like this occasionally happens when he is writing and thinking.

He has a sharp sense of incongruity and discordance, together with a Jewish self-deprecation and a black sense of humour; these are part of his creative sensitivity. The humour is a potent defence against misadventure and the pains of failure. But, it is sometimes an uncontrollable and alarming force which means that he can neither control his facial muscles, nor his tongue. Nor can he fully master its effect on his observational vigilance.

Although he is increasingly worldly-wise, the Detective is not a cynic. Indeed, he is driven by a moral passion to discover and uncover because he believes that it is his responsibility, as a scholar of political life, to try to assist the people to participate in a democracy with their eyes open. However, there are things that he becomes aware of when his own eyes are open. Particularly the status-seeking games, the egocentricity, the servile pursuit of favour at court, and the obsessive opportunism in the politics of the "greasy pole", which create in him a depressive sadness about the human condition, lower his energy level and (in spasms) completely cloud his judgement.

Over time, the Detective also notices changes within himself which affect his work. In particular, he notices that as he becomes more experienced, more observant and more skilful in "feeling" what is happening, so he also becomes less excited, less surprised and more world-weary. As the Detective now in a sense "misses nothing," so he begins to wonder whether he is actually in the process of losing something very important to his creative skill - the freshness of perspective with which the stranger or the novice can view the field.

As for the Patternmaker, he is at times a creative egotist. Pride in the concepts he creates, allied to a fascination with a multitude of alternative perspectives, can assist a sustaining self-belief fuelled by the wonderful things that pour out. But it can also be a terrible albatross, resulting in the phenomenon that (like the Emperor Joseph II's rebuke to Mozart) I think of as "too many notes."[12] The conceptual distinctions are valid, interesting and useful in themselves but, when combined with too many others, become incommunicable and almost unhandleable. This problem is compounded by the fact that the relationships under analysis are complex and multifaceted anyway, and in that feature alone difficult to communicate with ease and elegance.

In his battles with the self-sacrificing and ethically strict Patternmaker-realist, the Patternmaker-artist is often fighting to be publicly applauded. He finds it psychologically difficult to get rational control over his reactions to various threats to obliterate from public exhibition anything creatively "clever" he has sweated over. This became all too apparent in those first anxious months of research on the Labour Party Conference. And here let me explore further the disappointing experience described in Chapter Three.

The model of conference politics that I nurtured in that period involved a profusion of concepts and categories. It did begin to embody some important insights of the empirical investigation and seemed at first a very obvious development of the work. I thought it very valuable. Indeed, perhaps it was as an exploratory device, guiding what to look for in locating hidden power. And maybe it was also a practitioner's (how to do it) "power-maximisation" model. Whatever it was, I should have seen its limitations as well as its worth. Instead I had ambitions to develop a grand theory and to develop the model into a major theoretical framework. I don't have very clear memories of this now, but I know that I tried to develop and apply it in all kinds of ways. But, as a comparative exercise, it proved to be inadequate in covering the varieties of the forms of conference and the differences in political behaviour between them, and altogether it failed miserably.

In truth, though I do not know what I was doing with it, I do know that I had become infatuated with it and proud of it to the detriment of the main project. My reluctance to shed or sideline it nearly strangled the real research process and its theorising. Eventually, and slowly, I did allow new and different conceptual and presentational frameworks to emerge out of the empirical investigations of the British case which were directly applicable to it. Once involved in the new frameworks, the creative process was much easier and more satisfactory in its productivity. Many bits of the old model did find themselves integrated into the new one, but, as a clear statement, the loved one actually became whittled down to just one line in the conclusions of the book. I should have been aware of what was happening and made the decision to stop imposing the model much earlier. But I was very inexperienced and oh! how I loved that model and wanted people to see it.

Memories of that experience affected my feelings as I struggled with the patterning of *The Contentious Alliance*. This was painfully and carefully constructed to cover all aspects of the national relationship between trade unions and the Labour Party since the foundation of the Party. It succeeded sufficiently to be very well received, but I always wondered whether it was fully satisfactory because, anxious to illustrate two different sets of ideas (and two proud possessions) I broke one of the commandments of research presentation. The commandment is "Thou shall not try to present two conceptual frameworks at once". But, I had two. One framework covered the forces which pulled the relationship apart and those which held it together: the other framework covered the pattern of values and "rules" which governed the relationship. I thought that each in its way was too valuable to abandon.

It is an important banality that it is extremely difficult to say two things at once - except perhaps by way of irony which has limited utility in the form of analysis I am engaged in. You can do it in music (where even opposites can be expressed simultaneously [Storr 1989 p 246]). "Rhythm imposes unanimity upon the divergent; melody imposes continuity upon the disjointed".[13] You can also do it in a play or a film, where we can have hero, sunset and music at the same time [Lodge 1996 p 217]. But it is difficult to do anything quite like this in scholarly literature. Writing can only be received on one channel [Lodge 1996 p 217].

Eventually, I found an adroit way out which saved the study, and in some ways, added greatly to its value. I gave one of the frameworks (relating to divergent and unifying forces) a rather elaborate send off in Chapter Five of *The Contentious Alliance* - as a kind of contextual window - and then thankfully allowed it to move aside, leaving the field clear for the other framework which was more comprehensive and had greater explanatory utility. In the dead of night I still occasionally flirt with other ways in which the book might have been better structured, but so far (again, thankfully) I have not found one.

ALLIES, EDUCATORS AND MODELS

There is also something misleading about the description that I have presented here of the lone scholar. Whether acting as Detective or Patternmaker, I am always in dialogue with others, in one way or another. No academic really works alone, there is always some company, seen or unseen.

The unseen company is the more difficult to manage. Human life, including the meanings given to it, is essentially social. We are all part of a network and history of social influences upon our thinking, and those involved in academic research are part of a community of scholarly influences. I know that to be fully effective and creative I have to make myself aware of a web of hidden assumptions derived from a particular life experience and social milieu. I have also to wrestle with an accompaniment from the past; a self-inflicted tyranny of concepts - ideas, some of which I had in principle shed years ago, but to which I remain somehow in thrall.

I am not alone in another much more tangible sense. I gain a great deal from others - indeed I could not do without them. True, I do have a solitary style of work of which I am fiercely protective. I work to my own judgements, and one reason that I have never tried to employ research assistants is that I know that only by doing the most direct and the most laborious tasks of research myself am I able fully to take advantage of the associations and connections, peculiarities and problems which are stimulated in a creative process which envelops the work from start to finish.

During periods of absolute concentration and, particularly, during crises in the work, I try to create a space where I can withdraw from social interaction as much as possible - even if this produces, as it has produced, considerable social and domestic strain. But it is often neither feasible nor fully desirable, given my need for companionship, my family obligations and also my experience of the unexpected benefits of dialogue in the creative process.

Intellectually as well as psychologically, like everybody else, I feed off my interaction with my closest professional friends in ways which are deeply nourishing to the creative process - an idea here, an omission there, a piece of information, a way of presentation, a stimulant, a provocation, a spark. There is a friendly corrective dialogue ("I can't follow this. This isn't right. Have you considered this? Have you read that? ....." and so on). They can always see things that I cannot. ("Why is this here and not there?" No answer, except that that was where I thought of it.)

Of course, there is a sense also in which, when I am immersed in a piece of work, every conversation is explicitly or implicitly connecting mentally with the project (Is there something here that is useful? Is that like this? Perhaps that applies here as well? Maybe these can be linked?). And there is then a marked tendency for synchronistic encounters and chance inputs, which link into the intellectual stream of the work to become part of the creative "flow".

It is also the case that in the routines of my research, as I have already indicated, the most regular interaction, and often the greatest stimulus, is not the academic dialogue but the discussion with participants in my field of study. In particular, some of those that I met and interviewed became close friends, and have talked with me informally and productively for years.

Over time, these have given me an extended and sustained education about the nuances and distinctions of behaviour in the field. And also about political life in general. They too feed "the flow". With a small number of them, I share and test my interpretations as they share theirs with me. In this way my work, in recent years, characteristically develops in scruffy but priceless bits of paper at the side of the phone.

Others can give us much more than suggestions and understanding. They can offer us permanent models of creative work, not only in their own styles of work but in breaking out of mind-sets and developing the confidence to move to other positions.

I recognise now the extent to which not only did I have to gain an intellectual insight into the creative process, but, as a Detective and a Patternmaker, I had to develop the courage to allow spontaneity to take over, to plunge into the novel and the uncertain, away from the known and tried. The feeling that we might be thought ridiculously "way out" can be uncomfortable, especially if we are also fighting a battle for respect. Nerve is vital.

It has been said since ancient times that the best way to learn is to be an apprentice to "a master" at work. There continues to be a stream of thought in studies of creativity which emphasises role models, mentors and paragons in the training period.[14] A similar point has been made by and about scientists [Medewar 1990 pp 59-60], and also about reflective professional practitioners [Schon 1987 p13]. The models we adopt become a permanent accompaniment to our working process. It is a very important insight, but my point here would be that it can be taken further.

We are all to some degree and in different areas of our work, masters, one to another. We can all learn things from others that can improve the quality of our creative work.[15] That is why the honest sharing of our "private" research thoughts and personal creative experience is such an important project.

I learned much, as we all do, from our undergraduate teachers, particularly in the intellectual rigour and ethical commitment of their approach. I was particularly fortunate in my tutors.[16] But if I were to focus on the experience of enhancing creativity, I would point up one crucial influence. As a novice researcher, I was privileged to work with and watch a very innovative and uninhibited scholar, the late Peter Nettl, who had been commissioned to produce a critical re-appraisal of the Soviet Union [Nettl 1967] to coincide with the fiftieth anniversary of the

Bolshevik Revolution. Acting first as his research assistant, and then as part co-author of the book, I saw him weave his interpretations with a confidence and skill and a complete disregard for various conventional views on the USSR in a way which made my jaw drop. "Can you do that?" It was an uncomfortable, but also an instructive and a very liberating influence.[17]

From Peter Nettl I gained a model of confidence in the role of Detective and Patternmaker and in the search for originality. I also saw the benefit of a willingness to roam across boundaries into adjacent fields - a process not too difficult to accept in principle for a political scientist who began his degree as a sociologist, and then became more of a historian. However, in this respect, outside of the interplay between history and political science which gives depth and breadth to my work, the model proved difficult to follow, given the demands of time taken in huge and complex empirical investigations. Though, on occasions, I moved into areas of other disciplines in search of ideas and a greater depth of understanding (in relation to the examples noted in this study: role theory, bargaining in industrial relations, organisation theory and rules, symbiosis in biology and of course the creative process) I remained for much of the time blissfully but cursedly ignorant of some important and relevant work.

In a sense, the model also proved difficult to share in full. The style of my own creative work, in practice, emphasising as it does the creative benefits of even the most routine activities, together with the importance of the personal trust relationship with those I studied in the field, has not allowed me to act as mentor to my own experience "on the job" as much I might have wanted in principle. That is a pity and another good reason for attempting to share the experience here.

The story of my association with Peter Nettl had a tragic twist - which also became an important learning experience. He was killed in a plane crash and I was left with the manuscript. I found myself repeatedly having to make a wide range of clarifying interpretive judgements in response to the publisher's queries. All this done in a student telephone box, pushing coins in a machine and sweating profusely whilst long queues glared through the window. Sink or swim, there was not much room for indecision.

I swam.....

CHAPTER END NOTES

[1] This type is usefully distinguished from the "serialist" who sees writing as a preplanned and sequential process, corrected as it moves along. Lowenthall, D and Wason, P.C. 'Academics and their writing' *Times Literary Supplement*, 24th June 1977, quoted in [Phillips and Pugh 1987 p65].

[2] My own understanding of this process (which for years involved a sense that something creative, but in some ways mysterious, happened when I wrote) was clarified and consolidated by reading [Berthoff 1988].

[3] There is a suggestive passage in a book by Derek. L. Phillips, [Phillips 1971 p 158] , where he quotes from a paper by David Bakan entitled 'A reconsideration of the problems of introspection'. Bakan describes a process of sitting at a typewriter and typing whatever comes into his mind regarding a topic. In an oscillation between a mood of free expression and an analytical mood he generates a range of propositions. See on this also [Becker with Richards 1986 page 54] on free-writing - writing whatever comes into your head.

[4] 'Harnessed to the harpy: notes for aspiring writers' in [Boylan 1993 p 182].

[5] The phrase is used by Parnes in [Taylor and Getzels 1975 p 228].

[6] See on this [Atkinson 1990] who argues that, "What is conveyed is dependent upon implicit textual phenomona: the textual arrangements, the rhetorical figures, the choice of descriptive vocabulary, the selection of illustrative materials. These are all elements within a context of persuasion" (p 2). He argues also that a recognition of the rhetorical forms "that run through *all* scholarly and scientific discourse can only strengthen the awareness and discipline of our academic endeavours"(p 1).

[7] Parnes in [Taylor and Getzels1975 p 225].

[8] Kloos, P., 'No knowledge without a knowing subject' in [Burgess 1988 pp 221-241].

[9] There are many complex and intriguing epistemological and sociological problems which could be raised here, and this is obviously not intended as an exploration of them. It is simply an exemplification of a constant tension in creative work and the simple dialogue that goes on about it in my head from the two given positions. At times there is a broader mental dialogue over the wider theoretical problems - a dialogue which generates considerable uncertainty in relation to "knowledge". But generally I take the view that in the process of research too great a consciousness of epistemological issues and of the social influences over intellectual construction is not conducive to the motivation involved in creative research. A similar point is made by Trevor Pinch 'Reservations about reflexivity and new literary forms or why let the devil have all the good tunes' in [Woolgar 1988 p 180].

[10] "There are some enterprises in which a careful disorderliness is the true method" , [Melville 1985 edn p 371].

[11] This process is a common feature of creative composition, (see on this [Berthoff 1988 p 23) although not necessarily encumbered by the constraints of evidence and the scholarly obligations of the academic researcher.

[12] Actually he said, "Very many notes, my dear Mozart" [Watson 1994].

[13] Yehudi Menuhin quoted in [Storr 1989 p 244].

[14] Tardif in [Sternberg 1988 p 437].

[15] [Bandura 1986 p 104] quoted by Sethia, N.K., 'The role of collaboration in creativity' in [Ford and Gioia 1995 p 102].

[16] I was befriended before and during University by a lecturer in social and political theory, Justin Grossman, who was both enormously encouraging in a way that was vital to my self-confidence and important as a role model in his scrupulous concern for scholarship.

[17] I realise now I never actually saw him in the drafting process of his own beautifully crafted pieces - which was a pity.

CHAPTER 7

CREATIVE RESEARCH AND HEURISTIC THINKING

CONTRASTS OF THE CREATIVE MIND

My task in much of this chapter is to explore, and exemplify in detail, some of the ways that I most consciously and regularly intervene to shape and stimulate the creative process. It is the most generative dimension of the art of creative research - and it is often a rational, highly focused and clearly directed activity. However, to understand the place, and, in some cases, the development of these practices, we have to locate them in the broader context of my mental activities - activities which are mainly spontaneous, only intermittently directed and at times anything but rational.

I want to focus on these less-directed activities first. They are personified in the performance of a character whose role and behaviour is of a different order from those encountered in previous chapters. The character does not have a defined function, it is ubiquitous. At times it feels not so much like me playing a part, but more like an accompaniment - the contribution of somebody or something else.

THE CHATTERING MONKEY

This "something else" is speaking in my mind in a way which is difficult to describe (possibly why it is rarely described by academics). It is an activity which is not fully under control, in fact much of the time it is not under control at all. The fact is that there is talk taking place incessantly, in my head and I am nattering away in various other worlds like some demented old man on a park bench. Much of it is a repetitive and intermittently disconnected chatter, or a boring running commentary shadowing my activities. Often it is heavily laced with the most pointless forms of imaginative construction - the gramophone record of anxiety scenarios, the litany of life-time grievances, and the same old charge-sheet of personal failings. Parts of sentences and phrases come and go without being completed. A refrain of music is repeated a hundred times. Bits of day-dreams and fantasies are lovingly described. A wave of anger or remorse will suddenly flash out, interspersed with expressions of vituperation and obscenity.

More usefully, as far as creative research is concerned, sometimes part of this repetition involves explaining what I am doing to an unnamed audience, and what I say occasionally takes on new features, meanings and developments as I speak. Sometimes the talk involves rehearsing a difficult section of the work that I have (in theory) decisively put to one side. And the unrequested repetitive chatter seems to make a better effort of rewriting it, and planning its trajectory, than my consciously focused attempt.

An important part of the chatter also consists of a semi-regulated aggressive argument against various opponents. This dialogue - what Plato called a dialogue of the soul with itself -is as much spontaneous and spasmodic as it is ordered and organised, and it often takes, rather than is given, human form, as friends or known adversaries suddenly appear with questions and criticisms, arguments and rebuttals. The opponent is often not at all happy with any weakness in my work. Sometimes s/he has a bullying tone and I am under the white light of interrogation. At other times, s/he is a victim protesting at my unfairness. S/he challenges at any vulnerable point of my work whilst I (under attack) go back and forth desperately seeking to shore up the defence. This endless argument is sometimes conducted with far more ferocity than I ever mount in public.

If my opponent tends towards becoming the Destructive Critic, I seek to defend myself angrily and vigorously, and I try to filter and redefine the criticism so that it does not focus on my personal inadequacies nor question the temerity of my aspirations, but engages with the problems of the work. As I have grown more confident and experienced, despite the challenging tones, the dialogue is helpful and creative rather than destructive and undermining. One result is that I am repeatedly involved in what I now think of as a "creative retreat" as I am forced to admit inadequacy or error, then to adjust, change and take up my amended position without loss of face and with the same assertiveness with which I articulated a somewhat different position moments earlier. Then off goes the chatter again into another aggressive unregulated argument.

Often, bits of my solutions, possible connections and patterning, and a realisation of new problems, come to me in this dialectical form as the dialogue somehow dredges up a new insight, or puts together a fruitful combination of ideas in a way that expands the possibilities of the situation. It happens time and again when I am not at my desk; indeed, often when I have told myself that I have stopped working. Most typically, it is walking to the shop after I have decided to have a break. This "moving meditation" [Cameron 1994 pp 184-6] appears to be liberated by rhythmic activity and the change of scene.

Occasionally it happens at around four a.m., laid there in bed, eyes closed yet wide awake - forever it seems - agitated, but at the same time with an underlying sense of satisfaction at the way things arrive in the head, move, interconnect, and get pulled into something that is harmonious and meaningful. There is also the Saturday morning "lie-in," a planned rest which somehow becomes an irresistible yo-yo, in and out of bed as one idea follows another, incoherences get sorted out, and loose ends get woven together.

Something is also at work in the night as the mind seeks to order its experiences [Storr 1989 p 167]. There are times when I am suddenly being brought wide awake by a revealing thought or, out of nowhere it seems, am given a problem or a deficiency to rectify in the work. Creative artists in many different fields have testified to the productive importance of what emerges from an otherworld of the mind in sleep.

For years I have taken this as the strongest intimation of sub-conscious/unconscious creative processes operating whilst the conscious mind is at rest. It may be, of course, that some of this was a misperception. In the between time, half-awake and half-asleep, it is not a clearly defined experience, and could be a product of a conscious but non-directed mental process which occurs in the waking state. But that is not what it feels like. It feels as though it was part of the same process in sleep that produces the dialogues of dreams.[1] I simply do not know the full truth of all this. What has become vividly clear to me over time, however, is its importance and productivity in "the flow" of the creative process. In whatever way the phenomenon is defined and understood, part of creative effectiveness involves being in touch with, and understanding broadly how this spontaneous process works for us and feeds our creativity.

It involves having the confidence to live with, and to delight in, the free flow of a mind which, it appears, will *never* be silent. It simply will not shut up. It is a "chattering monkey". So it is for all of us.

Knowing how and when the chattering is likely to be most useful for us is a vital application of the injunction Know Thyself. The chattering is our burden and our distinctiveness as human beings. The mixture of sense and gobbledy-gook, surrealism and practicality, fantasy and reality, incoherence and logic is not simply a useless form of dementia. The creative muse is at work here. Day and night the chatterer seems to be sifting, filtering and coming up with offerings - sometimes useful, often a waste of thought, sometimes ridiculous, occasionally illuminating and exciting.

But the chattering monkey could not be enlisted as productively as it is were I not, consciously and deliberately, assisting "the flow" and feeding back into it in particular ways. Some of these ways have already been outlined in previous chapters, and I have drawn attention to the fact that the researcher can practise some consciously generative interventions in order to assist the creative process. I am going to add to that here by exploring in detail a series of interventions which cover the whole research process from inception to finalisation.

FROM HEURISTICS TO HEURISTIC THINKING

As noted earlier, I have called these interventions "heuristic thinking" to link it with the old scholarly tradition of study known as heuristic. Heuristics are often described in terms of precepts. Weber and Perkins, for example, point to the creative importance of the use of precepts of professional wisdom by successful inventors [Weber and Perkins 1992 pp 331-3]. Polya gives us "the wisdom of proverbs" in tackling mathematical problems creatively [Polya 1957 pp 222-5]. Occasionally, I do use precepts, but heuristic thinking involves more of a mode of thought, and a style of approach, than a series of precepts. I see it as a deliberate intervention in the mental process concerned with research - an intervention to stimulate and assist the mind in thinking in creative ways and taking creative opportunities during the research process.

We have already seen examples of this in previous chapters - particularly in the use of Critical Examination and the pursuit of peculiarities. The intervention seeks to change perceptions, generate alternatives, and enlarge possibilities in such a way as to assist in the emergence of original features. It is certainly not a mechanical procedure. It involves a mix of rules, reasoning, techniques and tactics, plus a metacognitive self-awareness which allows me to benefit more fully from spontaneous features of the creative process. Nor is it fully separated from the non-directed thought process described above; indeed, in some respects, as in the operation of the Awkward Sod and the Vicious Circle (described below) it builds upon them.

It also has a mixture of moods. Sometimes the style is one of gently teasing out and searching. At other times it is aggressive and provoking. Generally, it is playful and experimental in its engagement with ideas and information. It is also alert and receptive to the emergence of novelty and opportunity. It is sometimes self-challenging and, for a time, self-preoccupied, but its purpose is essentially focused on generating a creative response to the external world.

This heuristic thinking is concerned to stimulate and assist the creative process - not to verify or prove anything. I emphasise that it is concerned to get us there rather than to justify where we are. Indeed, it needs to be clearly distinguished from the reasoning of verification and the demonstrations of proof which must, at some later stage, be brought into operation. One has to distance the attention on verification, keeping it back a pace, allowing the creative Detective and the Patternmaker-artist the confident space to operate.

Only in the last four years have I discovered quite what it is that I do in this heuristic thinking and how it might be described and labelled. In retrospect I can see more clearly that out of my self-observation, out of my tracking of trial-and-error, out of my deepening understanding of the spontaneous creative process and out of my background reading of the literature, I had developed a gradual systematisation of my best practice.

These are not abstract suggestions. Nothing is offered here that I have not experienced in the research process and, where memory and record allows, it is offered with examples from my own work. I am making no claim for the primacy of any particular mode of work, practice or technique. Nor is the presentation here intended to be comprehensive. I am sure that there is much more that potentially might be used, but this is what works for *me*. That is the important test.

THE MODES OF HEURISTIC THINKING

The creative critic

Some of the important elements of my heuristic thinking occur before I formally begin, or have even clearly conceived of, the research project. The creative process begins in the critical mode. It is a matter of what I see as the limitations of the literature and how and why I deconstruct, critically "unravel", other people's work. What can emerge - when the criticisms are linked together - is the loose and sometimes very indistinct shape of something new.

So, to return to an earlier example, one part of my original research took off by unravelling MacKenzie's interpretation of his own data, looking for the inadequacies or limitations of what was portrayed as an "iron law" of Labour oligarchy.

In rebuilding another view of the relations between the Labour Party Conference and the Parliamentary Leadership I began by nitpicking at his conceptual language (eg by differentiating his use of the concepts of autonomy and freedom of action, authority and final authority) all of which he tended to fuse in support of his interpretation. I distinguished minute but significant differences of meaning, and then re-examined the evidence around them. The differentiation gave me some of the mental elements from which I shaped elements of a new construction which reordered the data.

I have now systematised exercises like this into a permanent feature of my creative working method in a way which, to a greater or lesser extent, is probably shared by most experienced researchers[2]. It is a routine process but, in terms of creativity, not to be under-estimated. Creatively, it is visualised as a process of finding room for alternatives which, joined together, will make up the outline shape of something new.

If anybody does work in my area of expertise - books, journals and serious newspaper articles - I attempt to work the material backwards in terms of their use of concepts, the adequacy of their data and the plausibility of their interpretations. I am particularly sensitive to the need to slay Giant Dichotomies (it is either this or that). In the field of Labour Movement studies, in political journalism and in discourse covering the distribution of power, such stark alternatives are often on offer.

I go through these exercises to find room for alternative perspectives from which I might later weave together something different. It is part of the craft of enlarging the possibilities appropriate to the task in mind. Thus, a contribution to a published symposium on Radicalism and Reconstruction after World War II was thematically structured by a critique that I had begun to assemble of Paul Addison's major study of the political impact of the Second World War [Addison 1975]. I took particular issue with the thrust of his argument that the 1945 Labour Government's policy was simply the implementation of a war-time consensus going back to 1940. My reconstruction was developed by first creating space and an outline shape out of the evidence that Addison had himself collected, noting possible alternatives in the way that the evidence had been used, and then following through with my own research which filled out and then sharpened the shape of a contrary interpretation [Minkin 1982].

If work is published by others relevant to the field of investigation, whilst I am actually involved in the process of research, it is often used critically to redefine or reshape the purposes of my own ongoing project. I attempt to unravel the new publication much as I did with the initial literature. And, because my domain expertise involves increasing command over the variations in group and institutional relationships, one of my responses is to examine whether the level of generality of the work done by others is inappropriate, unrevealing or imprecise.

I have become much more ready to mentally play with the idea that there are different patterns of behaviour in different areas of relationships involving the Labour Party. Thus my reaction to David Marquand's important views on Labourism [Marquand 1991 p 17] and Labourist culture was that the conceptualisation, and its level of generality, generated a misunderstanding about the potentiality for a transformation of the party.

As I followed this through in my own research, it became increasingly clear that there was not one static culture of Labourism but several cultures - and some of them discernibly undergoing significant change. From this perspective, Marquand's interpretation had failed to address the reality of complexity and counterflow. Out of this appreciation, I imagined and fashioned another interpretation of Labour's culture [Minkin 1991/92 pp 636-7].

The important point here is that although a distinction is sometimes made between deconstructive and constructive intellectual modes, and writers on creativity sometimes make the distinction between "the critical" and "the creative" approaches, in my creative process the two work together. Indeed, though critical thought can certainly be uncreative, it is doubtful whether creative thought can be effective without critical filtering. And crucially, at this early stage of the creative process, my own creativity often begins with a series of rigorous criticisms.

The critical unravelling process functions as a process of discrimination - a ground-clearing - rather than simply fault-finding and an exposure of shortcomings. Alongside the criticisms it always notes what is useful and what may be developed. Similarly, the deconstruction may well elicit new meanings and ambiguities in the text, but that is not its primary purpose. It is a procedure directed towards creating elements of a new structure and finding the emerging shape, or pattern, which will become the foundations of the creative outcome. The critical activity is a cumulative process building upon challenges to evidence, concepts and conclusions, delineating important gaps and unexplored areas, questioning interpretations, the level of generality and the scope of the enquiry. The significance of a speech is disputed, the characterisation of a position queried. Quotations become flags in the earth - markers of key positions.

What emerges is not only a tentative map of the terrain of the project, but also the outline shape (sometimes with bits in sharp focus, sometimes very vague) and in part, the girders and building blocks of the alternative perspective. This finding-the-shape-and-structures criticism, and the internal dialogue about the nature of the resulting contours (What is emerging here? Is there a pattern or patterns? What might link it together? What could be the organising theme? What further development can I see which could make it coherent?) become an essential part of my heuristic thinking oriented towards the possibility of inventing something new.

Working backwards from the end-state

It is widely agreed that research has to be built on a problem which is then pursued to a solution or conclusions. In the literature on creativity and on research, this is a constant theme. One source after another has testified that what comes first in research is the problem [Whitfield 1975 p 50]. I have myself emphasised the importance of problem-seeking as a springboard for the investigation.

However, in terms of the creative process, it is hard to generalise about what exactly constitutes the intellectual beginning of a project; the mental process is complex and variable in terms of entry points to the research. And there are even times when fruitful heuristic thinking reverses the commonly accepted assumption of the direction of thought from the problem to the conclusions. Certainly, in my own research, even before evidence is systematically collected, I am often toying with what my conclusions might be and how they might relate to the existing understanding.

Let me connect this with a point made by George Polya. "Analysis" to the ancient Greeks did not mean what we mean by it today. As defined by Pappus, it involved devising a plan starting from the unknown (or the conclusion) and working backwards towards the data (or the hypothesis) [Polya 1957 p 200].

Working backwards from the end-state where the answer begets the question can be a useful heuristic procedure. In my own research there are moderate and extreme versions of this way of working. It is not unusual for me to be looking at possible interesting conclusions in the light of partial evidence - sometimes just bits of evidence. What is going through my head is what restatement of the problem could lead to my giving this acceptable conclusion as the answer with this evidence? Or perhaps this answer could be given with more convincing evidence which looks as though it is available? [3] Sometimes, starting from this answer involves taking up an element of the evidence in the research which has hitherto had a subsidiary position in the project, then refining it and moving it nearer the centre of the study by raising its profile in the statement of objectives. In a more extreme version, very occasionally a particular conclusion is so alluring in its strangeness or dramatic attraction that I am drawn to it before I have accumulated evidence (although I know the field very well and have a sense of what might possibly be drawn from it and substantiated). The question that I am asking is, " What would I need to find for this conclusion to be clearly validated?".

On other occasions, in the middle of the research, the answer that draws me is to a question that I have not initially posed at all. One such example was my response to the (often crude) characterisation of an "inflexibility" which was everywhere in serious commentary on the Labour Party. The tone of those who referred to it was, "we all know that". I already had a wide range of questions and topics to pursue in a wide-ranging coverage of the trade union-Labour

Party relationship, and this was not a viewpoint that I had intended to challenge. Initially, I made no attempt to collect any direct evidence about it. My decision to do otherwise grew out of a reaction to editorials in the Sunday newspapers which took for granted Labour's inflexibility. I knew that they expressed a polemical rather than an informed position.

My own feel for the terrain, following a series of important reforms and changes in this period, was that a contrary case could be built. I began to frame a conclusion to the book which emphasised elements of flexibility in the Labour Party's relationship with the unions. As the Patternmaker-artist magnified this, it became a strong rejection of the idea of Labour conservatism. I decided that it was a striking and plausible "discovery," and moved backwards from the possible conclusion to stating the problem and then seeking the evidence.

The evidence accumulated aplenty and was impressive. It was not that there were no conservative features (as the Patternmaker-realist pointed out) but that there was also an extensive record of organisational change, of changes in financial and voting arrangements, of changes in policy and policymaking processes, and of shifts in the definition of party values - all of which suggested great flexibility. I tested the interpretation back and forth in relation to the evidence. By any reasonable standards (as experience since 1992 has born out)[4] the endemic inflexibility of the Labour Party was a myth if ever there was one [Minkin 1991/92 pp 634-7]. I then formally built the purpose, ie the problem, of asking how flexible this relationship was, into the project.

The awkward sod

There's another way of looking at my responses to McKenzie's study of political parties and to the charge of Labourist inflexibility. My responses can also be seen as one of a general heuristic type which I now call "Awkward Sod". The Awkward Sod is, in various forms, a routine companion of quality scholarship. It is also, under different descriptions, a conscious technique of creativity-generation.[5]

For years now, I have given this technique a personality, and used it (or has it used me?) as a heuristic procedure. In the theatre of the mind I am, in effect, married to a nagging revolutionary dogmatist who is always rejecting "them", always seeking a World Turned Upside Down, and always aspiring to reach a new state of perfection. The Awkward Sod is disloyal, disrespectful, anarchic and irrepressible. He can focus on some of my most fundamental beliefs, and even turn on my interpretations, patterns and conclusions, expressing a repudiation after I think that it is all complete and plausible.

In the imagination, everything can be reversed or transposed, including cause and effect. The Awkward Sod often starts a row in my head by saying sharply, "No it doesn't" or "No it isn't". If someone argues that "it goes up" the Awkward Sod says "it goes down". If they say it's new, he says it's old, if they say it is rigid he says it is flexible. The Awkward Sod makes big things small and small things big. He makes adverse influences into benefits and vice versa. He makes the determined outcomes chance, and so on. And sometimes when someone says "of course, this is here", the Awkward Sod says," I can't see a damn thing".

As might be expected, given my analysis so far, the Awkward Sod gets a particularly perverse pleasure from peculiarity. He gets excited at the slightest sign of evidence that appears to be odd or ill-fitting, taking any peculiarity to be a confirmation that established interpretations should be reversed or stood on their heads.

The Awkward Sod is actually wrong most of the time, and the contrary position that he advocates cannot be justified. However, he often agitates for, and energises, an alternative focus of investigation in the pursuit of evidence. Sometimes what is discovered in that exercise indicates, suprisingly, that the Awkward Sod is right.

Even when he is not right, there can be creative consequences of this confrontation with the Awkward Sod. He has set himself a task, and sometimes an uncomfortable task, of finding justifying arguments for the position to which he has committed himself. He has to do a scrambling, short-range search for something that will back him up. Sometimes, to my surprise (necessity being the mother of invention I suppose), what emerges out of nothing are some surprisingly perceptive comments on the data, and some equally surprising additional evidence dredged from "who knows where" in the store of knowledge. The Awkward Sod's position is found to have elements of plausibility which might fit a new interpretation.

Further, whether right or wrong, the Awkward Sod produces the most fundamental challenge to a variety of mind-sets, axiomatic beliefs and assumed connections. You have to reveal and give defensible form to your views in order to fight him off. On occasions, the views are revealed simply for what they are - prejudices. Thus, even when the Awkward Sod is unsuccessful in arguing his case, the hitherto accepted position may also be found to have weaknesses and be unconvincing. As a result, the situation is made more open to alternative possibilities.

Over the years, my experience of its success has given the technique of the Awkward Sod increasing respect in the mental dialogue. One particularly gratifying example lives brightly in my memory. It happened in 1983. I had been asked to prepare a chapter on Trade Unions and Political Communication for a book on political communication at the General Election [Crewe and Harrop, 1986]. At first sight, the most obvious feature of communication at the 1983 election appeared to be the failure of both the Labour Party and the trade unions to communicate their message. It might have been anticipated that I would present a general analysis of union activities with failure as the central theme. That, I think, is initially what I intended to do. However, the Awkward Sod kept focusing upon some bits of contrary evidence and asserting a contrary position. It encouraged me to dig deeper into the various areas of activity, and what emerged led me to go for this different diagnosis.

I was able to discern new techniques and a radical improvement in trade union communicational effectiveness underneath the tide of political adversity. I made this "communicational effectiveness" the central theme, in spite of what appeared, at first sight, to be obvious communicational ineffectiveness (and in the face of some disconcerting academic derision at a conference held in Essex) [Minkin 1986]. This was also one of those fairly rare occasions in the study of politics where a thesis can be empirically tested in later activity. Twelve months later, in the campaign to retain their Political Funds in ballots which were now obligatory under new legislation, to the surprise of many, union communicational effectiveness became blindingly apparent, and this development was then widely acknowledged.

A long term vindication of the Awkward Sod was contained in my evidence to the Home Affairs Parliamentary Select Committee "Enquiry into Political Finance" in 1993 [Minkin 1993]. Based upon years of investigation, much of it initiated with the aid of the Awkward Sod, I mounted a case, with example after example, which challenged the common-sense orthodoxy that trade unions used their financial power to control the Labour Party. I gave the committee not only explanations for the self-restraint involved, but six different kinds of acts of abdication of political power involving the financial relationship. These were abdications which appear to have gone completely unnoticed hitherto. When the mental dialogue is nicely balanced, the Awkward Sod brings up successes like that to argue "Go for it!".

In my novice days of early research I did not always pay full attention to the Awkward Sod. One example which caused me considerable uncertainty and anxiety was the constant reporting of "deals" over policy votes between the party leaders and the unions at the Labour Party Conference. These deals, it was said, were a direct trade-off between what the leadership wanted in one area, and what the unions were given in another. From one perspective, this all seemed very plausible. It fitted a particular view of political relations as a transaction, and it was compatible with the common view of how trade unions negotiated in politics. To accept this interpretation of the way that the relationships worked could be said to be the hall-mark of a sophisticated political analyst "in the know". What academic researcher would want to appear naïve?

Yet, naïvety (allied to independence of mind) can be a creative asset. There was something very peculiar here. As I came to categorise the various reasons for unions changing their anticipated votes in a surprising way, the Awkward Sod kept repeating naïvely but firmly, "There are no deals, there are no deals, there are no deals". After questioning and re-questioning the participants, I became convinced that the Awkward Sod was (in general) right. I rarely came across anything that resembled the kind of deal that had been suggested. Trade union relations with the Labour Party were governed by a much wider set of mutual considerations and obligations. Compromises yes. Adjustments yes. But the reasons why unions changed votes were, in general, not explicable in terms of specific "I'll give you this if you give me that" arrangements [Minkin 1978/80 p 157]. They were much more to do with a broad family reciprocity based on loyalties and alignments, shared values and party goals.

I slowly developed confidence in following the Awkward Sod with his apparently perverse fixation on the peculiar. Thus I was more amenable to following the claim of the Awkward Sod that Conservative Governments were, in the last analysis, he said, "always the best friend" of the trade union-Labour Party relationship, even though there was considerable evidence that successive Conservative Governments had tried to undermine and destroy the relationship. This was on the basis of seeing that one factor in forging the new unity of the relationship after 1970 was the behaviour of the Heath Government.

A review of the historical evidence did show that, at the key moments when the relationship was at its most fragile, particularly when the trade unions might have pulled out of the Labour Party in order to concentrate their political activity on the TUC's relationship with the Government of the day, a major unifying force was the hostile attitude of Conservative Government. I built this into a paper on *The Party Connection* and the interpretation has, so far, stood the test of time [Minkin 1978].

The book on *The Contentious Alliance* bore many marks of this mode of heuristic thinking, although it does not, of course, register the many failures. Were the links between the unions and the party breaking down, as was so widely assumed (and assiduously pedalled) in the 1980s? My Awkward Sod kept pointing to bits and pieces of contrary evidence. Eventually, after a lot of analysis, a whole pattern was laid in front of me which did show a strengthening of links overall [Minkin 1991/92 pp 651-3]. Or again, polls taken before the Political Fund ballots in the unions in the mid 1980s were widely thought to indicate a new weakness in members' support for the funds, therefore to suggest defeat for the attempt to preserve them. The unions, it was said, would be out of politics: the party would be bankrupt. Yet all the ballots resulted in majorities for political funds. Why? Initially I was as uncertain as everybody else. But on the basis of one peculiarity - a niggling, ill-fitting piece of evidence - and a persistent nag from the Awkward Sod, I set to work. After months of digging out alternative data and placing another perspective on the material, I could see, and show, that the polls were indicating both a new strength and a stability of support for the funds [Minkin 1991/92 ch 18].

The full utility of this dialogue with the Awkward Sod is not illustrated by the startling successes. Even if his dogmatic offerings are not fully vindicated, there are explorations and ideas which arise out of the mental conflict. Here I give just one example from many. My Awkward Sod was wrong in giving *the* dogmatic explanation for the unprecedented rise of the Left within the Labour Party Conference, and later on the National Executive Committee, from the late 1960s to the early 1980s as "just a pattern of luck". But after much argument with the Awkward Sod, and much focused investigation, an amended interpretation did place a novel emphasis on some un-noticed elements of chance whilst acknowledging the greater force of other factors in the situation [Minkin 1991/92 chs 6, 7].

Experimental mind-games

There is another regular heuristic thinking process that takes place in my work. It is the practice of experimentally re-writing history, asking the question "What if?" .

Counterfactual thought experiments, as they are often known, have a long history but a patchy usage. They can be played in various ways, in any field of thought.[6] Perhaps the most famous are the mind games of Einstein, which played a part in the genesis of his theory of relativity [7]. In the social sciences they have been used for a variety of purposes.[8] I use them mainly to stimulate a close examination of the territory from an unusual perspective, to challenge my own assumptions about the weighting to be given to the different forces at work, to open up alternative historical possibilities, and in the attempt to generate or reinforce a new interpretation. I change some fundamental feature of the problem area under investigation and reflect, "What would things look like if this had not happened at all, or had not happened under those conditions?"

Death, chance and murder

Much of this mental play is simply the routine curiosity of scholarship - a playing with "what if?" in order to loosen up the mental approach, and expand understanding of the area under investigation. It can be intellectually profitable because, having disturbed the accepted pattern, it encourages a detailed re-assessment of the different forces at work.

This was how I viewed it in 1973, when at a conference at Cornell University in the United States I drew attention to the importance of the sudden death of leadership figures in the recent history of the Labour Party, and speculated experimentally about the possible influence of these deaths on the rise of the Left in the party. The two most important figures in this conjecture were the Party Leader, Hugh Gaitskell from the right of the Party, who died suddenly of a mysterious illness in January 1963, and Les Cannon, the right-wing union leader who died from cancer after a short illness in 1970. But there were also other deaths of important Labour figures in this period.[9]

My remarks aroused a gratifying level of interest. Told later, privately, that some of those in attendance had close links with the intelligence agencies, I was fascinated, but blithely unaware of, another dialogue which, it later emerged, had been taking place in the security services of Britain and the US about the manner of the replacement of Hugh Gaitskell by Harold Wilson. Years later, as news of the "Spycatcher" MI5 plot against Harold Wilson first began to emerge, I came to wonder whether, in all innocence, I had fed into a dialogue between professional conspiracy theorists within the security services and into an attempt to smear the Labour Party and its Leader as a security risk.[10]

If you did not really understand the forces at work in the party in the late 1960s, I suppose that you might have taken the view (as apparently did some in the security services) that Gaitskell's death was "the single most important historic factor" in the party's continuing swing to the Left, and then arrived at the speculation that "Gaitskell might well have been murdered" to achieve this change.[11] And this might appear especially convincing if you had "information" that the KGB had planned to assassinate a Western Leader and replace him with one sympathetic to them.[12] This could be regarded as an example of creative, counterfactual reasoning, suggesting or reinforcing the usefulness of an hypothesis. I have to say that it never occurred to me at the time. Perhaps because although I had, and have, no expertise in security or medical matters, I did understand something about the forces at work in the Labour Party.

If the KGB knew that Wilson would be elected to replace Gaitskell, then they had remarkable powers of foresight. The more obvious candidate was a militant anti-Communist, George Brown. And if Wilson was an agent of the Communist Left, he must have been a very cunning man indeed with an astonishingly long-term Machiavellian attitude towards his version of the greater good. Although there were some fortuitous factors in the rise of the Left, it had, in my view, one major and convincing explanation - a hostile reaction on the part of the constituency parties and the affiliated organisations to the strategy of the Labour Governments of 1964-70 and of 1974-9, to their attitude towards the Party, and to the rejection of some key policies associated with the mainstream of the Labour Party and unions, as well as the Communist Party. These Governments were led, for most of the time, by Wilson.

As it happened, I spent many hours in the 1970s with Philip Williams as he prepared the biography of Gaitskell, discussing the Labour Party and playing at times, "what if?" games about Aneurin Bevan, Hugh Gaitskell and Harold Wilson. I do not recall any discussion of Gaitskell's death being suspicious, and in his biography Williams gave no credence whatever to any conspiracy theory. However, he did make the plausible historical speculation that the dead Leader might have caused less disillusionment and produced less adverse reaction on the Left and in the unions than did Wilson [Williams 1979 pp 761-2, 783-6].

Be that as it may, like other historians I continued to play my counterfactual game for my own varied purposes. It was a useful and regular exploratory exercise to follow through the many possible consequences of each death,[13] and to speculate on what might have been, in a probing enquiry which, at the very least, deepened my understanding of the field.

Human choice and the 50/50 decision

Another mind game, which encourages a flexible appreciation of alternative possibilities, involved experimenting with how the element of human choice can affect the causes and consequences of key historical events. In particular, it was sometimes both reasonable and helpful to imagine the consequences if a nicely balanced decision had gone the other way.

Take, for example, the "Winter of Discontent" in 1978-9 and its consequences for British politics and the union-party relationship. An election had been expected in the autumn. It was not called, and Labour was forced into an election in the Spring of 1979 after a winter of industrial action which undermined the electoral position of the Labour Party, and public support for the trade unions' relationship with it. Later, both the crisis in relations between the unions and the Labour Government, and Labour's electoral predicament in relation to the unions, came to appear, and were often presented as, virtually inevitable.

Now, there are many important questions which might be raised about the causes and consequences of this crisis, and many human choice variables which might be changed in terms of playing "what if?" games. Let us just take one that I have played with on occasions. What if Prime Minister Callaghan had not sung his silly song about leaving the bride "waiting at the church" at the TUC of September 1978 (indicating that he was not calling a General Election) and instead of waiting for the spring decided to call the General Election in October 1978? Crucially, what would have happened to the union-party relationship if the Winter of

Discontent had happened not under Labour but *under the Conservatives*?

The potential reverberations were varied and fascinating. Certainly one of Labour's great electoral negatives of the past 18 years - the memory and myth of that winter - would have been removed. The relationship might even have been seen in the early 1980s, as it was in the mid 1970s, as the constructive base for the management of inflation, and the re-establishment of economic advance under the "social contract" of that time. The relationship might well have generated a new unity, produced a new accord for Government, and been strengthened in electoral terms. The electorate's perception of the union-party relationship might now be significantly different, as might our view of its overall political value and its capacity for survival.

Playing these mind games makes the historical researcher sensitive to a range of possibilities, and feeds a healthy scepticism about anticipations of further developments on the basis of what is thought to have been past experience. The importance of human decision-making is highlighted at the expense of deterministic impersonal forces. Again, as with the first game, a nuanced understanding of the various institutions, processes, relationships and political tendencies within the party at any one time is heightened by the exercise of exploring the field in the light of these kinds of question.

Re-dating a historical development

Later, I came to appreciate that there can sometimes be more specific creative gains as a result of this form of mental experimentation. Re-dating a historical development, such that it takes place under very different conditions, can be a productive mental game. For example, dating a development, plausibly, as say ten, or even fifty years earlier or later. One such game that I played with was stimulated by my examination of the conditions and consequences of the Left-led revolt over intra-party democracy which took place in the Labour Party after the 1979 General Election.

What if the revolt over intra-party democracy had happened not in coincidence with the rise of Thatcherism, but, say, in the early 1940s, when, as far as it can be understood, the electorate was much more receptive to the Left's ideological case? What if a resurgent Left then had established new procedures on intra-party democracy? In raising these questions in my head and, to some extent, directly in my work, I found it useful in working systematically through various possible alternative trajectories in the history of the Party, and also in reflecting on what was endemic and what was conditional in the state of the Labour Party.

I was focusing particularly on a range of questions about change and stability. Could the developments have occurred at some point without promulgating a deep crisis and, perhaps, a defection from the Party? If the developments had led to major changes at an earlier stage, how persuasive now would be our contemporary theories and explanations of the culture, character and distribution of power in the Labour Party?

As it happened, my questioning on this also opened up a new and unexpected line of enquiry. I found a peculiarity. What was illuminated was the surprising numerical and organisational weakness of the Labour Left in the party in the post-war period of social radicalism when, from what was known of the changing political opinion at this time, the Left might be expected to have peaked in influence. In the changes in union leadership, in votes cast for the National Executive Committee, and in votes on the policy of "Progressive Unity" on the left of British politics, the Labour Left was nothing like as strong as might have been expected. Explaining that became a new, interesting and distinctive problem to be fruitfully pursued [Minkin 1991/92 pp 66-7].

Removing the typical

In my form of research, I often have to assess the variations and regularities of a limited number of cases. There have been occasions when I have been able to make, or confirm, a more illuminating interpretation by re-assessing the typical case. I have imagined that one of the instances considered absolutely typical was a maverick case or did not occur, and I removed it mentally. What does the pattern look like now? How might one better restate the pattern? Can one account for the exception? What can emerge from this process may be part new insight, part confirmation. One particular case stands out in recollection.

In the history and mythology of trade union power, it was often assumed (or asserted) that it was not unusual for the union leaders to threaten the Parliamentary leadership with financial sanctions if they could not get their own way. There was often an implication that "getting their own way" included policy issues. I have already made some reference to this mythology and will have more to say about it below. Here, I want to focus on the legend of Arthur Deakin, the Transport Workers' leader, who it was often said, publicly threatened the Parliamentary leadership with financial sanctions at the 1952 Party Conference. It was often cited as the conclusive proof. He was the General Secretary of the largest union, and at the core of the most senior group of union leaders in that period. There were no good reasons for suggesting that he was exceptional. And it was a public statement.

Up to this point, I had myself accepted this interpretation. But the rest of my research suggested that either the pattern of behaviour of union leaders had changed dramatically since the time of Deakin, or there was something not quite right about this "typical" case. In playing with the evidence in my head, I took the typical case out. The pattern of behaviour without it appeared so clear. Then I asked myself: Did he say what he was thought to have said at the 1952 Conference?

I re-examined the evidence about Deakin. A microscopic analysis of the speeches he made in 1952, and a detailed search through the evidence of his behaviour, suggested that the answer to the question was "No". There was never a clear threat. If there was a threat, in the one throw-away response he made to a heckler, it was in reaction not to the Parliamentary Leadership but to their dissident opponents. In any case the moment he was challenged publicly on the point he retreated. The case collapsed as the typical example of threatening the Parliamentary Leadership, and I could then proceed to map out the more plausible interpretation from an examination of the rest of the political behaviour of union leaders [Minkin 1991/92 p 99 n 69 and pp 516-9].

Analogies and metaphors

Attention is often drawn to the prominent role that analogies and metaphors have played in creativity.[14] Here I want to focus on the part that they play in the generation of my own creative work.

As may have already become apparent, metaphors fascinate me. In drawing attention to common as well as different features, they have, in my experience, three potential heuristic functions. As we have seen in the use of metaphorical self-images they can assist in self discovery. They can also illuminate aspects of the creative process itself (see the example below of "ecological balance"). And, most relevant here, they can assist in enhancing discovery about the substance of the field of enquiry.

My field is already cluttered with metaphor, some of which mislead more than they illuminate. Creative research is, in a sense, a constant battle against the mental tyranny of concepts and modes of expression. So there is a regular and important task in asking probing questions which filter the illuminating from the misleading. I ask all the time, "Is this metaphor useful? In what way is this supposed similarity unsatisfactory? If it is different from the picture emerging from the empirical investigations, what are the points of difference?". The demands of symmetry implicit in comparison may force us to see things in the similarities and differences that we had not looked for [Schon 1963 p 24]. But also, after a clearing exercise of this kind, we can also more easily ask "what else might this be like?".

The first port of call is usually the field of the academic discipline - in my case, the literature of political research. What else do I know of in this field which operates like this, or has features in common? What concepts have been produced that cover processes similar to this? Or, what has been produced covering some of these characteristics?

Although my work on the agenda of the Labour Party Conference began with a direct observation and a chance remark highlighting a problem, I recall not only playing with various phrases derived from the politics surrounding meetings and conferences and their study, but also from the metaphors of "agenda politics" which proliferated in studies of power in political systems. "Determining the agenda", "controlling the agenda", "shaping the agenda" were all in use to describe the way that particular sets of policy issues and questions came to dominate a debate. And the work done by political scientists Peter Bachrach and Morton Baratz around these processes, utilised the suggestive concept of "non-decisions," and invoked the idea of a hidden face of power [Bachrach and Baratz 1962], [Bachrach and Baratz 1963], shaping decision-making.

My empirical observations, and patiently grounded research on the conference, had already alerted me to many significant policy alternatives which had been submitted by affiliated organisations, but were in various ways sidelined or re-composed by the processes of agenda management. And, as I have also described, I was exploring the secret processes of managing this agenda. But all this was given theoretical and conceptual substance by the literature on "agenda politics" - a politics which, to my knowledge, has not hitherto been actually applied to literal, as opposed to metaphorical, agendas.

Wider than our own field, the whole world of similarities, in every field and discipline, is available for us to draw upon (in principle that is, and providing that we have the time). Inter-disciplinary boundaries are artificial in terms of the sources of illuminating analogies, problem-solving ideas or concepts. In terms of creativity, category lines are there to be broken. As Koestler pointed out, "decisive advances in the history of scientific thought can be described in terms of mental cross-fertilisation between different disciplines"[Koestler 1969 p 230]. More recently, Dogan and Pahre have noted that "a majority of the most important innovations in the social sciences are cross-disciplinary."[15]

The process of mental cross-fertilisation may usefully be appreciated through the work of William J.J. Gordon and the idea of "Synectics" - a term drawn from the Greek concept of "joining together of different and apparently irrelevant elements" [Gordon

1961 p 3]. Synectics emphasises the conscious use of analogy and metaphor in problem solving, and is potentially very fruitful in terms of its key heuristics - making the strange familiar and making the familiar strange [Gordon 1961 p 33].

We attempt (as I have already described) to make the familiar strange by finding ways to view it afresh, to come at it from an unusual angle, to see it in a different light. But also in another exercise, we attempt to make the strange familiar in order to aid the process of mental cross fertilisation. We can do this first by an atomization which might uncover elements hitherto unnoticed. And by stripping it down to its essential structure or pattern, we can also make it useable to identify a more general form. There can be underlying similarities not only with phenomena outside the immediate location, but also outside the discipline. These similarities may have been obscured by surface appearances. The use of these comparisons can not only give us new insight into the features, processes and relationships we are examining. At its richest, the identification of common or overlapping features or patterning, and the imaginative flexibility to utilise them, can feed into one of the fundamentals of creative process - combinatory play and synthesis.

Analogical reasoning can lead to the production of novel combinations of ideas hitherto seen as unconnected, even widely separated in different forms and fields.[16] This novel and unexpected synthesis from different frames of reference or universes of discourse is sometimes regarded as the archetypal creative product - what Koestler calls the bi-sociative fusion [Koestler 1969 p 45]. Even analogical images of wide scope can play an important part in generating a new synthesis. Darwin drew heavily on five such images - the irregularly branching tree, the tangled bank, wedging, artificial selection and human warfare in shaping the theory of evolution through natural selection[17].

It has been suggested that the capacity to make remote associations that are useful is an important creative ability[18]. Various authors, including Gordon, have also suggested the creative usefulness of what might appear to be irrelevant, or even far-fetched, analogies. Biology has been seen as a particularly rich source of direct analogy [Gordon 1961 p 56]. So, Brunel adapts the methods of the shipworm to the construction of the Thames Tunnel. Browne notices the spider's net and invents the suspension bridge. Watt takes from the shell of the lobster on his table the model of the pipes that will carry water under the Clyde [Smiles 1996 edn p 74].

However, Perkins has suggested that although these remote analogies do have a dramatic and impressive quality, and hence tend to dominate the literature, it is close analogies, or analogies from domains not so remote from one another, which are normally more fruitful for a creative thinker than the more remote analogies [Perkins 1983], [Nickerson, Perkins and Smith 1985 pp 98-9]. It is an interesting, if contested,[19] judgement. Certainly my own experience (for what it is worth here) seems to confirm Perkins. Where I have consciously sought for remote analogies that would have a heuristic function in illuminating the relationship under investigation, or would provide the overlap of patterning which allows combinatory play, then I have found myself forcing the similarities in a way that was artificial and unproductive.

In one of the first papers that I produced on the relationship between trade unions and the Labour Party, I referred to it as "a symbiotic relationship". This idea of a close living interdependence has a biological meaning in relation to animal or plant species. It was a reasonable and, in some ways, illuminating description. However, thereafter I spent some time on the literature in biology, hunting for a species which would produce at least a more revealing metaphorical allusion but also, I hoped, some creative new amalgam of ideas.

I have to say that I failed completely. I had some amusement, during the tensions of the 1974-79 Labour Government, with the report of an insect which, during and after copulation, ate the partner, but that was about as far as it went. The distinctiveness and rich complexity of the union-party relationship seemed to defy anything other than a crude analogy. However, creative insight came to me from another source.

In the research for *The Contentious Alliance*, I was struck by the array of vivid metaphors used in the rhetoric of those who commented upon, or participated in, the trade union-Labour Party relationship. I drafted an unusual opening to the book in which the metaphors became the means of introducing the reader to some of the key historical features of the relationship [Minkin 1991/92] pp 3-5]. Gradually, as my work progressed, I began to re-assess the metaphors in terms of their usefulness in characterising the relationship overall. I began this in the spirit of criticism and contrast rather than an acceptance of similarity. In particular, I found reasons to question whether the various commonly used "market" metaphors of the "transactional" relationship (deals, votes in exchange for money or favours, etc) allied to an economic model of power maximisation, were very useful in overall characterisations of this particular relationship. The points of similarity were relatively insignificant when compared to the differences.

I then began to appreciate that one of the metaphorical clusters and some of the most pervasive and sentimental of all metaphors -those relating to family life - were much less rhetorical than I had thought. Indeed they were the source of considerable insight into the ambivalent way that people actually behaved in the party-union relationship. There was, in practice, the mixture of common purpose and conflict, the striving for both bonding and autonomy, the destructive impact of open infidelity and the embittering hints of separation and divorce. All this accompanied by deep affection mixed with the occasional desire to murder!

In particular I was struck by the relevance of one similarity of patterning - the inhibitions and restraints inherent in the relationship. At an important stage in the project, I was influenced by these metaphors and this similarity in developing the explanatory framework of *The Contentious Alliance* in a way that I will illustrate in Chapter Eight.

Presentation as creativity-generation

As discussed earlier, to my initial surprise many years ago, I found that there was a remarkable tendency for creativity in the substance of a study to be generated out of preparing the presentation of it. The writing process was much more than simply a process of conveying prior thought. It was a creative process. But there was more than this. It has been alarming, and also illuminating, that significant creative developments occasionally simply "happen" in the process of finalising the presentation of my research.

What do I mean by "happen"? I mean here that, at a late stage in the drafting of the presentation - at "clean" draft stage, where the aim is for maximum precision - aesthetic arrangements, random order in footnotes, and the changing focus of checking items through the text, can break old associations of thought and suggest novel connections. It is an anxiety-ridden process at a stage so near completion deadlines, but an awareness of these "happenings" can, to some extent, be integrated into the researcher's art, making it more likely that they can become creative opportunities.

Aesthetics, order and focus

In tidying up the presentation, pursuit of the aesthetic sometimes offers new emphasis and new meanings to the substantive content. For example, if I examine just the sub-headings of my work and I ask, "are they elegant, economical and coherent across the book?" I find that I am sometimes producing and playing with new and plausible interpretations or reinterpretations of the data. Similarly, just the exercise of changing the sequence of particular sections occasionally offers a different emphasis to the thesis. I have then either to reject it or begin to play with it. Also, bringing two or three sections together from different parts of a text forces sequences around the remaining "holes" which may well trigger off new connections. Even, occasionally, the reconstruction of a single sentence can bring unanticipated beneficial consequences of the new contiguity.

The heuristic guidance here is that whilst you are preparing, focusing on, and carrying through any "final" presentational change in the text, you have to be alert to the unanticipated possibilities of the situation, keep your eye on the substantive connections and implications, and watch for the left-overs.

Aesthetically pleasing repetitions, counterpoints or juxtapositions can invite a search for the material to fit the attractive presentation, and this too can elicit hidden knowledge, and suggest new connections which may be of value. I am particularly attracted to alliterations in presentation. On occasions, these have also suggested productive lines of thought which creatively enhanced the substance of the work (see the influence of "relations rules and roles" discussed in Chapter Eight).

Stronger claims have been made, or implied, about the relationship between the aesthetic and the creative. Creative scientists, talking about their work, have sometimes used terms like "beauty and elegance" to describe what they have produced [Weschler 1978 p1]. Various distinguished scientists - Heisenberg and Einstein amongst them [Weschler 1978 p 1] - held that the aesthetic quality of a theory suggested its validity. It has even been argued that there is "a mysterious concordance" between aesthetic judgement and the "inner structure of reality" [Reanney 1995 p13]. Some have also argued that, in search of this quality, there is a scientific taste just as there is a literary or artistic one [Koestler 1969 pp 146-7] - a notion that "it feels right"[20].

From my research experience, occasionally something creatively fruitful can emerge out of judgements of incompleteness, lack of balance or lack of proportion in the framework. New lines of thought can open up by asking, "What is it that feels wrong here?" or, "What questions need to be asked in order for this to be developed in a way that feels right?". One major redefinition of the problem that I was pursuing over relations between trade unions and the Labour Party happened because of my dissatisfaction in handling what I felt to be a lop-sided framework (See Chapter Eight).

However, there are acute dangers that the aesthetic satisfaction "when a great and beautiful concept proves to be consonant with reality"[21] will in practice be subversive of the scientific pursuit of truth. It is possible for the symmetry of the created formulation to be at the expense of the portrayal of a complex and messy reality.[22] In any case, the criterion is unclear. Broken symmetry, even "wildness", can also be aesthetically satisfying[23]. As for social relationships, whatever the value of Einstein's observation that he could not believe "that God plays dice with the world,"[24] one could be forgiven for thinking that something plays dice with human affairs.

The warning here (and a constant reminder to myself) is that in creative research, there is always the danger of a "fix", when the evidence is made to fit, or the variations conveniently put to one side, as harmony and the sense of proportion are satisfied, or a good story emerges and the presentation is made to look smart and complete. Over the years, in my work, it has been over the possible temptations involved here that the Patternmaker-artist and the Patternmaker-realist have often come into intense conflict in my head.

The order of footnotes and endnotes in an analytical structure - particularly notes which have explanatory functions - can also hold heuristic possibilities. I am particularly aware of this because I have regularly to respond to a mysterious, last minute, "chinese whispers" effect on the endnotes of my books. This occurs partly because I have a "bifocal" mind which does not accurately register details when it probes ideas, but also because my work goes through so many reconstructions and re-types. It does not matter how many times I check them, the "whispers" still happen.

Of course, as my work is analytical and often breaks out of chronological sequences, the end notes, including some important explanatory endnotes, are in an order that I have not consciously structured for the relationship between them. They are ordered and numbered in relation to their place in the text. On occasions, in my articles, chapters and books, I noticed, as I checked the notes "vertically" as well as "horizontally", that these explanatory notes generated new connections. Sometimes they spark a hypothesis that demands pursuit, sometimes they clarify and deepen interpretations, sometimes they suggest new ones.

I am afraid that this is an area where I have no notes and only a weak memory of the examples - in part because the process involves a rewriting which obscures the original endnotes as well as the draft. But certainly one of the examples involved the radically new but complex explanation that I gave of the results of the Trade Union Political Fund ballots in the period 1984-5. As I have explained, with the assistance of the Awkward Sod, I had come to reject the commonly held view of the development of trade union opinion before the ballot successes. But it was only after I saw the sequence of the draft endnotes that I become clear about my explanation of the results. With the accidental pattern in mind I rewrote the text and adjusted the notes.

Another pattern, relating to the way that the Trades Union Congress and the Labour Party responded to the crisis after 1931, was clarified by a sequence of quotations which originally I had placed in the endnotes. According to legend, the TUC, seeking a new unity, moved "to take the helm" of the party. But what this account failed to register was the extent of the affirmation of autonomy and of distinct spheres of operation - the political and the industrial. The changes in procedure at this time involved a delicate balance of unity and autonomy. Again, my own understanding of that only became fully clarified after I had written the text, and was working through the endnotes in two different sections of a chapter. Problematic though it is, I have now grown used to this process, and I am now readier to regard scanning down the endnotes for connections as a heuristic procedure as well as a tedious necessity.

I have also become more aware that other kinds of routine and boring presentational tasks can have their heuristic value. Over time, I came to realise that in following errors of nomenclature in the text, I was noticing connections that I had not seen before. I now know that the more I change focus in pursuing particular items through the text, the more I tend to break myself out of the familiar grooves of perception and association. Thus, this too has developed into something of a heuristic procedure. Is there a pattern if I follow through the key examples of this procedure? Is there a pattern if I follow through this topic? Is there a pattern wherever this relationship occurs? Is there a pattern of behaviour whenever this person is involved?

One important example had considerable political significance. For reasons explained in the previous chapter, I had been alerted to look out for "non-decisions" - what the Conference had not been allowed to decide. At a late stage, I was checking a draft to try to achieve some standardisation in terminology and capitalization concerning "public ownership" and "nationalisation". As I worked through the references within different categories of agenda controls, I became aware (or re-aware, I am not sure) of the degree of agenda management of "public ownership" by the Labour Party Conference managers in the 1950s. What I found suggested to me that perhaps I ought to re-assess the extent of union and constituency party support for preserving, even *extending*, the public ownership policy. I moved back into examining the union mandates, finding strong evidence of support, but also a pattern of procedural manipulation in carrying out the mandates when it came to the Party Conference. Now I attempted a comprehensive analysis, following through, over the years, the handling of public ownership. The pattern then became absolutely clear.

Examining how this issue had been handled in its entirety in the period of the late 1950s and early 1960s, generated a radical new interpretation, focusing on the non-decisions of the Conference. It challenged the accepted view that there had been a real victory of Social-Democratic "revisionism" after 1960, [Minkin 1978/1980 pp 324-6] described as a victory for "the soul of the Labour Party"[Haseler 1969 p 253].

I was thus able to make much more sense than others of the powerful left-wing reaction in the Labour Party in the 1970s, a reaction which involved a reassertion of public ownership. In a sense it had always been hidden there.

The end of the beginning

Thus, the stage of creativity at which the clean draft is before me has lately grown to be a source of deep satisfaction and uplift, not just because there is an achievement in front of me, and difficult problems have been overcome, but because I often have a sense that perhaps some of the best is yet to come. Certainly the draft can change considerably after this point. At this stage, I see myself sometimes as though I was at the potter's wheel - all the clay assembled, the objective now clear, the shape has emerged, and elegance is now beginning to almost beautify the product. Sometimes, the image is of a composer/conductor, softening or heightening one passage, refining another. At other times, it is a weaver putting in the final threads, linking the patterns in an intricate tapestry.

However, I also see that something else can now be expected of this presentational, aesthetic and rhetorical process. In a variety of ways I have described, new connections will be made and new interpretations will be suggested. And my awakened sensitivity to the heuristic possibilities involved makes it more likely that I will notice, engender and take advantage of the new opportunities.

The heuristic moral of this section? I think of it in terms of an adaptation of Churchill after El Alamein, "Creatively speaking, the clean draft is not the end, it is not even the beginning of the end, but it is perhaps the end of the beginning."

Confronting the vicious circle

Talking as thinking

Before I move into the use of the next device, I want to extend a point made in the previous chapter about creativity and the process of expression. We might anticipate (and I certainly did as a novice researcher) that for the rational scholar, thought was prior to speech and action. Yet not only did I find that, in a sense, writing was thinking, but also that, on occasions, talking was thinking. What I mean by this is that, on occasions, particularly in an area where I am very knowledgeable, I say things that are illuminating and quite complex which I did not know that I had thought before I opened my mouth. Certainly, it did not involve a process of conscious formulation. Here is another odd but useful creative process that I do not fully understand. But, then, even the constructive creations of the Chattering Monkey are a bit mysterious to me.

Never mind. I tried to monitor the circumstances in which it happened to see what might be learned and repeated, but there seemed to be a variety of such situations. Certainly it could happen on occasions when the adrenalin was running, because the conversation was stimulating and, for some reason or other, the circumstances made me feel "clever" and gave me a sense of self-worth.

Perhaps more useful in terms of following good practice, it seemed to happen in the act of vigorously explaining and persuading, either face to face or talking to somebody inside my head, specifically as I sought to connect with the other's experience, with their interests, with their perspectives, with their level of knowledge and understanding, and with the angle of their questions. The focus and language of my explanation changed as I took up a different frame of reference, and something novel was encouraged to emerge.

I noticed this particularly in 1993 in the very early days of this project, when I first produced a framework for research analysis which emphasised the role of creativity. Then I had the task of trying to persuade various people to participate. Their response was of the order of "fascinated... but reluctant (for various practical reasons)". As I went through the repetitive exercise of persuasively explaining, to academics working in different fields, what exactly I had in mind, I learned more about what it was that I was proposing to do. Each time my explanations seemed to come out slightly differently in some features, as I attempted to connect with the interests and expertise of those to whom I was talking. I made distinctions and located new themes. In effect, I was developing ideas and enriching the framework as I attempted to talk persuasively about what I had in mind. At the end, what I had in mind was more than I had had in mind at the beginning.

Something similar happened that same year, but in this case it was talking in my mind. I fantasised about addressing a French political conference prior to preparing a paper for the real thing. I was explaining to them about the party-union relationship, and trying to convince them of the plausibility of my own distinctive perspective. I declaimed vigorously. In the process, the metaphors that I was using suddenly changed their function in the argument in a way that I had not anticipated, thus ordering my presentation in a way that took me by surprise.

This process of creative presentational development has happened so many times over the years that I now take it to be integral to my research process. I cannot command it, but it has heightened my sensitivity to the heuristic possibilities of various kinds of discourse in different situations. The heuristic rule I apply here is: try to connect with the mind frame of the people you are talking to, but be aware of what is happening *to your own* contribution as you do it. Experience suggests a simple application - that it may be useful from time to time to talk about your research, not to close colleagues, but to people who are experts in something entirely different. It may also be more useful than you anticipate to give a detailed answer to strangers who ask what seems to be a particularly stupid or ignorant question about your research (although, of course, it might well bore them to death).

The theatrical drama

But, in addition, and it is an important ingredient of the section that follows, the rules can also be applied more imaginatively to the formalisation of a variety of mental dialogues which build upon the natural processes of the Chattering Monkey. This theatrical drama can be organised in a way that can encourage the creative generation of ideas as the case is explained, argued and defended to different audiences.

The mental device I now want to introduce can have three functions. First, it is a process of rigorous scrutiny and filtering of ideas. Second, it can be a heuristic process generating new ideas and insight. But third, used as a final appraisal of all, it becomes a verificational process.

This mental theatre is a natural extension of the kind of dialogue which I have already described as spontaneously erupting in my head. Here it is formalised, and the characters are given a collective presence. From another perspective it could be regarded as a constructive utilisation of my paranoid search for invulnerability against the Minkin academic pogrom - a search made all the more necessary given the risks involved in the creative process.

Scrutiny and creativity

The "show" is staged like this. Periodically, I imagine myself inside, even captured by, a circle of rather vicious critics of different academic and political orientations who are out to destroy my work if they can. For some of them it is business, for others it is personal. To this audience I give the power of scrutiny. I present a particular thesis and its main arguments, or I define a concept and its usefulness. I invite, and listen mentally to, their criticisms - empirical and theoretical - and their alternative assumptions and positions.

So, I argue, say (using the evidence from the early 1920s and 1960s) that a series of industrial victories caused a shift to the Left within the party. They come back at me, "Crude, what counts as an industrial victory, and what was moving to the Left?" They point to other factors in the rise of the Left. They point also to movements to the Right which followed industrial victories in the 1950s. I restate my now much more qualified position in different forms and they launch new attacks. The process continues until I feel reasonably invulnerable in my thesis.

Or I test out a new concept. I assert that the various industrial and political freedoms involved in trade union activities can all be conceptualised as "integrity," and I give it a particular definition. "Plausible" they admit, but misleading because of this, this and this. The conceptualisation survives at one hearing, and goes into a publication [Minkin 1979] and some subsequent papers, but much later, after a new appearance before the Circle, it goes in the dustbin.

I try out a presentational device.[25] I say that I am integrating a personal soliloquy or problematic dialogue into the middle of the book, exploring how different interpretations might have been advanced at this point, and the text presented in contrasting ways . "Pretentious!" declares one. "Intrusive" says another. "Is it necessary?" "What does it do that can't be done other ways?" The idea is shelved, awaiting perhaps some expression in another form.

For me, this internal dialogue, where I am forced to confront the most awkward and piercing criticisms and questions, is valuable feedback from inside the mind. It often exposes weaknesses, and sometimes my positions have to be completely and reluctantly abandoned. More typical is that the dialogue suggests beneficial adjustments and adaptations which I can accommodate without losing face. (Indeed one of the points of this process is that, in a sense, I have made damn sure that it has all happened before it has got to my face).

Sometimes the adjustment is made with alacrity and a shameless immediate changing of position, sometimes it is made after vain and despairing attempts to bolster the position with inadequate arguments. As their criticism and my response together make my case stronger, my next mental recital of it within the Vicious Circle is all the more confident!

Recently, I have also come to see that there are prudential rules of engagement. My fear is that they might unite with the Destructive Critic and undermine the whole enterprise. So in the critical dialogue, however belligerent the encounter, the critics are not allowed to demean me personally and hurt my self-esteem (although it is not easy to stop them). This is such an anxiety-ridden confrontation that I have to keep feeling clever to deal with it.

The device is not just a scrutinising, filtering procedure. It has more clearly creative functions. The phased way that it operates within my mind is encouraging, not discouraging, to the creative process. It operates according to the deferment principles in which I have initially pursued the boldest possible overall interpretations and constructions - that is my starting point and the Patternmaker-artists's licence - knowing that after the Realist has had his say, so, once within the Circle, it can be adjusted, refined, and, if necessary, shed altogether under their fierce scrutiny.

The argument can have other beneficial creative consequences. As I attempt to perceive the study and its ideas as the Circle might perceive them, as I change my language and angle of approach, as I receive their damaging criticisms, and then try to answer them, as I attempt to argue and persuade, so this sometimes forces my mind out of grooves and I discover that I have reinterpreted my position; or I find new justifications on my lips, creativity through "talking as thinking". As in a real dialogue, it is always likely to spark off a connection with some other idea or experience apparently miles away. The Awkward Sod can occasionally make his useful appearance. The scene can dissolve into one or many productive soliloquies by the Chattering Monkey.

And verification

The technique also has another function. It can be used as a mode of verification. I have, so far in this study, concentrated on the heuristic rather than the verificational. Indeed, I would argue that in terms of guiding and managing of the creative research process, an immediate preoccupation with verification can be constipating.

Of course, I attempt to be as rigorous as possible in pursuing and checking evidence, and presenting coherent and well-grounded argument in a thesis of such plausibility that it will bear the closest academic scrutiny. If it is an obligation of creative research to search for originality, it is also an obligation of scholarship to be committed to the pursuit of truth and addicted to what T.H. Huxley called, "the slaying of beautiful hypotheses by ugly facts."[26] My Patternmaker-realist has first crack at that job. But not before the Patternmaker-artist has explored the possibilities, and given free flow to the informed imagination. Everything in its time and place in the consciously creative process.

However, in the end, and even after the Realist has been in action, I do become increasingly concerned about further rigorous scrutiny. I become anxious lest my political feelings and perspectives, and my search for originality, may have coloured the observations and interpretation. At this stage I become pre-occupied with the need for the case that I am making to be as powerful and water-tight as it can be made. Some of this is a fear of being "found out," some of it is a matter of living up to the moral self-image - creative but honest, truthful and scholarly. So, in the end, I utilise the Vicious Circle as the nearest equivalent that I have to experimental design in order to test and, if possible, to validate what I have to put forward; and of course, to counteract any research "pathologies."

I recreate the Circle with a mixture of outsiders and insiders, observers and participants in the field of study, and I then imagine this Vicious Circle providing different reviews of my finished work. How would they go about falsifying what I have to say? What weaknesses might they focus on? What bias might they detect? What counter evidence could they produce? If there are exceptional cases, have I justified their exceptionality, or could it be argued that they destroy the thesis? What other more plausible interpretation, concepts and frameworks, might be offered, and what could I argue with them in reply? I give the Circle a reviewing searchlight so that they have the best conditions to poke and delve into every nook and cranny of the work. The anxiety is, "What might the vicious bastards find?". If the finished project stands up to that degree of scrutiny (and it often fails) then it passes the experimental test and I am prepared to release it to the light of day - and of course to face the real critics.

There is another way of expressing this test. In creative scholarship, with its unpredictable sequences, its variable phases of discovery, and its sense that the project is dynamically alive, we always have to make an obvious but crucially important judgement about the end of the paper, article, chapter or book. Is it finished? I think of myself as having a good sense of this - a sense of ripeness, economy and completeness. But this may be because it is not unusual for the Vicious Circle to spot a vulnerable under-development, and sometimes an indulgent over-development, before I make my final judgement.

The Vienna panic

The Vicious Circle can take you by surprise just when you think they have finished their work. One occasion - known to me since then as "The Vienna Panic" - was in the final year of submission of the manuscript of *The Contentious Alliance*.

It had been a huge enterprise as I looked back on it. Twenty one lengthy and detailed chapters of it. Years of work on an old portable typewriter, mountains of evidence and the construction of an original explanatory framework for a multifaceted relationship. Now three or four chapters had been cleanly typed in their final versions by a hard-pressed secretary (servicing several academics) and the remainder were, I considered, just about ready. My wife and I had organised a brief winter holiday before the final submission of the book.

The day and evening before we left for Vienna, I was encouraging the Vicious Circle to monitor the text and felt increasingly satisfied with the results. But, as is sometimes the case, I was unable to switch off the searchlight during the night when it quietly continued with its survey, periodically waking me up with its darting criticisms. I was relatively unconcerned at this. It seemed that I had the critics foiled at every turn. I even seem to remember singing quietly at one point.

Suddenly, at around two a.m. "Oh God!", stomach churning, I sat bolt upright in bed. There was a significant incoherence between the interpretation in the framework Chapter Two and the detailed case study in Chapter Six. Panic; absolute panic.

Both were equally plausible, but they were different. The Vicious Circle warned that this was reprehensible. It made the rest of the book worthless, they said - the bastards!

It could not be ignored. What to do? The obvious chapter to keep was Six, which was based on a scrupulously tight analysis of the evidence. But Chapter Two - the framework chapter - had been typed.

In my work there is usually a Paragraph Two, or a Section Two, or a Chapter Two, which is the focus of the theorising for what is to follow. This paragraph, section or chapter has been (to put it bluntly) a pig to produce. But there comes a stage in the creative process when there is a delicate harmony and integration between this and the rest of the draft as it nears completion. Sections and themes now feed from, and into, each other. A mutual dependence has been created. It has, what I think of as an "ecological balance".

Harsh experience has now taught me to respect the ecological balance. The removal or change of any one significant element in the framework chapter, however justified in itself, can produce a major problem somewhere else in the draft, even a series of damaging reverberations. There is an acute danger of a thread unpicking throughout the book , running a ladder through the whole stocking.

The lesson here is that, at this stage of the process, amendments are a dangerous business, and the creative muse has either to be put under maximum restraint or given further time to mull it over. But, on this occasion, there was not the required time. In any case there was also the not insignificant consideration that I did not look forward to asking the secretary to retype Chapter Two again. Panic, panic; coffee, coffee!

For the first three days and nights of the "holiday" in Vienna, I wrestled with this problem, notebook in hand. I came to the view that I would have to face my stressed and overstretched secretary, and the framework chapter would simply have to be altered. At the same time, with a mental eye on all the other twenty or so chapters, I worked out carefully what that alteration could be, praying all the time that it would not produce yet more problems in other parts of the text. So far, to this day, it seems to be all right.

MEETING THE CHALLENGE

In this chapter I have described seven different modes of heuristic thinking - the reasoning, techniques, tactics and metacognitive sensitivities which contribute to disciplined creative interventions in "the flow". These are options open to the creative practitioner playing my game. They are presented here in a useful sequence, but in practice they can be followed in a variety of orders and interrelationships.

They are, of course, no guarantee of creative success. Failure is endemic in the creative process. And even success may be incomplete. Often the exercises simply result for me in bits and pieces of suggestive ideas which spend much time in suspended animation in the mind, or recorded in a File of Ideas.[27] Some of them are still there to this day. Nevertheless, the processes described here are my means of meeting the challenge, noted in Chapter Two, of constructing systematic creative play which can enlarge the possibilities of a situation and assist in achieving a better understanding of the world. As I have shown, they do make it more likely that, in any given situation, alternatives will be generated, novel or unexpected constructions will emerge, and something original and appropriate will develop.

CHAPTER END NOTES

[1] Very occasionally these dreams can themselves be helpful in taking my thoughts on my work a step forward. One recent experience was that in explaining the structure of a future book to someone in my dreams I moved a plan for a particular section so that it ordered the totality of the work in a way that was both rational and very promising.

[2] Something like it is described in relation to "the interrogation of primary sources" in [Burnham 1991 pp 18-9].

[3] [Torrance and Thomas 1994 p 109] make a slightly different point but it is suggestive of the same mental process. They point out that experienced researchers can often successfully write up "flawed research" by reconstructing new research aims "which the originally inconclusive results can fulfil". The notion of "flawed" here embodies an implicit assumption that the origional objectives are the proper ones. In practice in fieldwork

the objectives are often constructed and reconstructed in the process of research.

[4] See on this the Epilogue to the paperback edition of [Minkin 1992 pp 678-681]. Also [Minkin 1995].

[5] [Osborn 1993 p 279] refers to it as the vice-versa technique. [de Bono 1977 pp 124-130] refers to it as The Reversal Method.

[6] A book that I have not yet seen is Philip E. Tetlock and Aaron Belkin (eds) Counterfactual Thought Experiments in World Politics: logical, methodological and psychological perspectives, Princeton University Press, 1996, but there is an excellent essay by them, adapted from their introduction to the book, in Items Social Science Research Council, New York, December 1996, Vol 50, No 4 pp 77-85. They are concerned mainly with the grounds of valid causal inference rather than creativity generation but they do make the important point (p 79) that there are a variety of ways in which counterfactual argument may be enlightening.

[7] [Wertheimer 1945 p 169] His most famous mental experiment focused upon a question he had first posed at the age of 16, "What would I see, if I rode along with a ray of light?" There is a fascinating and suggestive series of games about time in the stories by Alan Lightman, [Lightman 1993]. Suppose that time was a circle bending back on itself so that the world repeated itself precisely, endlessly. Suppose that time flowed more slowly the further we were from the centre of the earth; suppose that time was a quality rather than a quantity and therefore we could not agree on its exact measurement; suppose that time ends on a known date; suppose there is a place where time stands still? etc. What might be learned about the effect of these changes on human motivation and behaviour?

[8] See on this [Tetlock and Belkin 1996 pp 79-82]. Also [Gould 1969 pp 195-207], [Fearon 1991 pp 169-195], [Hawthorne 1991]. [Stretton 1964 p 252] suggests that the chief value of accumulating "pasts" as imagined alternatives is in provoking questions and sometimes consoring answers rather than by finding and proving causal relations.

[9] The leading Leftwing MP, Aneurin Bevan died in 1960, a few months after an operation for cancer, and the Party's General Secretary, Morgan Phillips, died in January 1963, after suffering a stroke in 1960 at the height of his powers.

[10] On this see [Dorril and Ramsay 1991], [Leigh 1988].

[11] See on this [Pincher 1981 pp 77-9]. Also [Wright with Greengrass 1987 pp 362-4].

[12] According to [Wright 1987 p 362], a KGB defector, Anatoli Golitsin, told MI5 that before he left he had heard that there was to be a top level KGB political assassination in Europe to get their man in post. For a different perspective on the Golisin "revelation" and how it was used see [Leigh 1988 pp 79-86].

[13] The tragic pattern continued later with the death of the leading intellectual, Tony Crosland in 1976, and more recently in 1994 with the death of the Party Leader, John Smith.

[14] [Gordon 1961 pp 36-56], [Jubak 1992], Langley and Jones in [Sternberg 1988 p 199], McReynolds, P. 'Motives and metaphors: a study in scientific creativity' in [Leary, 1990, p 136], [Schon 1963 pp 35-44]. See also [Perkins 1981 pp 89-91] for a qualified view.

[15] [Dogan and Pahre 1990 p17] citing the work of Deutsch, Platt and Senghaas in [Deutsch, Marcovits and Platt 1986].

[16] Koestler gives the examples of Gutenberg combining the techniques of the wine press and the seal, and Kepler marrying physics to astronomy [Koestler 1969 p 208].

[17] Gruber in [Wechsler 1978 p 130-2].

[18] Mednick, S.A. 'The associative basis of the creative process', Psychological Review 69, 1962, pp 220-32, cited by Andrews in [Taylor and Getzels p117], also by [Nickerson, Perkins and Smith p 91].

[19] See on this [Poze 1983]. See also Parnes' view that remote analogies are "seldom reported" is more accurate than "seldom contribute". Parnes in [Parnes 1992 p 194].

[20] Gruber in [Wechsler 1978 p 138]. Note also the comment of Watson about the double helix, " ..like almost everyone else she....accepted the fact that the structure was too pretty not to be true" [Watson 1968 p 164].

[21] Einstein in a letter to Freud, quoted in [Leytham 1990 p102].

[22] As Hammersley warns, the contemporary emphasis on textuality can privilege the rhetorical at the expense of the scientific or rational reducing the attention paid to the quality of argument and the use of evidence. Atkinson, P. and Hammersley, M. 'Ethnography and participant observation' in [Denzin and Lincoln 1994 p 257].

[23] Morris, P. 'On broken symmetries' in [Wechsler 1978 pp 55-70].

[24] Quoted in [Koestler 1969 p 146]. Others, in the light of quantum mechanics or turbulent fluid flow, would deny that the universe is necessarily an orderly place.

[25] I might have been bolder in some of this if I had known more about some of the recent exploration of textual expression in sociology. For a very innovative and entertaining example of new literary forms see [Mulkay 1985].

[26] Quoted in [Koestler 1969 p 146].

[27] I do not keep a differentiated File of Ideas. Laurel Richardson [Richardson 1994 p 526] differentiates Observation Notes, Methodological Notes, Theoretical Notes and Personal Notes in a way that could be useful. I have a Reminders File and, as noted, a Summaries File, but otherwise I do find it useful to keep the ideas in one potentially inter-active context.

CHAPTER EIGHT

THE CREATIVE DEVELOPMENT OF IDEAS

A reader of the previous chapter on heuristic thinking might well have got the impression of a range of modes of operation, neatly programmed platoons of imaginative devices, which are brought into battle in methodical formation. That, of course, is the aspiration, but, alas, the truth is that my real work practice has been a much messier and more uncertain affair. For a start, it has been a learning process. The development of the researcher's art has involved a pragmatic combination of tried and tested old routines, explorative new initiatives, and various fire-fighting responses designed only to deal with the immediate problem.

I am by nature (and anxiety) one who looks ahead. Hence, my work does have some important pre-planned approaches, and recognisable stages which I follow though as systematically and as rigorously as I am able. However, it is also often a scramble back and forth across the project and text, dealing with emerging possibilities and unanticipated problems as various new developments occur. At times, rather than feeling like a planned method of assault, it feels like searching for structures to prop up a dangerously unbalanced edifice, or exploring various ways to fill the huge and glaring hole that I have myself opened up, or trying to find a way to move backwards out of an indefensible trench.

Also, I have said little so far about how these modes of heuristic thinking fit into the longer term gestation of a project. Nor have I said anything since Chapter Three about the way that ideas around a particular set of problems emerge, interact and develop over time - sometimes over more than one project. So those are now the objectives in this chapter, where I will be exploring the process of change and development in my understanding and interpretation of the relations between trade unions and the Labour Party.

As I explain the emergence of the explanatory framework which covered this relationship, we will gain another perspective on the role of the Patternmaker, and further insight into other mental activities involved in creative research.

THE ASSOCIATION OF IDEAS

There are inherent limitations upon any attempt to trace the linkage and transmutation of ideas over time. Not only is it a complicated interactive process, it is also, at the closest inspection, fleeting and difficult to discern. Catching elements of the moment of association, even when one is alert to the process and its typical patterns, is an operation fraught with uncertainties. The brief moment which constitutes the development is often only partly available to conscious thought, and not as clearly registered as the completed new connection that has now been made.

"The phantom is through the mind and out of the window before we can lay salt on its tail, or slowly sinking and returning to the profound darkness which it has lit up momentarily with a wandering light".[1]

However, if we just focus on the most conscious processes of these micro developments, there are some typical general patterns that seem clear to me and can be described.

There is most obviously a characteristic development which arises out of a dialogue with colleagues. A position is taken, a counter position or qualification is argued, information is exchanged, meanings are changed, a position is redefined. A similar process can, and does, go on regularly in the head where the talk can be even more flexible - as I described in the operations of the Chattering Monkey. But, there is also what I think of as a "right angle" effect in dialogue, real or imaginary. I am in a discussion on one topic, and a point is made whereupon my mind suddenly shoots off to the side to make connections with something else, perhaps far away, with which it is associated in my mind. The "right-angle" process can happen with books, with files, with notes or any source of information, and its apparently mysterious quality and unpredictability is a constant source of wonder and creative satisfaction to me.

Associations of ideas which trigger such productive connections can happen in a variety of ways which have been categorised into "laws" or principles since the period of the ancient Greeks[2]. In more modern times there has been a special emphasis on the association of ideas in the work of William James [James 1901 pp 550-605]. For me, it is useful to think of the associations in terms of four main types. There is an association by contiguity (of space or time), there is an association by similarity or analogy, there is an association by contrast or incongruity, and there is an association by cause and effect [Thoughless 1958 edn p 130].

Some elements of this categorisation are questionable in terms of overlap (associations categorised as contrast or incongruity, and cause and effect could be said to be forms of contiguity). They leave me dissatisfied also in terms of the uncertainties of my experience of the way that connections take place. But I find it a useful list, nevertheless, and a list which itself can be a systematic way of creatively generating ideas [Osborn 1993 pp 108-18]. (What is this near to? What is this like? What is this unlike? What other cause might produce this effect?)

The process of connection seems to vary considerably in its character and completeness. Typically, a new meaning or connection suddenly emerges "in the head". But, at other times, some insight or experience appears to be "sort of" interesting or just feels vaguely suggestive. (There is something here: what is it?) Such intimations can hang around in the back of my mind, or in the Ideas File, before a useful connection is fully perceived -sometimes long afterwards. There are also occasions when it seems as if the full connection is almost engineered. (This looks good and relevant. Perhaps it is connected with this? Perhaps it would work if I put it here? What could I connect it with? Where can I put it?)

Ideas around an initial connection may multiply in a variety of forms. At times the connection is followed fairly quickly by a thickening and consolidating process of accumulating other material around the idea. I see a connection and then another. I think of this as a "cluster" effect. Causes and consequences are played with. A mental sweep around begins, in which other connections are made with the cluster.

Something of that kind happened to me recently in relation to an analysis of "New Labour" prepared for the Jean Jaures Foundation. I was writing the article alongside beginning the preparation of this study of creativity. Associations of ideas moved back and forth between the two pieces of work. For example, the Foundation's line of questions about the newness of "New Labour" set me on a heretical line of thought about the political costs of modernisation. Ideas accumulated about the costs of various enterprises generally considered beneficial. I examined the causes and consequences of the costs. This line of thought then crossed projects and fed back into this study of creative research. It connected with the sense of long term struggle conveyed in Chapter Three, and led, in the end, to the reference to personal costs and the role of Faust in the life of the researcher.

There is also, sometimes, a longer term pattern that I have come to recognise - what I think of as the "Roman Candle" effect. The ideas change at quickening pace, pulling in one cluster, then another, and then suddenly petering out - only to be re-ignited much later as some other input acts as a fuse.

Transmutations in a pattern of ideas around a problem may recur for weeks, months, even years, triggered sometimes by a single connection, sometimes by an accumulation of connections, before the association of ideas comes to what feels like mature synthesis.

Those then, are some of the general patterns of the micro process of association of ideas, or at least of the ones of which I am most aware. I suppose that something like this goes on in all our minds. The examples give only a "bitty" and untethered insight, but at this distance memory does not allow anything else.

The memories are unclear and they can shift as you seek to make them clearer. I am very aware that memories of the various changes that have taken place in my ideas have themselves changed whilst preparing this study, as one draft followed another - moving towards more accuracy, I think, but who knows? Certainly my long-term memory of the chronology of these interconnections - even with a variety of notes and props that I still have - is here at its most fallible as it seeks to make sense of the experience. It does mean that long term, retrospective introspection is utterly unsuited to any attempt to put in place the detailed nuances and the micro developments. And I shall not attempt the exercise. My analysis has therefore had to move up a level of generality.

Nevertheless, I think that it provides a useful and necessary contribution in highlighting in context some of the heuristic processes already described, in illustrating the lengthy process that can be involved in pursuit of the solution to a complex problem, and in tracing the variety of influences which affect the course of creative patternmaking. If there is still a degree of uncertainty about the absolute accuracy of parts of the story, and an inevitable degree of artificial fluency in the dramatic reconstruction, there is certainly enough truth and insight here to illustrate the major turning points and influences, and to provide a sense of the creative movement through time.

BACK TO THE PROBLEM

I left the description of the core of my research problems in Chapter Three at the point where, nearing completion of a long term project, I was beginning to pay increasing attention to its inadequacies in terms of the problem-focus. In particular, I was seeing the traditional problem-focus on the Parliamentary leadership as a misdirection. And I was pondering the unanswered question of why, in spite of the facilities available to them (and in contradiction of the myths) trade union leaders did not seek to maximise their power over the Labour Party.

Even in the periods of democratic revolt, the unions made little attempt to dismantle the controls existing at the Party Conference, or to challenge constitutionally the still wide policy discretion left to the Parliamentary Leadership. The union leaders tended to build new linking committees in order to extend dialogue and enhance unity rather than seek to establish overall control. The core problem, which in myriad ways generated much of my later work and its offshoots, was "why?"

I have described already, albeit very briefly, the most important and original feature of my book on the trade union-Labour Party relationship. The *Contentious Alliance* was the solution that I gave to this problem. Eventually I came to see the relationship in terms of a pattern of inhibitions and unwritten "rules." I described how this was based on role playing, and a differentiation of functions and spheres of the industrial and the political. It was also based upon a core of fundamental values shared by the Labour Party and trade union leaderships. This framework enabled observers to see the party-union relationship in dramatically different terms to those in which it was often viewed. And it proved to be readily recognisable to the players. At no point after the publication was I confronted by a serious criticism from the participants that something important had been misunderstood or distorted in this framework.

Now, if I were to be asked how this emerged, and where the ingredients came from, I would point not to one moment of inspiration, not one source or one technique, nor to one consistent, systematic, linear process, but to a variety of sources and influences involving a complex and lengthy creative development.

Phase I: Entrances

I knew that the renegotiation that was taking place in my perspective on the problems that I had been examining in the book on *The Labour Party Conference* might lead, at some time in the future, to an even larger long-term project. There had been no major study of the relationship between trade unions and the Labour Party for many years, and in that time it had become the most controversial relationship in British political life. Given the scale of what might be involved, initially I aimed only to produce papers on various facets of the relationship.

I had an intriguing question to explore and knew some of the other questions that I wanted to ask. This questioning did not take place in an intellectual vacuum. What was happening around me generated and influenced the "flow" of the creative process. Others had already written in this area. Positions had been taken on the trade union - Labour Party relationship, most strikingly with differences of opinion on the positive and negative possibilities of enlarging the scope of trade union political action. Further, I was always operating in a mental dialogue with contemporary perceptions which fed into my work. There was a deepening conflict within the Labour Party of which the unions were an integral part. The period when I carried out this research was one in which the power of the unions aroused constant public controversy.

The contrast between what I was observing and unearthing, and the views that were being put forward in books, newspapers, television and radio broadcasts, and journals, provided many entry points and opportunities for the creative critic to map out alternatives, and to mark out a shape for a fundamentally different perspective.

Phase II: Peculiarities and inhibitions

The "take-off" of the project followed what I came to see as a familiar trajectory. It followed a series of peculiarities. Indeed this whole case study might be seen as variations on a theme of peculiarities. In seeking the answers to the first general peculiarity of trade union restraint, I picked up on a specific peculiarity of trade union attitudes towards political finance in order to take the analysis forward.

The sophisticated political analyst will always tell us that "those who pay the piper call the tune." Endless columns of newsprint have told us for years that this was how the Labour Party worked. Affiliation money and electoral fund payments were paid; policies and party management decisions agreeable to the unions were produced. This was common-sense. Who would want to argue with it? But, to my initial surprise, and in spite of the mythology, there did not seem to be any clear examples of a direct reciprocity in exchange for trade union financing of the Labour Party. Certainly the practice was neither obvious nor widespread. In fact, there seemed to be regular and clear cases of it not happening.

I was particularly struck by the oddity that succeeding General Secretaries of the Transport and General Workers Union reacted with affronted horror when I asked whether they, as the landlords of the Labour Party, had ever threatened financial sanctions in connection with the Labour Party's failure to follow their policy line. Given what everybody said about what followed after paying the piper, why was there this sense of outrage? Strange.

I began to play with a line of enquiry that such union leaders, far from being power hungry "politicians" seeking to control both the Labour Party and the Government, were in practice constrained by a range of inhibitions. The regularity of these inhibitions began to appear striking. This was probably related to a general distinction which other writers had noted between the spheres of the industrial and the political, but how exactly was it related? I probed further. What kind of considerations were involved?. How far did the inhibitions spread across the range of trade union involvement? Did the inhibitions affect all union leaders regardless of factional allegiance and regardless of period? Under what circumstances, if any, did the inhibitions break down?

It was around this time that there was an extraordinary, synchronistic encounter on Stalybridge railway station. It was mid-morning. There was a deserted platform. I became suddenly conscious that the leader of the engineers union, Hugh Scanlon, stood only about ten yards away from me. In the past I had found him to be a very busy and elusive man, pleasant but difficult to engage in a long discussion. I had been thinking about how I might get into a longer meeting. I now began a polite conversation and, after some initial hesitation, he invited me to sit with him on the train. (I'm not sure that he had much of a choice without being very rude).

It gave me an unusual and, in the end, very congenial opportunity to raise some crucial personal questions and receive some revealing examples of the self-restraint exercised by union leaders within the Labour Party. In our discussion, he immediately challenged point blank the description of a famous crisis meeting between union leaders and the Labour Prime Minister, Harold Wilson, in 1969, where Wilson is reported to have said at one point of heated exchange, " Get your tanks off my lawn, Hughie".[3] That was startling in itself but, crucially, Scanlon also argued, with profound emphasis, that the atmosphere was not like that and that his behaviour would not have provoked such a comment.

I questioned all this very closely, not focusing on the details of the Downing Street meeting but concentrating instead on why exactly he would not have provoked such a comment. In the light of his answers, we then examined some other situations where he and other union leaders had the opportunity, but not the inclination, to use their political muscle to the full. In this discussion, various clues emerged as to the considerations involved in this propriety and restraint, the scope of the inhibitions, and the degree to which they affected a union leader who then regarded himself as the epitome of the assertive union Left of the Party.

Later, armed with these clues, I began to assemble from different areas of the relationship with the Labour Party, a range of cases where unions and union leaders might have exercised power but did not do so. In the light of what union leaders, including Scanlon, had said about their motivation, I then sought various explanatory categories in which to put the cases. I thought that I could see some interesting patterns emerging although they were not strong enough, or inclusive enough, at this stage to make me secure in my judgement overall.

Somewhere around this time I was invited to give a paper at a Conference in the USA. Should I plunge into this as the framework? My hesitation in producing the framework was initially held back by some psychological uncertainty at going public on this judgement. Union leaders at this time were seen as politically aggressive. Jack Jones, the General Secretary of the Transport and General Workers Union, was portrayed as Prime Minister Jones. I knew that I could easily mount a critique of some of the crudest characterisations, but could I substantiate a complete, across-the-board rebuttal in a framework which ran so counter to the common-sense of the time?

As I remember that period, I was in an anxious quandary. The Patternmaker-artist was probably pushing the pattern to the extremity of its strangeness, the Realist would then be trying to rein it in and securely ground it. The Destructive Critic was, I do remember, saying something like, "it is not ready yet; they will find big holes in it; they will laugh at its naïvity; you will look foolish".

At one point I remember vividly that I was worried enough about the work appearing vulnerable and incomplete to consider moving back to a previous analytical format which had gone down well at a past conference in the USA.

Unusually, I was visited by two organisers of the conference. (It was to be a serious business - and well financed). In these circumstances, having to say something about my paper in advance, I found myself describing it enthusiastically in ways that committed me to the new framework. At the time they did not seem very impressed, but there I was - stuck with it. Eventually, in the paper, I compromised in the format by adding the new analytical framework on to the old framework, i.e. having a different mode of analysis for different recent historical periods.

In introducing the new analysis, I emphasised the broad restraint with which the trade union leaders operated in the Party, and the consequent ambivalence in their behaviour. Mainly from the examination of peculiarities, I diagnosed a group of principles that had guided their behaviour and were the source of their inhibitions. These I conceptualised as "priority," "integrity," "unity," "constitutionality," and "community." As it happened, at the conference itself the paper was very well received and the conceptualisation then underpinned my contribution to a book on Eurocommunism and Eurosocialism [Minkin 1979]. With increasing refinements and detours, it was the subject of various articles, lectures, and papers over the next few years.

Phase III: Crisis

There came a point when I began to focus the research seriously onto issues, themes and chapters of a new book. However at this point my diagnosis of union inhibitions became severely tested as there developed a period of crisis in the union-Labour Party relationship following "the Winter of Discontent".

Crisis situations offer illuminating examples of the behaviour of office holders, institutions and procedures operating under stress. This was a particularly acute crisis period, with some previous behaviour patterns tested to the full during the "Campaign for Labour Party Democracy" revolt of 1979-81, the Bennite campaign for the Deputy Leadership in 1981, the defection of the "Social Democrats" from the Party in 1981, and the disastrous election campaign of 1983. I had to make sense of some unprecedented developments. This meant that in each area of the study, and in relation to each category of consideration which had led to the inhibitions, I had to re-assess the relevance of my analytical framework. In particular, I had to address the allegation, made regularly at this time, that the unions were in the vanguard of this political revolt - a course of action which was unlikely, given my explanatory framework.

As I examined in detail what was happening after 1979, it became clear that there was a grotesque misrepresentation of the role played by the unions. Virtually the entire media was carrying the myth that the passing of new constitutional amendments against the recommendations of the Party Leadership, at the Party Conferences of 1979 and 1980, and the Special Conference of 1981, had been supported by the unions. But if you broke away from the tyranny of prejudice, you saw immediately that the unions were divided on these issues. More than that, following strong signals from the Awkward Sod, and after much digging, I eventually plunged through the mystification to find out (and to point out) that the union majority had actually voted *against* the amendments [Minkin 1991/92 p 195].

The media focus on the union leaders - particularly their obsession with the *bête-noir* union leader Clive Jenkins - was obscuring the fact that revolts were occurring in spite of them rather than because of them. To this day, regardless of the evidence, the myth of the leading role of the unions is perpetuated[4]. Yet the crucial fact was that, in the main, in this crisis period, the old inhibitions and considerations were still a potent force, even though weakening at some levels in some of the unions. My framework was vindicated.

Throughout this period, Arthur Scargill's leadership of the National Union of Mineworkers was also seen as central to the Labour politics of the time, and typical of a new style of Leftwing unionism assertively seeking a controlling influence over the Labour Party. But behaviour of the union leaders was much easier to understand if Scargill was treated as the exception that highlighted the rules by which the majority of other union leaders, Left and Right, operated. He was exceptional in how he defined his role, and he was exceptional in how he was defined and treated by others. Indeed, Scargill became for me something of a yardstick against which to contrast the behaviour of the others, a model that enabled me to understand and confirm the definition and force of the inhibitions at work in the party-union relationship. (In 1996 he still played the same role, as the founder of the Socialist Labour Party.)

Phase IV : Relations, rules and roles

As a new period with a new mood developed in 1983, once again I began to build the shape of the new book based upon the exploration, theorising and argument of the past few years. At the same time I continued to research the crisis period from 1979 to 1983. As I did so, there began to emerge a new development in my thinking about the relationship. It was a slow shift of perspective towards the idea of seeing the relationship as regulated by pervasive unwritten "rules" - rules which affected the political leaders as much as they affected the union leaders. The change in perspective was shaped by many influences, including the fact that some elements of the new perspective had been present for years in my thinking about the Labour Party.

I had noted (as had other scholars in the field) the existence of customs - unwritten "rules" covering the discretion on policy left to Labour leaders under the terms of party's constitution. Also, trade union leaders had occasionally spoken to me in terms of what might be called prudential rules which regulated their priorities. In addition, already in place were two important contributions to my long-term thinking which had come out of the investigations of peculiarities. There was the early tracing of an important web of unwritten rules covering trade union voting in the Party's National Executive Committee elections, and there was the diagnosis I had made of the power of those rules in limiting political factional considerations. There was also the observation of a pattern of rule-governed reciprocity in relation to the protection of the autonomy of the Party on the one side, and the unions on the other.

So here were pieces - ideas living separately. Something had to re-order and re-focus my perspective in such a way as to produce a new framework for these pieces. I do not recall any sudden illumination on this. There appears, in retrospect, to have been a wide range of influences slowly producing this effect - as I shall show.

One interesting feature was that an aesthetic attraction to a particular title played some part in the reorientation of my thinking. In an early paper I had been attracted to "Relations, Rules and Roles " - a title adapted from a philosophical work - and I had used it as a rather neat sub-heading, in an article in 1978 without properly thinking through its implications. "Relations, Rules and

Roles" kept running through my mind over the years. It was alliterative and it had a nice sense of completeness. So here was always the seed of a greater emphasis on rules. But there was also the slow influence of my understanding of some little noticed peculiarities of trade union behaviour during the crisis period of the early 1980s.

There was something particularly strange about the way in which union leaders responded to the role played by the National Executive Committee of the Labour Party on industrial disputes. During this period the political Left were either the controlling majority or they were a powerful minority on that governing committee. They were disposed to be very supportive of workers and unions involved in industrial action. You might have expected union leaders to welcome this approach, would you not, but in fact, there was, in general, on the part of union leaders, a deep and rule-governed opposition to the NEC "interfering" in these disputes. So the NEC was not expected, indeed not allowed, to give support unless it was clearly requested by the union leadership.

Thus, what I had expected to be an automatic acceptance by the union leaders and the TUC of the expression of solidarity turned out be heavily constrained by notions of trade union "freedom" from "political interference". It became obvious from the behaviour of the union leaders, and an exchange of letters with the General Secretary of the Party, that there were some very strictly monitored rules on this.

However, what may have been the key "dislodging" influence in changing my perspective was that I also began to note that the Parliamentary Leadership seemed to have their own areas of rule-governed (if in some cases resented) inhibitions about what they said and did in the Party. The "liberation" described later by some of the defecting Social Democrats was widely reported, but not fully appreciated in terms of the norms of the union-party relationship. I linked this with some previous observations. In the previous decade I had written about the "sense of guilt" expressed from within the Parliamentary Leadership after 1970 (which seemed to be about crossing boundaries of the acceptable - breaking understandings as well as making policy deviations). I connected this sense of boundaries of behaviour with a previous diagnosis that certain areas of industrial policymaking had long been closed to initiatives from the politicians. Thinking about the sense of "liberation" now consolidated my perception of the importance of a pattern of rules-governed inhibitions for the political as well as the industrial leadership.

As a result of these various experiences, influences and thought processes, I now found myself mentally playing inside elements of a new framework of unwritten rules. The big question for me became, could I satisfactorily connect all the elements of the framework and increase its inclusivity? Could I possibly pattern the entire relationship - indeed the history of the relationship since 1918 - as rule-governed reciprocity? I became re-aware that writers on the Labour Party had occasionally referred to the relationship with the unions as involving "codes of behaviour," but, as I looked at it again, much of this appeared rhetorical and was unspecific[5]. Now the Patternmaker-artist aspired to lay out a complete framework of such codes.

The decision did have some potentially daunting risks. The scale of it was huge in terms of detail, and the framework to be negotiated through the intricate dialectic of the parts to the whole. I could have finished up in a swamp of material. I could have faced a huge and unfillable gap in evidence. Or I could have been defeated by some monstrous incoherence. However, by this stage I had invested so much intellectual effort, the prospect of where it might lead seemed so alluring, and the sense of trajectory was so powerful in the way that it was pulling me, there did not really seem a choice. I took whatever risks there were in the confidence (or perhaps hope) that I would deal with it. I went for the big framework.

Phase V: Analogy and metaphor

An analogy and a cluster of metaphors played their parts in influencing and reinforcing my decision, and also in filling out the configuration of ideas.

I had been very conscious of the influence of the norms and procedures of the British Constitution on the behaviour of the Labour Party and the development of its internal democracy - particularly since Labour became the alternative Government in 1922. But, I now started to play with the question, "Could it be that the form of the British Constitution, with its minimal statute law and its proliferation of unwritten conventions, was a workable analogy for the Labour Party - trade union relationship?". I had also (as I have indicated) been playing for some time with the various metaphors of "family" life in the Labour Party's relationship with the unions, and toying with their possible implications in terms of inhibitions and restraint.

The fact was that I had had a disconcerting discussion with a close academic friend, Leo Panitch, about a quotation from a trade union leader relating to "divorce" in the relationship, that I had used in a conference paper. This discussion had caused me considerable angst because I realised later that, though I had been at the meeting where the words were spoken, I had used Leo's particular report of the union leader's remarks without attribution. Feeling that I may have done him a disservice, I could not get it out of my mind - which in the end was probably just as well. It kept bringing the notion of the family to the fore in my thinking, as I became increasingly aware that the metaphor did accord with (and affect) behaviour in the relationship.

So I began to integrate the two ideas, the analogy and the metaphor, into the notion of a multifaceted and comprehensively rule-governed relationship with conventions and protocol accompanying a minimum of formal written regulation. I was now seeing the inhibitions as part of a pattern of unwritten rules, affected by both independent and mutual interests in a common enterprise, on the model of a family.

Once alerted, I started to dig further back in time, and could see how the rule-governed relationship might have evolved, both as a response to the distinctive functional needs of the political and trade union leadership, and their joint participation within the British system of government.

This digging backwards took on a new dimension as I began to enquire into the process of role socialisation. Who, or what, defined the roles? How and when did it happen that union leaders adopted particular rules? What agency or processes continued to socialise new union leaders into the codes of conduct?

This exploration turned my attention to the behaviour of the Trades Union Congress bureaucracy in the 1920s and subsequently. And as the 1920s turned out to be an illuminating and seminal decade, I attempted the delicate task of embodying the framework chapter in an historical era - thus explaining not only what the rules were, but why and how the rules had arisen.

A close colleague, Bob Fryer, then came up with a further illumination of the trade union perspective by giving me a range of insights into how the analogous historic behaviour of the unions in their industrial relations may have increased the general appeal to them of unwritten, rule-governed behaviour in the political field.

So after much experimentation, testing, failing and adjusting, and after much play with evidence and ideas, the jigsaw began to come together. As always at these moments of culmination, I wondered how it was that I (as well as everybody else) had managed to miss so much of this complex inter-connection. It now all now seemed so obvious. Why had it taken so long?

Phase VI : Problem reframing and the challenge to the settlement

Yet it was to take even longer. At this stage I might well have attempted finally to pull the book together for publication. Certainly there was a variety of social pressures to do so. However, I had not quite bargained for the extent to which crisis and dramatic change would become almost an endemic feature of the Labour Party in this period. There were unprecedented new developments following the ten-yearly Political Fund ballots imposed by the Conservative Government. There were changes in Labour Party organisation, financial arrangements, policymaking, party ob,jectives and policy - all of which had important repercussions for the relationship with the unions.

But it was more than just the scale of the general changes in the field. Having now seen the extent to which the Parliamentary Leadership was involved in a variety of inhibitions based on "rules," I had come to judge the explanatory framework as aesthetically unsatisfactory. It felt lopsided in its present form. It was plausible, indeed convincing as far as it went, but it was still focused primarily on the trade union leadership with the behaviour of the political leadership to some extent tacked on, at various key points, to exemplify the fact that some of their behaviour was also rule-governed. Further, over the years, my appreciation of the considerations governing trade union participation had become very subtle, and I had a range of detailed examples categorised under the different considerations and rules. But, my understanding of the political side of this relationship was much less developed. Consequently, parts of the framework were very disproportionate in the degree of explanation and exemplification that was involved.

In effect, what was happening was that my exploration and theorising had outgrown the original problem-focus. The lopsidedness of the framework now seemed to impel a new perspective. It led me to reframe the problem and to synthesise two different focuses. The investigation was no longer focused upon the question "why did the union leaders not attempt to maximise their power?" (although that remained the primary and the most intriguing question of the entire work) but on "why did both sets of leaders obey unwritten rules?".

Having reframed the problem, and now searching for a substantively satisfactory and aesthetically pleasing overall framework, I needed as full a set of answers on the political side as I had on the union side. This led me to the obvious question of whether the same categories of consideration affected the political side as affected the union side? It proved to be no easy question to answer without more detailed exploration of the politics of the past sixty years.

That was the enterprise I now embarked upon. In itself it would have been a hard enough task, but whilst I was involved in it something else became apparent. The rules that I was examining -

the rules that had held the relationship together as a "settlement" for so long - were beginning to be challenged from the political side in a way that had not been seen for sixty years, and in some respects longer. Not all the rules were challenged, and perhaps not even the most important, but enough were being changed to add a new complexity to the analysis. Oy!!

Now, if at this stage the reader is beginning to feel somewhat fatigued by these twists and turns, it will give just a little of the flavour of my own state of mind at this time. The Pilgrim feared that he was never destined to pass through the gate. Holding the project together in these circumstances became a major problem and a source of deep anxiety and stress. This appeared to be a never-ending-always-changing story. Would the bloody thing ever be finished? Could any framework capture this degree of complexity and flexibility? Would it be any good if it did? The task had turned into a huge burden. After each setback, love turned into flashes of hatred and thoughts of a speedy separation. Yet I knew that publishing at this stage would have produced an impressively researched analytical framework but one which had not realised its full potential. It would be caught, as it were, in mid-flow. I could probably hide the inadequacies, but I would know. Furthermore, it would have thwarted a further major new understanding which added an important development to the framework.

Phase VII: Values

I began to see something that had escaped me and others for years. Not only were the rules related to the role responsibilities of the "politician " and the "union leader," but they arose out of some particular shared values. The factors which had brought about the inhibitions of trade union leaders, I now began to see not just as trade union-based considerations, but as values which were held in common (albeit with some important variations in definition and emphasis) with the political leadership.

Thus, my theorising of the development of power relations in the party now became more closely entwined with an understanding of developments in its political traditions and its social theory. The values were now clarified as freedom, democracy, solidarity, unity and (for the moment) priority. As I arrived at the definition of these values, so I filled out their meaning for groups in the different wings of the Labour Movement, and I detailed the stages at which those traditions had significantly changed.

Into view now came the outlines of a framework in which the considerations affecting the behaviour of the Parliamentary leadership could dovetail within similar categories to those governing the behaviour of the trade union leadership. I was now knee-deep in historical cases and examples relating to the behaviour of the Parliamentary leadership, and I do remember a sense of elation at one point because it looked as though the whole thing, in outline, would work! Certainly it appeared to enhance our understanding of the history of the relationship, and behaviour within it, in terms not previously proposed.

I was now playing day and night with the big picture of these five major values from which were derived a vast network of unwritten rules regulating the roles of politician and union leader. It involved a complex *quid pro quo* - a mutual understanding between the union leaders and the political leaders, who themselves obeyed unwritten rules.

The attempt to ensure historical precision, coherence, and a degree of elegance in the presentation of this framework was a huge enterprise which at one point exceeded my capacity to hold the ideas in my head, let alone to play with them. In some desperation, and for the first time in my work, I resorted to a mapping exercise on a huge sheet of paper. I had then to alternate the extraction from the map of first overviews and then fragments, in order to cope with, and play mentally with, the data. The whole and the parts of the pattern had to be coherent, and had also, of course, to remain firmly grounded in, and justified by, the evidence. The shape of what emerged had also to be creatively negotiated around my critical responses to a range of positions in the existing literature.

In handling all this I made many false moves, and I had to make many adjustments to the definition of values, the statement of a "rule", and the playing of the roles - particularly to take account of exceptional cases. I had also to deal with the familiar analytical problem that some actions could be classified within more than one category - in this case, under more than one rule. In addition, some rules were affected by more than one value. Simply to ensure a degree of elegance and comprehensibility to the analysis, I had to emphasise some actions, rules and values at the expense of others, whilst as far as possible remaining faithful to the evidence and its complexity.

Not until a very late stage did I begin to question whether or not the consideration of "priority" (a concept that I had been using since my first paper, and a very real consideration) was of the same order as the other values which underpinned the "rules." Indeed, arguably it was not a value at all. Reluctantly (because it was aesthetically disturbing to the pattern) I had to disconnect "priority" from the values and represent it as a distinct and separate category - "a working principle".

Phase VIII: The framework

So, at last, years after the first glimmerings of the problem, my work culminated in 1991 in a comprehensive explanatory framework of the relationship over a long period of history - a theory of power based upon values, roles and rules, with the new developments in the rules noted alongside the old, and both linked to a mass of detailed evidence. The framework also formed the basis of an in-depth exploration of the main areas of the relationship, and of many controversial features of the Labour Party and its recent history. It laid the basis of a variety of original interpretations and explanations.

In summary, as I have shown, the development of the framework had been an incremental process involving constant reconsideration and amendment, characterised by some imaginative play with a variety of perspectives but also by slow, painstaking investigation, construction, failure and reconstruction. There was never one sudden huge leap forward, although there were various points of new insight. And there were important uplifting moments of accomplishment when novel and appropriate configurations of ideas came (or were fused) together. But these too were repeatedly adjusted and refined.

As for the final framework of unwritten rules based on values as well as roles, this came in the way of a slow reorientation of perspective rather than a sudden planned movement. There was a gradual realisation that, over time, and in the light of a variety of experiences and understandings, I had incrementally arrived somewhere with new and exciting possibilities. This promise was then explored as far as it could realistically be taken - an adventure with various elements of risk.

The resulting configuration of ideas had been a long-term process, germinating within one major study, passing through several smaller studies, and ending in the completion of another large scale project. It had been fed by my changing understanding of a relationship which was itself undergoing extensive change. There had been many detours - some into papers and articles which only lightly touched the general thrust of this line of thought, others in direct off-shoots. There had been points at which I might, under pressure and sheer fatigue, have wound it up as complete, leaving the intellectual loose-ends, nagging problems and under-developments covered over, unexplored.

In spite of a variety of pressures, I deferred the closure. Had I not done so, our understanding of this field of study, and the understanding of those who participated in it, might, I think, have been that much the poorer.

CHAPTER END NOTES

[1] Writer in *Times Literary Supplement* 31.12.24 quoted by [Wallas 1926 p 105].

[2] See on this [Osborn 1983 p 114].

[3] [Jenkins, 1970 p 140]. This story is endlessly recycled. But note that the diaries of Barbara Castle, the Secretary of State for Employment, who attended the meeting, confirm Scanlon's report of the atmosphere, and give a softer version of Wilson's comments on the tanks, "... there are two types of Prime Minister I have made up my mind I will never be: one is Ramsay MacDonald and the second is Dubcek. I'm not going to surrender to your tanks Hughie". Note that in this version there is no mention of them being "on the lawn" [Castle 1984 pp. 661-2].

[4] The myth was perpetuated in Episode One of the recent BBC four-part TV documentary *The Wilderness Years*, 3. 12. 1995.

[5] The exception was Alan Flanders, who had written an article on "Trade Unions and Politics" (reprinted in *Management and Unions*, Faber, London 1970 pp 224-37). Some of his general arguments may well have lodged in my mind, although I seemed to be discovering them afresh and I finished with a very different interpretation of the reciprocity of the relationship and of the particular case that he made.

CHAPTER NINE

INSTABILITY, AUTONOMY AND THE CREATIVE PROCESS

TRANSMUTATIONS

In this chapter, I want to explore in some depth a point made earlier (and exemplified to some extent in Chapter Eight) about one of the startling dimensions of the creative "flow" - the transmutations of the research project itself.

The nub of it is this. In field research, there is a phenomenon that nobody warned me about when I began as a post-graduate. *The damn thing - the project - won't stand still.* Thus, the decision on the shape, and even the purpose, of the project was not, for me, a once-and-for-all decision. I had also to calculate, periodically, whether or not to stick with the charted course or to explore and navigate a change of route or even a change of destination.

This was not intellectual sloppiness, nor was it an inability to make decisions. Nor was it simply wrestling with the consequences of Murphy's Law - that what can go wrong will go wrong - although I would not underestimate this as a factor in the trajectory of research. As the joke goes, "What makes God laugh? Tell her your plans".

As will have become very clear from the analysis presented in the previous chapter, some of the instability was a product of the particular subject matter of my research and of recent behaviour in the field itself. I am a research worker who analyses contemporary developments. If it is true, as Mao said, that it is too early to understand the significance of the French Revolution, it has to be conceded that judgements on recent events are even more tentative and subject to constant re-evaluation in the light of new evidence and new perspectives.

I am also a research worker in a field of rapid change. In recent years my project area has been subject to the most extensive upheavals and radical reform for seventy years. New developments produced new evidence which cast new light and doubts upon past, even recent, interpretations. An essential element in the social value of the project is that these very recent changes be made understandable. This is a challenge to the researcher which cannot be ducked.

So the intellectual management of projects in this area of investigation became a specially complicated exercise. At times it could be a navigator's nightmare. In the face of a multidimensional relationship in constant flux, with new peculiarities emerging, the case for flexibility and repeated adjustment became irresistible.

Those are the distinctive features of my field of study, but, as will already have become clear, there are other destabilising and transforming forces at work, over and above these singularities of the area of work. The destabilising forces produce, at times, an exciting but nevertheless uncomfortable sensation that, in its transmutations, the project is behaving as if it had a dynamic of its own.

In the early days of doing research, I assumed that all this movement involved some inadequacy on my part. However, I now accept that I am a very rigorous scholar and I was simply untutored in, and inexperienced about, this aspect of the creative process in field work. I found that this experience was not just a feature of my own research. Certainly it has been noted in creative literary activity.[1] And it is a wider phenomon. William Gordon suggests that this is a regular occurrence in creative activity, which he calls "autonomy of (the) object,"[Gordon 1961 p 138] where the product begins to feel as though it has a capacity to act as an entity separate from the mind that created it.

But here, for a university academic, is a particularly acute problem. Gordon's advice as a theorist and practitioner of creativity is that "In the course of the creative process, the individual responsible for the creative activity must permit what has been constructed to live its own life - to lead on."[2] However, if this is persuasive (as it often is for me), it is in some tension with what is sometimes understood as rigorous and controlled research, and it also lives very unhappily within an important element of the present research culture which emphasises clarity of purpose in grant applications and adherence to completion deadlines for assessment. Certainly, it runs counter to the advice one might instinctively give to a student who appeared to be allowing the focus of the thesis to meander. Experience as a supervisor suggests that in some students it can be a sign of lack of self-discipline and the ability to focus - a means of escape and distraction. In others, it is an unwillingness to commit and to take an explicit view. All the more reason, therefore, that we are clear about the forces genuinely engendering this instability.

We have to make an educated assessment of whether any particular movement is likely to be productively creative and best treated in *this* project, or is a potentially interesting avenue but one with low priority, or is simply undisciplined drift. Only after making this judgement can we possibly establish an appropriate degree of control and move in the right direction.

So, what are these influences and developments? Why doesn't it stand still?

DESTABILISING FORCES

There have been seven general destabilising forces at work in my research which I have grown to understand and monitor as carefully as I can. Some of them are implicit in what has already been said, but it is important to pull them together here, before assessing their implications.

Shifting sands

However systematic I was in playing the role of the Detective, the information was not necessarily acquired in the most useful order. Further, the information overall tended to be variable in its detail and its quality. Thus, my judgement of the evidence - on verbal testimony in particular - could vary considerably as my knowledge of other evidence increased. As a result, there was a back and forth movement and adjustment across the study over time, rather than clear, phased stages of information gathering.

Sometimes I faced problems of the inaccessibility of anticipated data. A source might not be open to me, records might be missing, an important official might not be prepared to talk, an insecure individual or group might freeze me out. I therefore had the task of changing the emphasis or direction of my search. Conversely, the deeper I dug, over a longer period, the more likely it was that new and important evidence came to light, and a new understanding was reached. Sometimes, well into the study, there has been the sudden availability of new and valuable sources - a finding, an available observer, a missing link uncovered. It is also one of the inescapable truths of creative research that serendipitous findings and synchronistic meetings cannot be planned. Neither can the sudden appearance of peculiarities which can lead to a beneficial re-appraisal and renewed investigations. The project can thus, at times, move off at unexpectedly rewarding angles. It can also involve an unexpected regression deeper into history, or a move sidewards in pursuit of causes and explanations, in a way which can be a distraction, but can also be an exceptionally fruitful detour.

The very least that happens as a result of these processes is that the analysis enlarges and "thickens" at some points, and diminishes and "thins" at others, in ways which were unanticipated when the project commenced. But on occasions an important productive and creative reshaping of the project can take place.

In short, although exploration of the field, and the gathering of information, is a first stage process, it is not confined to that stage, and at various stages, the emergence of relevant evidence, and the non-availability of expected information, can reshape the contours as well as the content of the project.

Varying levels of generality and complexity

There is also a process in my work involving a shifting level of generality and complexity. In political analysis, a project seeking to investigate a relationship has initially to be pitched at a given level of generality. So, for example, an analysis of the relationship between the National Executive Committee of the Labour Party and the Shadow Cabinet might well be pitched, initially, at the level of main committee work rather than delving into the details of the feeding environment of sub-committees, bureaucratic support and individual assistance.

Sometimes I have found the anticipated level of generality to be appropriate, but often, in my experience, as the investigation proceeds, variations in the level have to be renegotiated from time to time. On occasions, this involves a move upwards as it becomes clear that the detailed evidence that has been expected is unavailable or unreliable. Much more often, in my experience, there is, if the digging is assiduous, more information than anticipated and also evidence of variations in each sub-domain. The result is therefore a seductive pull towards further differentiation.

This can produce the disorienting sense of getting lost in the complex diffusion of variations, or the feeling of getting submerged within a project which is becoming more complex as it micro-differentiates. But this complexity can also involve more subtlety and illumination - often the discovery of different patterns of power in different areas of the relationship (organisational/ financial/ constitutional/ policy) - opening up the possibility that the investigation can fruitfully be deepened and extended.

Generating problems

Creative research is a problem-generating activity. Problem discovery cannot be a scheduled activity. It can happen at any time. Further, as immersion in the project deepens, knowledge around key problems increases, and the quest becomes more educated and refined, so shifts can take place in the perception of the problem under investigation. Because of this, as noted earlier, it may help in the creative process for the crystalisation of the problem not to take place too early in the project.

In my long-term, "core" projects, there have been three major changes in the way that the central problems were defined. The first shift came gradually but fairly early in my first major project, as I shifted from an international comparative framework and focused upon the "how" and "with what effects" of agenda management, also shifting the focus of "what variations" from an international assessment to an historical appraisal.

The second major shift was more profound, as I came to see that the focus of the original problem on the behaviour of the Parliamentary leadership required a change to question the more significant peculiarity of trade union restraint. This shift towards explaining the activities of the union leaders took place before I had finished the first long-term project, and eventually it became the core problem of the next. A very fertile problem, it turned out to be. But it, too, underwent a change in the middle of the project when it became clear that the focus on the union leaders now needed to be synthesised with a focus on the Parliamentary Leadership in order to solve the problem of why they both obeyed unwritten rules.

Core problems can also generate subsidiary problems. (What were the mechanisms of socialisation into the rules, and how had they developed?) They can generate application problems. (What was the effect of the inhibitions and rules on Leftwing trade union radicalism and what was the effect on Rightwing defection? What was the effect on party stability and flexibility?) And there can also be significant independent problems, as particular segments of a multidimensional relationship in the problem area generate their own concerns. (Why were the unions successful in securing a "yes" vote in all the political fund ballots?) In all these ways problem generation can modify, broaden or redirect the focus of the project.

Stages of discovery and interpretation

Discoveries, judgements of what may yield discoveries, and evidence suggesting new interpretations, can come at various times throughout the research process rather than arriving in a cluster, or at a given stage. This feature alone feeds a dynamic quality into the research project.

What we discover and what we interpret, can change or expand what we plan the objectives to be. At times, the first look at a body of detailed evidence can be so illuminating as to pull the project along a rather different route from that which was planned. Much later, as I write it up, the project sometimes takes on shapes and a direction which are, in a sense, drawn from what is in front of me rather than planned. What is anticipated to be the last look and "tidying up" of the presentation can also produce something new, or at least something provocatively alluring, in the substance of the work. The creative flow is being fed up to the last punctuation mark and footnote by processes which are a combination of chance, observational vigilance, conscious intervention, and the benevolent uncertainties of creative thought.

Outside interventions

Whilst I am engaged on planning the research and then carrying out the project, other scholars in the field are not inactive. The research is shaped not only by my reaction towards what they have written before I began the project, but what they write whilst it is under way. Some of this is illuminating, corroborative or congruent and can be fused into my own project in a way that strengthen its purpose, but some of it throws up new areas of concern which heighten their relevance, or are in tension with my own developing perspective in ways that cut across the analysis and have to be addressed.

As I have explained, there is a creative process to the engagement with critics, or potential critics, and with findings that run counter to our own evidence. This engagement may produce, at the least, a new edge to the interpretation or a new elaboration. But, as we have seen, it can also result in a significant adjustment and a detour in pursuit of a novel rebuttal.

Conceptual development

Crucially, the creative development of the conceptual framework, is just that, a development. As I have illustrated, the development arises primarily from the fieldwork and is subject to a complex creative interaction of influences and ideas. It is not something that comes to me complete and polished at the beginning of the project, and is then applied to the study. The development of my own theorising, and the resulting conceptual framework, arises out of the changing data and the (at times slow) transformation of my perspectives and understandings.

So, (whatever I might say to a funding agency) I now appreciate much more clearly that, as with any creative enterprise, the end is never in full sight at the beginning, and that it is a disadvantage to be too fixed in one's ideas of how the problem is best handled.

As the framework develops, so the project takes on further unanticipated shapes. The polished explanatory framework can suddenly highlight particular areas in unexpected ways. Sometimes it exposes a gap or an inadequacy. Sometimes it can provide a new insight which involves re-examination of an area which was thought to be well covered, or not worth covering.

Changing researcher

Finally, the appearance of movement in the material is in a sense misleading. To some extent, the movement is in the mind of the researcher. But, I don't think that there is anything mysterious (nor scientifically reprehensible) about it. The point is that in any research process over a period of time, researchers - you and I - do change. We change in understanding, and we change in perspective. We also change all the time in our competence and confidence. As we change, not only do different parts of our project come to interest us more than others, but sometimes we feel more able to tackle problems which initially appeared to us too difficult. Non-directed thinking, and the creative sub-conscious processes, are often responsive to these developments in the ideas that are pursued, and the problems that the mind gets preoccupied with.

This personal development, with its tendency to shift the focus of interest, can be an indulgence, but it must not be discounted as of no constructive research value, particularly if this is a difficult or protracted piece of research which requires the curiosity, creative flexibility and sustained motivation in pursuing problems of the kind that I have described above.

ASSERTING CONTROL

Each of these influences is likely to interact with the others in ways which are difficult to anticipate. This may open up new possibilities but also produce new problems. It can test the scholar's judgement and the Juggler's skill to the utmost. In handling this unstable, shifting, moving entity, there does develop a sense of the dynamic autonomy of the object, enhancing the feeling of a powerful and unremitting "flow" which is not simply going on in the mind but also in the project itself.

This sense of autonomy is obviously at its greatest in a multifaceted project based on long-term fieldwork, but I have noticed this affecting also independent field research projects with much more limited ambitions and time scales. Indeed it has been evident, to some extent, in every project and paper that I have been involved in. I can see also how some of it could affect other forms and methods of research.

If so, it is a fundamental prerequisite of the art of research that we understand these dynamic and creative factors in the research process - and, after a clear judgement, seek to assert what rational conscious control we can, and at the time it is needed. This may be only to thwart the seductions of a particular change, and stick with the project and its objectives. But it may also be a preliminary to the conscious risk strategy of navigating in a new direction.

Certainly, this flexibility of navigation and the constant adjustment of objectives has been productive in both my core projects. Indeed, in general, I have now learned - as indicated in Chapter Eight - that some of the most creative developments of my work have been when I accepted the sense of autonomy, took a sensible risk, and navigated with the flow. It is an experience which, as noted, has strong resonance in the literature on creativity, and it is also congruent with that element in the work of Schon on the reflective practitioner which emphasises "conversation" with, and "listening" to, the "message" of the materials.[3]

Of course, as the film director Sidney Lumet suggests in another creative sphere, much depends on the quality of the materials and the quality of the preparation that went into their assembly. If you are letting the material tell you "what it's about ... the material had better be good" [Lumet 1995 p 16].

Over the years I have, I think, developed a keen ear for listening in this way, a shrewd feel for the quality of the material, and a sensitivity towards the genuine and productive detours and departures of the project (as opposed to various pathologies, in misleading cloaks, that deflect the scholar from the disciplined task).

However, the management process is variable in its form. It can involve a clear reponse to a clear option, or an almost automatic, and barely noticed, crossing of a watershed. Sometimes, as in the pursuit of fascinating but postponable distractions, it is possible to come to a decisive, immediate judgement of priority.[4] But, decisions can involve a tumult of clashing considerations and emotions. At such times one can feel like the Fiddler on the Roof - trying to continue to produce beautiful and meaningful music whilst desperately holding the balance between conflicting imperatives and options. In the end there may be no easy guidelines as to which way the experienced creative researcher should move, only the exercise of professional judgement.

Certainly, in making movements one way or the other, a creative scholar can make misjudgements. As with most dedicated researchers, I have had occasional problems with over-absorbtion in particularly interesting areas, with the deflections of fascinating intellectual byways of the subject, and with the dangerous process of an infinite regression backwards in the search for a satisfactory explanation.

There is a story here which is familiar to research supervisors. In my field, the 1920s is a particularly interesting period in terms of the shaping of the Labour Movement (and of electoral alignments). It is full of seminal developments and the closure of important alternatives. As I regressed backwards in the search for explanations of the development of first The Labour Party Conference, and then The Contentious Alliance of the unions and the Party, I did produce new interpretations which enriched the explanatory framework but I twice got stuck in this period. I was fascinated by the unusual features and precedents that shaped future actions and constraints. At one point I found myself unable to stop filling out the explanations for *that* period, becoming almost completely absorbed in it at the expense of the main project. It took a forceful managerial exercise to pull myself out of it.

One of the most difficult decisions of this kind that I had to take in *The Contentious Alliance* concerned the Miners Strike of 1983-4. In many ways the political responses to the strike vividly highlighted and confirmed the range of behaviour patterns I had traced in the book, and so I began to use it as a case study. There was a very important story to be told in detail about the multiple crises affecting the NUM's relations with the Labour Party, but so prolonged was the dispute, and so important were its reverberations, that the scale of the case study in the book began to seem inappropriate. In short, as the material accumulated so the case study outgrew its place in the text. In the end, I took the traumatic decision (I had done an awful lot of work on this - about 25,000 words) to abbreviate the important references to the strike in this book and to turn the case study into a separate book. So far this book has not progressed because it is too overlaid in my mind with the terrible desolation of the mining villages. At some stage, I will achieve enough distance from it to regain the motivation.

Focusing and Prioritising

In dealing with these difficulties, and exercising judgement about how to deal with them, the only clear prudential precept is that we have to be constantly aware of what is happening to the work -and to ourselves - and why.

In making judgements I now see the need, at times, to go through a formal self-interrogation exercise (a systematisation of my own processes influenced by reading de Bono) in which I stop digging, sit myself down as it were, and keep asking myself, again and again, four fundamental focusing and prioritising questions.

> Where am I? (What exactly is the movement that I am making here? For what purpose?)
>
> How did I get here and why? (A retracing of steps with explanations and justification for major movements. When did it move? Why did it move?)
>
> What are the costs and benefits of movement? (A rational judgement involving a calculation of the practicabilities and the likely reverberations of any change, an assessment of the risks and priorities involved - particularly in relation to any deadlines, but also a judgement which is heavily influenced by vivid scenarios coloured by anxiety on the one hand and aspiration on the other.)
>
> Where is it now most productive to move in terms of the overall project? (Back on the original path, or on with the new trajectory?)

I do not always perform this exercise in time, nor am I as systematic in practice as I am in principle. Sometimes it is an agonizing process, sometimes it leads to a very quick decision. But the point is that I am very aware of what needs to be done. On the basis of this judgement, I make the decision, move one way or another, shed this or adopt that, and I *try* to stick to it.

THE DYNAMIC PROCESS: IMPLICATIONS

The experience of this dynamic process, as I have described it here, has many implications for the management of research. Let me just focus on the most important of these implications. In terms of creativity, I came to accept that all this movement made a difficult but also rewarding contribution to the creative process, opening new possibilities of a rich and original outcome.

As far as my personal management of research projects is concerned, I also came to regard it as normal that my statement of objectives, with its accompanying diagnosis and references, would be amended many times, and in its final form it was often virtually the last thing that I wrote. I think of this as The Overture as Finale.[5]

I also drew from this experience a deeper and more profound lesson. I came to see the creative process of political research as analogous to my political experience. Creative research, like politics, involves compromises between aspirations and practicability. It fuses imagination with realism. It is both the exaltation of the possible (a phrase of Martin Buber) and the art of the attainable, involving a sensitive internal dialogue, and a persistent experimentation, concerned with what can, and what does not, work. It is an experience which mixes rational planning and routine procedures with a willingness to navigate uncharted seas, improvising around much wreckage and often in stormy conditions.

In this journey, the utopian with eyes glued to the sky-line, lacking adequate steering and with a poor means of anchorage, is unlikely to arrive safely. On the other hand, the cautious and pragmatic formalist who is without vision and the willingness to defer closure, can not travel very far. The creative designer of research dreams, to be effective, combines both vision and realism, and is both a risk-taker and a patient pragmatist.

DISCIPLINE AND CONSTRAINT

What I have described here also has some broader implications for the contemporary management of academic research. There is clearly a problematic relationship between this sensitivity to the autonomy of the object and the strict contemporary emphasis on a manageable research project which is methodologically sound, well planned, well focused, and available for assessment "ON TIME"[Bell 1987 p1].

Of course, it is easy to see the practical problems that would be caused if simply following all the possible transmutations of the creative process was adopted as an unqualified practice in research management. It should never be an *unqualified* practice, and I am certainly not arguing for sloppy, aimless scholarship. It is a disciplined responsibility of the research navigator. The research project must be accompanied by what Nickerson, Perkins and Smith, call "executive review" [Perkins 1981 p 69]. This involves, as I have indicated, both the sensitivity gained by experience in the research process and, from time to time, a systematic mental monitoring of process, position and priority before a judgement is made on what would be the productive course to take.

These days, for post-graduate research students, such a review has to be carried out with an alert awareness of time and risk in relation to the academic demands of publication, the strictly enforced discipline of the date of completion (including penalisation of the department in the event of non-completion) and the search for a job. In these circumstances, in the production of a thesis there has to be a strong "health warning" given against allowing the moving, generating, transforming process to get out of control. The reality may be one of enforced limitation. There may have to be less depth to the field work and the reflection upon it. The problem definition may have to be closed early. The level of generality, and the scope of the investigation, will have to be strictly judged in relation to the time available. The conceptual development may have to be judged as the best reached at that stage, and the researcher's own changing interests within the research focus will have to be held strongly in check.

The drawback is that once an intellectual position has been announced in a research presentation, psychologically, and in terms of the justification of a future problem-focus, it may not be so easy, in present circumstances, for those who want to continue in academic research to return to the enquiry for re-examination. To that extent, these are serious new constraints on creative scholarship.

However, some of the processes described here do not have to be responded to by postgraduate researchers within the immediate project, and can be used as a rich source of future output in a continuing academic career. Thus, the sudden emergence of new peculiarities at later stages, the regressions into history and into broader explanatory influences, the fascinating curiosities of various intellectual byways, the new insights which the framework gives into behaviour within sub-areas, the new interpretations which evolve or are intimated in the process of preparing the presentation, the contestation of positions taken by other scholars in adjacent territory, the exploration of application problems, and a multitude of suggestive but unexplored connections can all be used to generate either useful spin-offs or future investigation. Indeed, they can be suggestive of lines of thought and enquiry which last throughout the academic's life.

THE CHANGING CULTURE: IMPLICATIONS

Having made these points, it is appropriate here to make a brief but broader appraisal of the potentially serious repercussions for all involved in research, of some of the recent developments in the research culture.

British Universities are involved in a complex and far-reaching series of changes and adjustments, some of which are radically affecting the purposes and conduct of research. The resulting problems have been the subject of much recent controversy which has covered a wide range of issues relating to the purposes of Universities - a canvas broader than my focus here. More relevant is that some of this discussion has touched upon the potential constraints upon creativity and innovation.

In particular, attention has been drawn to financial limitations upon potentially innovative" blue skies" research, also to the pull towards academic orthodoxy involved in the focus on mainstream journal publications, and the problems of a loss of control by researchers of the agenda of problem-seeking. What I want to add, and to point up briefly, are some other features which may affect the creative research process as I have analysed it here. These features again relate mainly to time and risk.

The quantity and quality of research productivity in British Universities is now assessed by a "research assessment exercise", which operates within time-cycles (four years in the social sciences) which make little concession to the individual scholar's life cycle of creative production, and may (or may not) match the scholar's rhythms of creative energy. As indicated, the time-frame of assessment and the demands of completion may interfere with the researchers own choice of creative priorities in managing particular projects: they can, at certain points, inhibit the choice of topic, the form of the project and the decision on how to develop it. There can be, implicitly, a discouragement of persistence in seeking the full flowering of ideas and in pursuing the best possible solutions.

The conditions of risk-taking have changed, with potentially adverse consequences for creative scholarship. Today the risks in choosing the "hard" or more time-consuming problem, in deferring completion and in seeking to pursue something that is almost at the margins of your capacity to tackle, have become significantly greater as they are measured against the costs of failure to make targets.

Personal impressions and consultations with colleagues suggest that, overall, there is now a much heavier pressure on researchers than previously to focus on completion of the immediately publishable. Responses to the new situation do vary by disciplines, research scholars and crucially, local research managers. The worst was summed up in a recent article by the Professor of Organisational Analysis at the Manchester School of Management who offered the view that, "The changes invite and reward academics who willingly restrict their work to duties and activities that provide the greatest measurable, visible output for the lowest risk and least effort".[6] If you were seeking a definition of an anti-creative culture, that description would have much to recommend it.

Add to this a further consideration concerning mental pressure and the quality of this research time. Those bureaucratic circumstances which hamper the mental process of creativity - conditions that Wallas warned about in the 1920s [Wallas 1926 pp 86-93 and 147-9] - have become significantly worse. Researchers are pressurised, not only by the universal increase in work load, but by a new weight of paperwork and administration concerned with applications, admissions, submissions and various quality assessments[7] .

Of course, it has to be recognised that some of these innovations and pressures had their initial individual justifications. Resources are scarce and, in making their claim upon public expenditure before a much more critical public, Universities have to show the effectiveness with which they carry out various functions. In research, as in other activities, the universities must be able to demonstrate the relevance of their role in answering social needs. Thus, some new mechanisms for the assessment of quality, and some greater control over research activity was, to some extent, inevitable. As a result of these changes, submission rates for Ph.D students, which were low, have now been raised.[8] Today, under various pressures, some academics are probably producing more than they would have done.

But as to quality, that is another matter. In the wake of the latest Research Assessment Exercise the official view was that there had been a rise in the quality as well as the volume of research in the past four years.[9] Others, however, have given a more qualified[10] or critical[11] appraisal of the exercise, and there is no consensus about its effects.[12]

On the overall picture I am in no position to make a detailed judgement, but in the light of my analysis here I do raise a note of deep concern. In terms of time, risk and bureaucratic duties the working conditions for research are much more adverse to research scholarship than in the past, with potentially damaging effects on the working judgements of the individual researcher. There is a danger that, in combination, and in the way that they have developed, the recent changes affecting the conditions and management of research may act as growing constraints upon research creativity - thus limiting the potential quality of what is produced.

I began this study with a discussion of the limitations of the dialogue in the old research culture. I end here with a much greater emphasis on the dangers of a degeneration of that culture, pointing out what might now be threatened or lost by constraints on the creative impulse of the researcher.

CHAPTER END NOTES

[1] "Books do not always obey the author's orders and this book.... quickly became obstreperous" [Tomalin 1994 p xvii].

[2] [Gordon 1961 p 139]. In Neil Simon's autobiography there is an interesting argument between Simon and the choreographer Bob Fosse over the musical *Sweet Charity*, after which Simon reflects "I felt, even with the plays that I wrote, that a show has a mind of its own, and it's wrong to push it in a direction it doesn't want to go" [Simon 1996 p 231].

[3] Bamberger, J. and Schon, D.A., 'Learning as reflective conversation with materials' in [Steier 1991 pp 190-1].

[4] James A. Stimson tells us of a device that he uses. He writes to himself what he describes as "a quick and dirty research memo on the distracting questions" so that he feels free to forget it. 'Pursuing a belief structure: a research narrative" in [Shively 1984 p84].

[5] "The last thing one settles in writing a book is what one should put in first". Pascal, quoted by Oliver Sacks in his introduction to [Sacks 1986 p ix].

[6] *Times Higher Educational Supplement*, Nov 10, 1995.

[7] There has been a "marked growth of paperwork and administration" [AUT 1994].

[8] Since the introduction of penal sanctions there has been a dramatic rise in PhD completions. Hill, T., Acker, S. and Black, E., 'Research students and their supervisors in education and psychology' in [Burgess 1994 p53].

[9] Brian Fender, the Chief Executive of the Higher Education Funding Council, was quoted as saying that, "Researchers have produced a remarkable improvement in quality", *Times Higher Educational Supplement* 27/12/96.

[10] An Editorial in the *Times Higher Educational Supplement* 20/12/96 commented that the quality of research "has probably not diminished".

[11] For a very critical and sceptical view of the Research Assessment Exercise see Hugh Willmott " Publish and Be Crammed", *Times Higher Educational Supplement*, 20/12/96. He argues that "in practice the RAE is less effective as a means of improving research focus and quality than as a method of dividing, degrading and sweating the work of academics". Anthony Wright an MP who had been an academic, has described how he saw "former colleagues under enormous pressure to write things they don't want to write and which no one will want to read", "Perspective" *Times Higher Educational Supplement*, 29/12/95. Noel Malcolm has described an "overproduction of unnecessary publications" which are of questionable value in terms of originality. Noel Malcolm 'Sinking in a sea of words', *Independent on Sunday* 21/7/96, reprinted from *Prospect*. In the past two years as I prepared this book I heard a wide variety of comments from researchers in line with these judgements.

[12] In a recent study by Ian McNay, four-fifths of Heads of Department said that the quality of their staff's work was better than five years ago, two-

thirds of staff thought that their own output was better, but only a third of researchers said that the overall quality of research in higher education had been improved by the RAE. 'Research's damaging split', *Times Higher Educational Supplement*, 30.8.96.

CHAPTER TEN

OVERVIEWS AND AFTERTHOUGHTS

ENTRANCES AND EXITS

So, at the end of this singular journey into the mind of one researcher and into one scholar's version of creativity, what has been achieved, what has been discovered, and where has it arrived?

I have argued that, over time, in a learning process on the job, the researcher develops a professional art. I have illustrated how modes of activity and particularly ways of thinking can be pursued in such a way as to make this professional art a creative art. Thus, what has been achieved has been a detailed confirmation that research - even research on worldly, sensitive and familiar areas of political life - can involve a creative artistry, as interpretations and concepts are produced, the theoretical and presentational patterns are generated, and previous understandings are transcended.

What I hope has also been achieved is the sharing of an experience of the mind at work - distinctive in some respects, but more general in others. This has illustrated, in a variety of ways, the advantages to be gained by following the methods of this study in portraying the mental activities of research without succumbing to the kind of fear-filled defensiveness which obscures the real process. It has also suggested a range of insights into the role of the mind in actively creating, as well as exploring and investigating, the meaning of the world that is being researched.

I have argued that in this activity the central task of a creative researcher is to expand the possibilities of any given situation. This expansion is particularly assisted by reflection based on observational vigilance and precepts, reasoning, challenges, tactics and techniques which are directed towards stimulating the creative process and taking creative opportunities - what I have described as heuristic thinking. This creative activity of the researcher is a special kind of learning and re-learning, involving varieties of "serious play". In this play, an experimental and toying activity of the mind, the researcher's objective is to produce a new and better understanding of the problem-field of enquiry.

What has been made clear is that in seeking to create this new and better understanding, it is not enough to follow established procedures - important though these may be. There has also to be an engagement of imaginative vision. On the other hand, it is not enough either, simply to think the unthinkable. Nor is this simply an exercise in free artistic expression. As with all scholarship, creative research is grounded in methodical, scrupulous, precise enquiry. The creativity involves an interplay between what can be imagined, what can be grounded in the data, and what can be made practicable in relation to the problem. The artist has to be in responsive dialogue with the realist. In this sense, the serious play of creativity in research involves not just imagination but disciplined imagination, with a mixture of freedom and focused mental application.

I have emphasised the crucial importance, in my own work, of the pursuit of "peculiarities" in stimulating productive play, and in generating creative outcomes. I have indicated that there is a constant process of problem-seeking as well as problem-solving. I have illustrated the importance of sensitivity to patterning in creative research. I have also exemplified the use of various modes of the heuristic thinking which can assist in the playful generation of creative thought and an expansion of possibilities. In all this, I have sought to demonstrate that we, who aspire to be the creative scholars of research, need not wait for the random assistance of the muse in our work. We can help ourselves. The mental approach that we take towards research, the attitude we take towards our own mental processes, the mental dialogues we indulge in, and even the cast of characters we assemble in our minds, can engender self-awareness and facilitate the creative generation of ideas in a way that can improve, even transform, the quality of what is born out of the project.

What has also emerged from this study is the multi-dimensional character of the creative experience. I have highlighted and explored this complexity in various ways: describing different perceptions of the creative "flow", noting the importance of the span and quality of time, and explaining the psychological dimension of creative scholarly activity. I have portrayed the emotional as well as the rational, the non-directed as well as the directed elements of the mind at play. I have also contributed some indications of the various processes and influences which can affect the long term development of ideas in research, and the extraordinary transmutations which can occur in the research project - indicating also the way that these have to be managed.

At its best, creativity in research has been shown to arise out of a total engagement of the personality as well as the intellect, the use of the critical as well as the creative faculties. It can be a lengthy engagement, from the initial speculative thoughts and preliminary observations right through to the final tidying and fine-tuning of presentation - a presentation which can itself turn, or be turned, into a creative inter-relationship with the substance of the study.

Viewed in retrospect, the creative process, as analysed here, can be seen to have involved an intricate blend of mental attitudes and activities, with many tensions and some paradoxical features. There was method and planning but there was also flexibility and receptivity. There was realism, pragmatism, logic and hard graft; but there was also an engagement of vision and imagination, even perhaps a theatre of the mind. There was rigour but without rigidity. There was an outward focus on investigating and understanding the world that was studied, but this was beneficially combined with an inward focus on understanding the self and experimenting with the mind.

There was the classic research scholar's concern to achieve an easy familiarity with every nuance of the terrain that was under investigation. There was, more unusually, at times a creative co-partnership with those whose behaviour was being studied. But these activities had to be coupled with a sense of distance and role, and with the renewal of a freshness that could refashion perspectives. There was a mental promiscuity with these perspectives but a fidelity to the evidence. There was a dedication in the pursuit of this evidence and an effort at demystification, in "telling it like it is". But there was also a fascination with the peculiar and the strange, and repeated efforts to pattern and play mentally with a world that was appropriately strange, in an attempt to make better sense of it.

In this play, the creative researcher is often involved in a delicate mental dance, to and fro. At times it is a careful measured process, on other occasions it is spontaneous and performed in the twinkling of an eye. It is a movement into complete engagement, then a movement to detachment, an involvement with all the details and the entrails, the behaviour and the relationships, of the subject under observation - then a laid-back reflection on that experience. It involves a period of deep immersion and penetration into the complexity of a problem, then on occasions a lapse of time or a shift of focus away to other activities before an insight, a new perspective, or the intimation of a solution returns the researcher to the task.

In portraying these different characteristics, dimensions, perspectives and movements, I have attempted to convey honestly the nuance, feeling and flavour of a range of features not normally put on show for detailed public examination. In some ways I think that I succeeded in this communication, in others perhaps not.

Looking back over the text, I have to say that both creative style and heuristic thinking are probably over-emphasised at the expense of the necessary but more humdrum routines of any research inquiry - including any creative inquiry. Also, try as I might, it proved almost impossible not to over-systematise the representation of my mental processes compared with how they were in practice. The result has been to make the author look far more organised and far more creative at work than he is. It is not a con-trick. It seems to be just a fact of the chosen focus, the attempt at accessibility and the introduction of a degree of recommendation.

The study has been necessarily misleading in other ways also. What I have presented here is not quite what I set out to do, even if the general trajectory and the main diagnosis and themes were clear. The reader will not be surprised at this stage to learn that I found the precise objectives and the shape as I proceeded, and that I rewrote The Overture accordingly.

It was itself a creative process and also a process of self-discovery. My views on the nature and importance of different mental processes changed draft by draft. Some activities were uncovered that had become so automatic I had lost sight of their significance.

Long forgotten examples, of this or that, came back into consciousness, whilst other cherished examples appeared, on investigation, to be misconceptions or faulty memories. In the process, elements of my psychology, my intellectual techniques and personal style became clarified. New possibilities emerged as I reflected, remembered, read, wrote and thought again.

All in all, I had begun with a confident assumption that I understood a lot - an unusual amount perhaps - about the way that I thought and worked. But as I watched and reflected on my process, as I read more deeply into the literature on creativity, and as I organised the material, I came to realise how little I knew, and consequently how limited was my appreciation of the available options. That discovery provides a reinforcement of the case to be made for this form of enquiry and for a dialogue on this kind of agenda.

THE PERSPECTIVE AND THE CONTEXT

The agenda and the analysis which has accompanied it, will, of course, be received by different people in different ways. Each will read into it something different, take from it what is useful to them, and reject what is unacceptable. That is how it should be. Some may, perhaps, find the perspective taken here on creative research difficult to accommodate within the new time-constrained, cost-conscious, tough-realism, commercial-academic culture.

My response is fully to acknowledge that today's university research is being conducted in much more adverse and limiting circumstances than when I began thirty years ago and could choose much more easily what, how, when, where and whether to publish. I took it for granted then, as did most others, that the fundamental purpose of university research was not the pursuit of institutional competitive advantage but the furtherance of scholarship and learning.[1] That fundamental purpose is always worth reasserting and defending, but I am not surprised that, in the face of contemporary pressures, and the transformation of British higher education, other criteria have begun to take precedence. As a result, for many the masks have now been drawn tighter; an unnatural face often says ruefully, defensively, and pessimistically " That is the name of the game".

If so, in that game, we each set our own aspirations and standards, we make what space we can, and we do what we can to live up to them. In general, it is better to seek a greater vision, and to set high aspirations and standards, than lower ones, although there must always be a judgement of the practicabilities and the risks involved. This is the exaltation of the possible combined with the art of the attainable. But, the definition of the game is what we all make it. Even within the present difficult national and international context, we can change some of it. Indeed, at this moment in history it might be strange if we did not.

THE CREATIVE ERA?

We have moved into an era marked by powerful forces engendering new elements of what Arieti has termed a creativogenic culture [Arieti 1976 p 303] - a culture particularly suited to the promotion of creativity. Indeed, in spite of various obstacles and countervailing features, you could say that we are beginning to live in a creativity-generating society. It is a society which is receptive to, and being stimulated towards, an increasing level of creative activity, and growing interest in the exercise of creative ability.

This society is marked by constantly activated development and an extraordinary pace of change and innovation. It is a society increasingly in need of a multiplicity of flexible problem-solvers to deal with the emergence of new and unpredictable social, economic and political problems, as well as with those old problems to which the world has not yet found solutions.

It is also a highly competitive global society where there is a constant search for means of utilising and expanding natural assets - particularly human talent. It is an information-age society, increasingly focused upon the production and reproduction of ideas. It is a knowledge-intensive society, where we are able to know much more of many things, more quickly as we bring them into our mental play. It is a society where life-long learning involves greater adaptability for the individual in shifting the area of expertise and the mode of problem-solving. It is a society where workers require metacognitive qualities as well as technical qualification.[2]

It is a society where there are both economistic and humanistic new calls upon creative expression. Human capital and socio-economic productivity are now inextricably linked [UNDP 1996 pp 43-79], and an increasingly important economic and social role is being played by the cultural sector with its emphasis on the utilisation of creative ability. At the same time there is also a strong international reassertion of the value of human development and human well-being independent of considerations of market competitiveness or economic growth [UNDP 1996 p 223]. Further, in an increasingly reflexive society, where changing the self often becomes a personal project, there is a turn towards continuous self-observation as individuals seek to construct for themselves a satisfactory sense of identity [Giddens 1991 pp70-80]. Such perspectives on productivity, human development and the construction of identity are likely to involve a greater receptivity to the value of developing to the full the creative expression of our latent human potentialities.

These various developments for different purposes have contributed to a strong surge of interest in the nature and management of creativity. The focus on creativity is there in a new appreciation of the need for a creative, as well as a vocationally trained, workforce in "a country of innovative people"[3]. It is there in the shift towards utilising the insights of creativity research in organisational and corporate settings.[4] It is there in Singapore's new turn towards creativity and an "intelligent island".[5] It is there in the ecological concern for creative re-use.[6] It is also beginning to feed into a broader social appraisal of the forces for beneficial change - as in "the Creative City"[7] and the emphasis on "Creative Altruism" and "Creative Collaboration" [Goleman, Kaufman and Ray 1993 pp 160-161].

It would be very surprising if the universities were not drawn into a greater response to these intellectual currents concerning creativity - particularly as their staff are amongst those most likely to be in the forefront of (and to investigate) new life-style reflexivity, as well as being important sources of creative ideas. It would perhaps be even more surprising if universities were to ignore the relevance and potential significance of this development for the definition of their social role.

Creativity is not, and will not be, a quality expressed in the activities of any one sector, institution or social group, but the universities, as one element of their increasingly pluralistic identity, can legitimately emphasise their function as centres, facilitators and producers of creative expertise in all its diverse forms. A comfortable and natural marriage could be made between creativity and the university mission for excellence.

A CREATIVE RESEARCH CULTURE

Here we return to the focus on research. The generation of an appropriate research culture would involve a renewed awareness of, and respect for, the creative process in research, and a more vigorous concern to protect and nourish the appropriate culture for creativity.

Such a culture would be sensitive to the relations between means and ends in the pursuit of quality in research. The nature of creative research is such that systems for the assessment of quality can become subversive of some of the ends they are intended to serve, as attention is paid to the performance indicators at the expense of the potentiality of the performance. Bearing this in mind, more consideration might be given to a loosening of some of the risk-inhibiting rigidities and to raising some of the short-term-focused constraints which can hamper creativity.

A more general and obvious point about this culture is that we are more likely to encourage the creative process if we discuss it, publicly value it, and encourage our post-graduate students in the belief that they are engaged in it, rather than ignore or undervalue it. Increasing attention is now rightly paid to research students and the quality of their training. New emphasis has been placed upon the importance of learning about writing strategies, particularly knowledge-transforming approaches.[8] Alongside this, a place could be found for introducing a new dimension to the dialogue of research training which focuses more broadly on the creative process.

This emphasis on the dialogue of research is where my diagnosis began and where it has once again emerged - but with a new consideration. Creativity involves a rich expression of individual human talent. On those grounds alone, in our educational institutions it demands respect and nourishment. But creativity - individual, collaborative and collective - has also become a social and economic imperative of the age.

A new agenda of discourse on creative research would involve an appreciation of the diversity of creative activity, and an understanding of the various currents of thought about the creative process. It would acknowledge that, in tune with the broad diversity of academic and social purposes in which universities engage, creative research can take a variety of forms. Every project will have its own constraints but also its own possibilities. Whether in pure or applied research, within the purposes of the project, the art of the creative researcher lies in maximising those possibilities.

A new focus on creative research would involve also a humanising of our image of the thinking intellectual doing research - broadening our understanding of what is actually involved in the creative activity of the mind. This would be sensitive to the variety of the mind's contributions to creative productivity, as well as being committed to the rational procedures and methods of academic enquiry.

It would emphasise, in particular, the importance of self-knowledge in relation to those abilities, qualities and self-images which facilitate our personal creative performance. It would be appreciative of the possibilities involved in, and the mental space required for, a productive theatre of the mind. And it would be much more willing to engage with the idea of applied creativity and creativity-generation.

THE SIGNIFICANCE OF FAILURE

The final point to which I want to draw attention has been a sub-theme of this study from first page to last. It is by no means a discovery of mine, nor is it a novelty. Described in different ways it often emerges as an intellectual insight in the literature on creativity, on the development of scientific understanding and on educational philosophy. What it amounts to is the normality, and potential value, of "failure" - that multiplicity of misdirections, misunderstandings, mistakes, and misadventures which generally characterises the creative research process.

That may appear a startlingly unfashionable note to end on. It may even, perhaps, seem perverse in present circumstances. Such an emphasis lives in uneasy tension with the contemporary productivity-measured, results-assessed culture. But it is, in fact, strikingly relevant to the understanding and the management of high quality research.

What I have to say here should not be mistaken for fatalistic acceptance, or for a withdrawal from responsibility - as my own story makes clear. Nor is it a celebration of sterile research, or of poor decisions - of which I have had my share; although it does involve an appreciation that the more creative and complex a process of research, the more it is likely to involve human misjudgement. What I do want to make clear are a range of hard-earned understandings about the nature of such research.

In the process of trial and error that is the research journey, a "steady stream of failure"[9] contributes to creative success. As I have indicated throughout this study, failure, though endemic, is not necessarily a disaster, nor need it be a full stop. It can even represent an opportunity.

From its inception, the research process can involve a range of uncertainties. Even a researcher who is a "genius" may be mistaken in assessing what is likely to be confronted, may be unclear which of the many alternative paths are to be explored, and may at crucial junctures find him or herself somewhere contrary to where was anticipated. The compensation is that discoveries and suggestive possibilities can emerge at any stage of the research process. In this context, failing to keep to the plan or failing to keep to the timetable are common experiences. Playing with the new possibilities - altering course, changing strategy, reframing problems, deferring closure and taking more time to secure better solutions - are often virtuous qualities of the creative process, not inadequacies which deserve to be penalised. The greater the research aspiration, the more problematic is the mode and time of arrival. Arriving at unexpected destinations, or the right destination by the wrong boat, is not unusual in creative activity [Koestler 1969 p 145].

So, as we come to reconsider the whole business of quality in research, and of its procedures of assessment, we might remind ourselves of what the very creative Nobel Prizewinner Peter Medawar said in his Jayne lectures on scientific thought,

> "I reckon that for all the use it has been to science, about four-fifths of my time has been wasted and I believe this to be the common lot of people who are not merely playing follow-my-leader in research" [Medawar 1968 p 32].

Researchers who understand the creative process appreciate that, in this context, there are failures that can be regarded as "heroic".[10] They know that they must struggle with the emotion of the different kinds of failure. They may even sometimes gain an invigorated psychological impetus from the experience. They try to focus on the causes of trouble and disorientation, learning about the dangers to avoid and the weaknesses to correct, understanding what is not effective and what might yet work. And they seek patiently to evaluate, toy with, and take advantage of, the possibilities inherent in the position where they have arrived.

One writer on jazz and creativity has called this constructive sensitivity to failure "the aesthetics of imperfection".[11] It is a particularly important perspective in curiosity-led creative research, where every exit can be an entrance and where we can rarely be quite sure of the ultimate social value of the new understanding that has been generated.

This aesthetic accepts - even glories in - the fact that uncertainty, misconception, error and disorientation are in the nature of the creative journey, and are inescapable elements of our common endeavour. As John Ziman has written,

> "What is surprising is not that each of us makes many mistakes but that we have made such remarkable progress together" [Ziman 1978 p 41].

These are considerations relating to the creative process which ought not to be lightly disregarded in the pursuit of rigid performance indicators. Nor is it useful for this reality to be hidden behind masks. Their honest public acceptance at this time is the means by which we heighten our commitment both to creative research and to our mutual education.

CHAPTER END NOTES

[1] A point made by Martin Harris 'Circling around the Dearing ring' *Times Higher Educational Supplement*, 19.7.96.

[2] On this see particularly the Danish approach to skill development decribed in Ray Marshall and Marc Tucker [Marshall and Tucker 1993 edn pp 204-5].

[3] Speech by Tony Blair MP, Leader of the Labour Party, to the Keidanren, Tokyo, 5/1/1996. Employee creativity has become an important topic in management literature [Scott, R.K. 1995].

[4] [Ford and Gioia 1995 p 7], [Fryer 1996 p 1]. At the 1994 International Creativity and Innovation Networking Conference around a third of the papers were concerned with organisational management. Jacynthe Bedard (Ed) *Trans-Sphere Proceedings* (No place or date).

[5] James Kynge 'Efficiency, hard work...now for a spot of creativity', Financial Times, Weekend 26th/27 October 1996.

[6] [Papanek 1995], [McHarry 1993]. [Giddens 1991 p223] makes the point that, as proponents of deep ecology assert, "a movement away from economic accumulation might involve substituting personal growth - the cultivation of the potentialities for self-expression and creativity - for unfettered economic growth processes".

[7] [Landry and Biancini 1995], Peter Hall 'Creative cities' in [Hardy, Malbon and Taverner 1996 pp 107-113].

[8] See on this the proposal in [Torrance and Thomas 1994 p 120] and their stress on the importance of an understanding of the knowledge-transforming approach to writing.

[9] [Runco and Albert 1990 p 266]. In this sense, as one scientist has put it, "Making mistakes is the key to making progress", Dennett in [Brockman and Matson 1995 p 137].

[10] Simonton in [Ford and Gioia 1995 pp 88-93].

[11] See Weick, K. E., 'Creativity and the aesthetics of imperfection' in [Ford and Gioia 1995 pp 187-194]. From an idea by Ted Gioia [Ford and Gioia 1995 pp 54-55].

BIBLIOGRAPHY

EDITORIAL NOTE

This bibliography is constructed in three sections.

The first of these lists all works cited in the text in alphabetical order of author in conformance with the Author-Date (Harvard) System of referencing.

The second lists publications by the present author to which direct reference is made in the text. It is arranged in chronological sequence. These publications are extracted for convenience from the main bibliographical sequence under Minkin, L.

The third lists twelve books which the present author has found particularly interesting in understanding creativity. This list is aranged alphabetically by author.

Works cited in text

Adams J.L. 1987, *Conceptual Blockbusting*, Harmondsworth, Penguin

Adams, J.L. 1988, *The Care and Feeding of Ideas*, Harmondsworth, Penguin

Addison, P. 1975, *The Road to 1945: party politics and the second world war*, London, Jonathan Cape

Albert, R.S. and Runco, M.A. 1990, *Theories of Creativity*, London, Sage

Anderson, E. 1978, *A Place on the Corner,* Chicago, University of Chicago Press

Anderson H., ed, 1959, *Creativity and its Cultivation,* New York, Harper and Row

Arieti, S. 1976, *Creativity: the magic sysnthesis,* New York, Basic Books

Association of Univesrity Teachers (AUT) 1994, *Long Hours, Little Thanks: a survey of the use of time by full time academic and related staff in the traditional UK universities,* London

Atkinson, P. 1990, *The Ethnographic Imagination: textual constructions of reality,* London, Routledge

Bachrach, P. and Baratz, M. 1962, 'Two faces of power', *American Political Science Review,* 1962

Bachrach, P. and Baratz, M. 1963, Decisions and non-decisions: an analystical framework' *American Political Science Review,* 1963

Baker, T.L. 1994, *Doing Social Research,* New York, McGraw-Hill

Bandler, R. 1985, *Using Your Brain for a Change,* Moab, Ut, Real People Press

Bandura, A. 1986, *Social Foundations of Thought and Action: a social cognitive theory,* Englewood Cliffs, NJ, Prentice Hall

Bargar, R.R. and Duncan, J.K. 1990, 'Creative endeavour in PhD research: principles, contexts and conceptions', *Journal of Creative Behaviour,* Vol 24, No1

Barnes, J.A. 1977, *The Ethics of Inquiry in Social Science: three lectures,* Delhi, Oxford University Press

Barnes, J.A. 1979, *Who Should Know What?: social science, privacy and ethics*, Harmondsworth, Penguin

Barron, F. 1963, *Creativity and Psychological Health*, Princeton, NJ, Van Nostrand

Beauchamp, T.L., Fadden, R.R., Wallace, R.J. and Waters, L. 1982, *Ethical Issues in Social Science Research*, Baltimore, John Hopkins University Press

Becker, H. with Richards, P. 1986, *Writing for Social Scientists: how to start and finish your thesis, book or article*, Chicago, Chicago University Press

Bell, C. and Encel S., eds, 1978, *Inside the Whale*, Oxford, Pergamon

Bell, C. and Newby, H., eds, 1977, *Doing Sociological Research*, London, Allen and Unwin

Bell, C. and Roberts, H. 1984, *Social Researching: politics, problems, practice*, London, Routledge and Kegan Paul

Bell, J. 1987, *Doing Your Research Project: a guide for first time researchers in education and social science*, Buckingham, Open University Press

Bereiter, C and Scardamalia, C. 1987, *The Psychology of Written Composition*, Hillsdale NJ, Lawrence Erlbaum

Bergson, W. and Wettersten, J. 1984, *Learning from Error: Karl Popper's psychology of learning*, La Salle, Ill, Open Court Publishing

Bernard, H.R. 1994, *Research Methodology in Anthropology: qualitative and quantitave methods*, London, Sage

Berthoff, A.E. (with Stephens, J.) 1988, *Forming, Thinking, Writing,* Portsmouth, NH, Boynton/ Cook

Bevins, A 1996, 'Blair's awkward squad could shatter Labour unity', *Observer* 7.4.96

Blaxter, L., Hughes, C. and Tight, M. 1996, *How to Research,* Buckingham, Open University Press

Boden, M.A. 1990, *The Creative Mind,* London, Weidenfield and Nicolson

Boden, M.A., ed, 1994, *Dimensions of Creativity,* London, MIT Press

de Bono, E. 1977, *Lateral Thinking,* Harmondsworth, Penguin

de Bono, E. 1993, *Serious Creativity,* London, Harper/ Collins

de Bono, E. 1993, *Teach Your Child to Think*, London, Harper/ Collins

Booth, W.C., Colomb, G.G. and Williams, J.M. 1995, *The Craft of Research,* Chicago, Chicago University Press

Boylan, C, ed, 1993, *The Agony and the Ego: the art and strategy of fiction writing explored*, Harmondsworth, Penguin

Brannigan, A. 1981, *The Social Basis of Scientific Discoveries,* Cambridge, Ma., Cambridge University Press

Brenner, M., Brown, J. and Cantor, D. 1995, *The Research Interview: uses and approaches*, London, Academic Press

Brockman, J. and Mason, K., eds, 1995, *How Things Are: a scientific tool-kit for the mind,* London, Weidenfield and Nicolson

Bulmer, M., ed, 1982, *Social Research Ethics,* New York, Holmes and Meier

Bulmer, M., ed, 1987, *Researching Organisations*, London, Routledge

Burgess, R.G. 1984, *In the Field: an introduction to field research*, London, Unwin Hyman

Burgess, R.G. 1988, *Studies in Qualitative Methodology: Vol 1, conducting qualitative research*, London, Jai Press

Burgess, R.G. 1990, *Studies in Qualitative Methodology: Vol 2, reflections on field experience*, London, Jai Press

Burgess, R.G., ed, 1994, *Postgraduate Education in the Social Sciences: processes and products*, London, Jessica Kingsley

Burnham, P. 1991, *The case for Methodological Glasnost: rethinking how research methodology is taught to political science graduates*, Working paper 50, University of Warwick, Department of Politics, May 1991

Burnham, P. 1992, 'Method and myth in political research: a practical guide for research students' *Politics*, Vol 12 No 1

Byson, L., ed, 1948, *The Communication of Ideas*, New York, Harpers

Cameron, J. 1994, *The Artists' Way* London, Souvenir Press

Cannon, W.B. 1945, *The Way of an Investigator*, New York, Norton

Carey, J., ed, 1995, *Faber Book of Science*, London, Faber and Faber

Castle, B. 1984, *The Castle Diaries*, 1974-70, London, Wiedenfeld and Nicolson

Charlesworth, M., Farrall, L., Stokes, T. and Turnbull, D. 1989, *Life Amongst the Scientists: an anthropological study of an Australian scientific community*, Melbourne, Oxford University Press

Cox, C.M. 1926, *Genetic Studies of Genius,* Stanford, Stanford University Press

Crewe, I. and Harrop, M. eds 1986, *Political communications: the general election campaign of 1983,* Cambridge, Cambridge University Press

Crewe, I. and Harrop, M. eds 1989, *Political communications: the general election campaign of 1987,* Cambridge, Cambridge University Press

Crick, F. 1989, *What Mad Pursuit: a personal view of scientific discovery,* Harmondsworth, Penguin

Cropley, A.J. 1967, *Creativity,* London, Longman

Czikszentmihalyi, M. 1975, *Beyond Boredom and Anxiety: the experience of play in work and games,* San Fransisco, Jossey Bass

Czikszentmihalyi, M. 1988, 'Society, culture and person: a systems view of creativity' in Sternberg 1988

Dane, F.C. 1990, *Research Methods,* Pacific Grove Ca, Brooks/ Cole

Dellas, M. and Gaier, E.L. 1970, 'Identification of creativity: the individual' *Psychological Bulletin,* No 73

Denzin, N.K. and Lincoln, Y.S. 1994, *Handbook of Qualitative Research,* Thousand Oaks, Ca, Sage

Deutsch, K.W., Markovits, A.S. and Platt, J. 1986, *Advances in the Social Sciences 1900-1980: what, who, where, how?* Cambridge, University Press of America

Dewey, J. 1910, *How we Think,* Boston, Ma, Heath

Dilts, R.B., Epstein, T. and Dilts, R.W. 1991, *Tools for dreamers: strategies for creativity and the structure of innovation*, Capitola, Ca, Meta Publications

Dogan, M.and Pahre, R. 1990, *Creative Marginality: innovation at the intersections of social sciences*, Oxford, Westview Press

Dorril, S. and Ramsay, R. 1991, *Smear! Wilson and the secret fourth estate*, London,

Emerson, R.M. 1983, *Contemporary Field Research: a collection of readings*, Boston, Little Brown

E.S.R.C. 1995, *Postgraduate Training: Guidelines...*, Swindon, Economic and Social Research Council

Entwistle, N. 1988, *Styles of Learning and Teaching*, London, David Fulton

Fearon, J.D. 1991, 'Counterfactuals and hypothesis-testing in political science' *World Politics*, No 2, January 1991

Feldhusen, J.F. 1995, 'Creativity: a knowledge base, metacognitive skills and personality factors', *Journal of Creative Behaviour*, Vol 29 No 4

Flowers, L. 3rd edition 1989, *Problem-Solving Strategies for Writing*, San Diego, Ca, Harcourt Brace

Ford, C.M. and Gioia, D.A. 1995, *Creative Action in Organisations: ivory tower visions and real world voices*, London, Sage

Ford, D.Y. and Harris III, J.J. 1992, 'The elusive definition of creativity', *Journal of Creative Behaviour*, Vol 26 No 3

Forrester, K. and Thorne, C. 1993, *Trade Unions and Social research: the casualties and victims of social research*, Aldershot, Avebury

Foster, G.M., Scudder, T., Colson, E. and Kemper, R.V. 1979, *Long-Term Field Research in Social Anthropology,* New York, Academic Press

Freeman, J., Butcher, H.J. and Christie, T. 1968, (second edn 1971) *Creativity: a selective review of research*, London, Society for Research into Higher Education

Freud, S, see Strachey J, ed

Fryer, M. 1996, *Creative Teaching and Learning,* London, Chapman

Gardner, H. 1993, *Creating Minds,* New York, Harper/ Collins

Getzels, J.W. and Czikszentmihalyi, M. 1976, *The Creative Vision: a longitudinal study of problem finding in art,* New York, John Wiley

Ghiselin, B. 1954, *The Creative Process: a symposium*, Berkeley, Ca., University of California Press

Giddens, A. 1991, *Modernity and Self-Identity: self and society in the late modern age,* London, Polity Press

Gioia, E. 1988, *The Imperfect Art: reflections on jazz and modern culture,* New York, Oxford University Press

Glaser, B. and Strauss, A.L. 1967, *The Discovery of grounded theory,* Chicago, Aldine

Glover, J.A., Ronning, R.R. and Reynolds, C.R., eds, *Handbook of Creativity,* NY, Plenum Press

Goleman, D. 1996, *Emotional Intelligence: why it can matter more than IQ*, London, Bloomsbury

Goleman, D., Kaufman, P. and Ray, M. 1993, *The Creative Spirit*, New York, Penguin

Gordon, W.J.J. 1961, *Synectics: the development of creative capacity*, New York, Harper and Row

Gornick, V. 1984, *Women in Science: portraits from a world in transition*, New York, Simon and Schuster

Gould, J.D. 1969, 'Hypothetical history' in *Economic History Review*, Second series, 22 August 1969

Gouldner, A. 1973, *For Sociology: renewal and critique in sociology today*, Harmondsworth, Allen Laine

Green, B. and Gallway, W.T. 1986, *The Inner Game of Music*, London, Pan

Guilford, J.P. 1968, *Intelligence, Creativity and their Educational Implications*, San Diego, Ca, Knapp

Hammond, P.E., ed, 1964, *Sociologists at Work: essays on the craft of social research*, New York, Basic Books

Harding, S., ed, 1987, *Feminism and Methodology: social science issues*, Milton Keynes, Open University Press

Hardy, S., Malbon, B. and Taverner, C. 1996, *The Role of Art and Sport in Local and Regional Economic Development*, Proceedings of Regional Studies Association

Haseler, S. 1969, *The Gaitskellites: revisionism in the British Labour party, 1951-64*, London, MacMillan

Hawthorne, G. 1991, *Plausible Worlds: possibility and understanding in history and the social sciences*, Cambridge, Cambridge University Press

Hertz, R. and Imber, J.B., eds, 1995, *Studying Elites Using Qualitative Methods*, Thousand Oaks, Ca, Sage

Horowitz, I.L. 1969, *Sociological Self-Images: a collective portrait*, Oxford, Pergamon

Howard, K. and Sharp, J.A. 1985, *Management of a Student Research Project*, Aldershot, Gower

Isaksen, S.A. et al 1993, *Understanding and Recognising Creativity: the emergence of a discipline*, Norwood, NJ, Ablex

Jackson, B. and Marsden, D. 1966, *Education and the Working Class*, Harmondsworth, Pelican

James, J. 1994, *The Music of the Spheres*, London, Little, Brown and Co

James, W. 1901, *Principles of Psychology*, London, Macmillan

Jenkins, P. 1970, *The Battle of Downing Street*, London, Charles Knight

Jewkes, J. 1948, *Ordeal by Planning*, London, MacMillan

Jubak, J 1992, *In the Image of the Brain*, Boston, Ma, Little Brown

Jung, C.G. 1984 edn, *Modern Man in Search of a Soul*, London, Routledge

Kagan, J., ed, 1967, *Creativity and Learning*, Boston, Houghton Mifflin

Kanter, R. M. 1977, *Men and Women of the Corporation*, New York, Basic Books

Kirby, D. and Kuykendall, C. 1991, *Mind Matters: teaching for thinking*, Portsmouth, NH, Boynton/ Cook

Koestler, A. 1969, *The Act of Creation*, London, Hutchinson

Landry, C. and Biancini, F. 1995, *The Creative City*, London, Demos/ Comedia (Paper No 5)

Leary, D.E., ed, 1990, *Metaphors in the History of Psychology*, Cambridge, Cambridge University Press

Lee, R.M. 1993, *Doing Research on Sensitive Topics*, London, Sage

Leigh, D., *The Wilson Plot: the intelligence services and the discrediting of a prime minister 1945-76*, London, Heinemann

Leytham, G. 1990, *Managing Creativity*, Dereham, Peter Francis

Lieberman, J.N. 1977, *Playfulness: its relationship to imagination and creativity*, New York, Academic Press

Lightman, A. 1993, *Einstein's Dreams*, London, Hodder and Stoughton

Lodge, D. 1996, *The Practice of Writing*, London, Secker and Warburg

Lumet, S. 1995, *Making Movies*, London, Bloomsbury

McHarry, J. 1993, *Re-use, Repair, Re-cycle*, London, Gaia

McKenzie, R. 1955, *British Political Parties*, London, Heinemann

MacKinnon, D.W. 1962, 'The nature and nurture of creative talent', *American Psychology*, Vol 17

MacMillan/ Free Press 1968, *International Encyclopaedia of the Social Sciences*, London/ Glencoe

Marshall, R. and Tucker, M. 1993 edn, *Thinking for a Living: education and the wealth of nations*, New York, Basic Books

Marquand, D. 1991, *The Progressive Dilemma*, London, Heinemann

Maslow, A.H. 1976, *The Farther Reaches of Human Nature*, London, Penguin

Medawar, P. 1963, 'Is the scientific paper a fraud?' (broadcast transcript) *The Listener* 12 September 1963

Medawar, P. 1968, *Induction and Intuition in Scientific Thought*. Philadelphia Pa, 1968 Jayne Lectures of the American Philosophy Society

Medawar, P. 1990, *The Threat and the Glory: reflections on science and scientists*, Oxford, Oxford University Press

Melville, H. 1985 edn, *Moby Dick or The Whale*, London, Oxford World's Classics (Chancellor Press)

Merton, R.K. 1957, *Social Theory and Social Structure*, New York, Free Press

Metzger, D. 1992, *Writing for Your Life: a guide and companion to the inner world*, San Fransisco, Harper

Michels, R. 1962 edn, *Political Parties: a sociological study of the oligarchical tendencies of modern democracy*, New York, Collier Books

Mills, C.W. 1959, *The Sociological Imagination*, New York, Oxford University Press

Minkin, L. 1967 *The Soviet Achievement* (with Nettl, J.P.) London, Thames and Hudson

Minkin, L. 1974 'The British Labour Party and the Trade Unions: crisis and compact' Symposium on Trade Unions and Political Parties, *Industrial and Labor Relations Review*, October 1974.

Minkin, L. 1977 (with Seyd, P.) 'The British Labour Party' in Patterson, W.E. and Thomas, A.H. 1977, *Social Democratic Parties of Western Europe*, London, Croom Helme, pp101-152.

Minkin, L. 1978 'The Party Connection: divergence and convergence in the British labour movement', Symposium on Trade Unions and Political Parties, *Government and Opposition*, October 1978.

Minkin, L. 1978 *The Labour Party Conference: a study in the politics of intra party democracy*, Harmondsworth, Allan Lane.

Minkin, L. 1979 'Leftwing trade unionism and the tensions of British labour politics' in Brown, B., ed, 1979, *Eurocommunism and Eurosocialism: The Left Confronts Modernity*, New York, Cyrco Press

Minkin, L. 1980 *The Labour Pary Conference: a study in the politics of intra party democracy*, (revised paperback edition with epilogue), Manchester, Manchester University Press

Minkin, L. 1981 'The politics of the block vote', *New Socialist* Vol I, No 1, September/ October, 1981.

Minkin, L. 1982 'Radicalism and reconstruction: the British experience', Symposium, La Reconstruction de l'Europe 1944-49, *Europa*, Tome 5, No 2, 1982.

Minkin, L. 1986 'Against the tide: trade unions, political communication and the 1983 General Election' in Crewe, I. and Harrop, M., eds, 1986, *Political Communications : The General Election Campaign of 1983, Cambridge,* Cambridge University Press

Minkin, L. 1989 'Mobilisation and distance' in Crewe, I. and Harrop, M., eds, 1989, *Political Communications: The General Election of 1987* , Cambridge, Cambridge University Press

Minkin, L. 1991 *The Contentious Alliance: trade unions and the Labour party*, Edinburgh, Edinburgh University Press

Minkin, L. 1992 *The Contentious Alliance: trade unions and the Labour party* (paperback edition, with epilogue), Edinburgh, Edinburgh University Press

Minkin, L. 1993 Memorandum of Evidence to the Home Affairs Committee enquiry into the *Funding of Political Parties,* London, HMSO, 20/7/93.

Minkin, L. 1995 'The New Labour Party: continuities, innovations and uncertainties' in Blair, A. and Minkin L., *La Renovation du Party Travailliste en Grande-Bretagne*, Paris, Fondation Jean Jaures

Moyser, G. and Wagstaffe, M., eds, 1987, *Research Methods for Elite Studies*, London, Allen and Unwin

Mulkay, M. 1985, *The Word and the World: explorations in the form of sociological analysis*, London, Allen and Unwin

Murdock, M.M. and Ganim, R.M. 1993, 'Creativity and humour: integration and incongruity', *Journal of Creative Behaviour,* Vol 27, No 1

Nettl, J.P., with Minkin L as part co-author, 1967, *The Soviet Acheivement*, London, Thames and Hudson

Newell, A. and Simon, A.H. 1972, *Human Problem Solving*, Englewood Cliffs, NJ, Prentice Hall

Nickerson, R.S., Perkins, D.N. and Smith, E.E. 1985, *The Teaching of Thinking*, Hillsdale, NJ, Lawrence Erlbaum

Oakeshott, M. 1962, *Rationalism in Politics and Other Essays*, London, Methuen

Ochse, R. 1991, 'Why there were relatively few creative women', *Journal of Creative Behaviour*, Vol 25 No 4

Olson, T. 1965, 'Silences: when writers don't write'. *Harpers*, October

Osborne, A.F. 1993, *Applied Imagination*, Buffalo NY, Creative Education Foundation

Papanek, V. 1995, *The Green Imperative*, London, Thames and Hudson

Parnes, S.J. 1992, *Source Book for Creative Problem Solving*, Buffalo NY, Creative Education Foundation

Perkins, D.N. 1981, *The Mind's Best Work*, Cambridge Ma, Harvard University Press

Perkins, D.N. 1983, 'Novel remote analogies seldom contribute to discovery', *Journal of Creative Behavour*, Vol 17, No 4

Perkins, D.N. 1986, *Knowledge as Design*, Hillsdale NJ, Laurence Erlbaum

Pesut, D.J. 1990, 'Creative thinking as a self-regulatory metacognitive process - a model for education, training and further research', *Journal of Creative Behaviour,* Vol 24 No 2

Phillips, D.N. 1971, *Knowledge from What: theories and methods in social research,* Chicago, Rand McNally

Phillips, E.M. and Pugh, D.S. 1987, *How to Get a PhD: a handbook for students and their supervisors,* Buckingham, Open University Press

Platt, J. 1976, *The Realities of Social Research: an empirical study of British sociologists,* London, University of Sussex Press

Pincher, C 1981, *Their trade is treachery*, London, Sidgwick and Jackson

Polya, G. 1957, *How to Solve it,* New York, Doubleday

Popper, K. 1959, *The Logic of Scientific Discovery,* London, Hutchinson

Poze, A. 1983, 'Analogical connection - the essence of creativity', *Journal of Creative Behaviour,* Vol 17, No 4

Prensky, R.A. 1980, *Creativity and Psychopathology,* New York, Praeger

Prince, G.M. 1968, 'The operational mechanism of synectics', J*ournal of Creative Behaviour,* Vol 2 No 1

Quinn, S. 1995, *Marie Curie: a life,* London, Heinemann

Reanney, D. 1995, *Music of the Mind: an adventure into consciousness,* London, Souvenir Press

Richards, D. 1968, 'Elite interviewing: approaches and pitfalls' *Politics* 16(3)

Richardson, L. 1994, 'Writing: a method of inquiry' in [Denzin and Lincoln, 1994]

Roberts, H., ed, 1981, *Doing Feminist Research*, London, Routledge and Kegan Paul

Roberts, R.M. 1989, *Serendipity: accidental discoveries in science,* New York, John Wiley

Rose, L.H. and Hsin-tai Lin, 1984, 'A meta-analysis of long term creativity training programmes', *Journal of Creative Behaviour,* Vol 18 No 3

Rothenberg, A. and Hausman, C.R. 1976, *The Creativity Question,* Durham NC, Duke University Press

Runco, M.A. and Albert R.S., 1990, *Theories of Creativity,* London, Sage

Russell, B. 1956, *Portraits from Memory and Other Essays,* London, George Allen and Unwin

Sacks, O. 1986, *The Man who Mistook his Wife for a Hat,* London, Picador/ MacMillan

Sandblom, P. 1992, *Creativity and Disease,* London, Marion Boyars

Schaffer, S. 1994, in Boden 1994

Schatzman, L. and Strauss, A.L. 1973, *Field Research: strategies for a natural sociology,* Englewood Cliffs, NJ, Prentice Hall

Schon, D.A. 1963, *The Displacement of Concepts*, London, Tavistock Publications

Schon, D.A. 1987, *Educating the Reflective Practitioner,* San Fransisco, Jossey-Bass

Schonfield, A.H. 1979, 'Explicit heuristic training as a variable in problem solving performance', *Journal for Research into Mathematical Education,* Vol 10 No 3

Scott, R.K. 1995, 'Creative employees: a challenge to management', *The Journal of Creative Behaviour,* Vol 29 No 1

Shakespeare, P., Atkinson, D. and French, S. et al 1993, *Reflecting on Research Practice: issues in health and social welfare,* Buckingham, Open University Press

Shively, W.P. 1980, *The Craft of Political Research,* Englewood Cliffs, NJ, Prentice Hall

Shively, W.P. 1984, *The Research Process in Political Science,* Itasca, Ill, F.E. Peacock

Simon, N. 1996, *Rewrites: a memoir,* New York, Simon and Schuster

Smiles, S. 1996 edn, *Self Help - with illustrations of conduct and perseverance,* London, Institute of Economic Affairs

Stanley, E., ed, 1990, *Feminist Praxis: research theory and epistemology in feminist sociology,* London, Routledge

Stanley, E. and Wise, S. 1983, *Breaking Out: feminist consciousness and feminist research*, London, Routledge and Kegan Paul

Stanley, E. and Wise, S. 1993, *Breaking Out Again: feminist ontology and epistemology,* London, Routledge

Steir, F., ed, 1991, *Research and Reflexivity*, London, Sage

Sternberg, R.J., ed, 1988, *The Nature of Creativity: contemporary psychological perspectives*, Cambridge Ma., Cambridge University Press

Stevenson, R.L. 1920, *Essays in the Art of Writing*, London, Chatto and Windus

Storr, A. 1976, *The Dynamics of Creation*, Harmondsworth, Penguin

Storr, A. 1989, *Churchill's Black Dog and Other Phenomena of the Human Mind*, London, Fontana/ Collins

Strachey, J., ed, 1969, *Standard Edition of the Complete Works of Sigmund Freud*, London, Hogarth Press

Stretton, H. 1964, *The Political Sciences*, London, Routledge and Kegan Paul

Taylor, C.W. and Barron F., eds, 1963, *Scientific Creativity: its recognition and development*, New York, Wiley

Taylor, I.I. and Getzels, J.J. 1975, *Perspectives in Creativity*, Chicago, Aldine

Tetlock, P.E. and Belkin, A, eds, 1996, *Counterfactual thought experiments in world politics: logical, methodological and psychological perspectives*, Princeton, NJ, Princeton University Press

Tey, J. 1951, *Daughter of Time*, London, Heinemann

Thompson, C. 1995, *Born on the Wrong Side*, Bishop Aukland, Pentland

Thoughless, R.H. 1958 edn. *General and Social Psychology,* Cambridge, University Tutorial Press

Tomalin, C. 1994, *Mrs Jordan's Profession,* Harmondsworth, Penguin

Torrance, E.P. 1965, *Education and the Creative Potential,* Minneapolis, University of Minnesota

Torrance, M.S. and Thomas G.V. 1994, 'The development of writing skills in doctoral research students' in [Burgess 1994]

United Nations Develoment Programme (UNDP) 1996, *Human Development Report,* New York, UNDP

Vernon, P.E. 1970, *Creativity,* Harmondsworth, Penguin

Vincent, D. 1981 *Bread, Knowledge and Freedom: a study of nineteenth century working class autobiography,* London, Europa

Wallas, G. 1926, *The Art of Thought,* London, Jonathan Cape

Watson, D., Ed. 1994 *WordsworthDictionary of Musical Quotations,* Edinburgh, Chambers

Watson, J.D. 1968, *The Double Helix,* London, Weidenfield and Nicolson

Webb, S and B 1932, *Methods of Social Study,* London, Longman Green

Weber, R.J. and Perkins, D.N. 1992, *Inventive Minds,* New York, Oxford University Press

Weisberg, R. 1986, *Creativity:genius and other myths,* New York, Freeman

Welsh, G.S. 1975, *Creativity and Intelligence: a personality approach*, Chapel Hill, Institute for Research in Social Science, University of North Carolina

Wertheimer, M. 1945, *Productive Thinking*, New York, Harper

Weschler, J., ed, 1978, *On Aesthetics in Science*, Cambridge Ma, MIT Press

Whitfield, P.R. 1975, *Creativity in Industry*, Harmondsworth, Penguin

Williams, F. 1993, 'Thinking: exploring the "I" in ideas' in [Shakespeare *et al* 1993]

Williams, P. 1979, *Hugh Gaitskell: a political biography*, London, Jonathan Cape

Williams, R. 1976, *Keywords: a vocabulary of culture and society*, London, Fontana

Winks, R.W., ed, 1968, *The Historian as Detective: essays on evidence*. New York, Harper and Row

Wolcott, H.F. 1995, *The Art of Fieldwork*, London, Gower

Woolgar, S., ed, 1988, *Knowledge and Reflexivity: new frontiers in the sociology of knowledge*, London, Sage

Wright, P. with Greengrass, P. 1987, *Spy Catcher*, Richmond, Victoria, Australia, Heinemann

Ziman, J. 1978, *Reliable Knowledge: an exploration of the grounds for beief in science*, Cambridge, Cambridge University Press

Publications by the author (Minkin, L.) to which direct reference is made in the text

1967 *The Soviet Achievement* (with Nettl, J.P.) London, Thames and Hudson.

1974 'The British Labour Party and the Trade Unions: crisis and compact' Symposium on Trade Unions and Political Parties, *Industrial and Labor Relations Review*, October 1974.

1977 (with Seyd, P.) 'The British Labour Party' in Patterson, W.E. and Thomas, A.H. 1977, *Social Democratic Parties of Western Europe*, London, Croom Helme, pp101-152.

1978 'The Party Connection: divergence and convergence in the British labour movement', Symposium on Trade Unions and Political Parties, *Government and Opposition*, October 1978.

1978 *The Labour Party Conference: a study in the politics of intra party democracy*, Harmondsworth, Allan Lane.

1979 'Leftwing trade unionism and the tensions of British labour politics' in Brown, B., ed, 1979, *Eurocommunism and Eurosocialism: The Left Confronts Modernity*, New York, Cyrco Press.

1980 *The Labour Pary Conference: a study in the politics of intra party democracy*, (revised paperback edition with epilogue), Manchester, Manchester University Press.

1981 'The politics of the block vote', *New Socialist* Vol I, No 1, September/ October, 1981.

1982 'Radicalism and reconstruction: the British experience', Symposium, La Reconstruction de l'Europe 1944-49, *Europa*, Tome 5, No 2, 1982.

1986 'Against the tide: trade unions, political communication and the 1983 General Election' in Crewe, I. and Harrop, M., eds, 1986, *Political Communications : The general election campaign of 1983*, Cambridge, Cambridge University Press.

1989 'Mobilisation and distance' in Crewe, I. and Harrop, M., eds, *Political Communications: The General Election of 1987*, Cambridge, Cambridge University Press

1991 *The Contentious Alliance: trade unions and the Labour party*, Edinburgh, Edinburgh University Press.

1992 *The Contentious Alliance: trade unions and the Labour party* (paperback edition, with epilogue), Edinburgh, Edinburgh University Press.

1993 Memorandum of Evidence to the Home Affairs Committee enquiry into the *Funding of Political Parties*, London, HMSO, 20/7/93.

1995 'The New Labour Party: continuities, innovations and uncertainties' in Blair, A. and Minkin L., *La Renovation du Party Travailliste en Grande-Bretagne*, Paris, Fondation Jean Jaures.

Twelve books that the current author has found particularly interesting in understanding creativity

Boden, M. 1990, *The Creative Mind* , London, Weidenfeld and Nicholson.

de Bono, E. 1977, *Lateral Thinking,* Harmondsworth, Penguin.

Getzels, J.W. and Csikszentmihalyi, M. 1976, *The Creative Vision: a longitudinal study of problem finding in art,* New York, John Wiley.

Ghiselin, B. 1954, *The Creative Process: a symposium,* Berkeley, Ca., University of California Press.

Gordon, W.J.J. 1961, *Synectics,* New York, Harper and Row.

Koestler A. 1969, *The Act of Creation* , London, Hutchinson.

Mills, C.W. 1959, 'On intellectual craftsmanship' in *The Sociological Imagination,* Oxford, Oxford University Press.

Nickerson R.S., Perkins, D.N. and Smith, E.E. 1985, *The Teaching of Thinking,* Hillsdale, NJ, Lawrence Erlbaum, 1985.

Osborn, A.F. 1993, *Applied Imagination,* Buffalo NY, Creative Education Foundation.

Perkins, D.N. 1981, *The Mind's Best Work,* Cambridge, Ma, Harvard University Press.

Storr, A. 1989, *Churchill's Black Dog and other Phenomena of the Human Mind,* London, Fontana/ Collins.

Weber, R.J. and Perkins, D.N. 1992, *Inventive Minds,* New York, Oxford University Press.

INDEX OF CITED AUTHORS

EDITORIAL NOTES

This index lists authors cited in either the text (eg 34) or the endnotes (eg 34n6).

It does not include the editors of collections except where their own contribution(s) has been cited.

Surnames beginning Mc or Mac are listed as if spelt Mac.

Abelson,: 88n8
Acker, S: 312n8
Adams, J.L: 90, 92n14, 101
Addison, P: 219
Albert, R.S: 37n3, 104n34, 328n9
Amabile, T.M: 41n16, 52n50, 89n9
Anderson, E: 70n8
Andrews, F.M: 50n41
Arieti, S: xxiin5, 48n34, 91, 105n36, 323
Armbruster, B.B: 40n15
Association of University Teachers: 312n7
Atkinson, D: 9n13
Atkinson, P: 13n19, 190n6

Bachrach, P: 239
Bakan, D: 177n3
Baker, T.L: 5n6, 70n8, 129n9
Baldamus, W: 20n31
Balzac, H: 93
Bamberger, J: 303n3
Bandler, R: 101n28
Baratz, M: 239
Bargar, R.R: 11n17, 87
Barnes, J.A: 151n21
Barron, F: 41n17, 86, 92, 92n14, 99n23
Beauchamp, T.L: 151n21
Becker, H: 5n9, 99n26, 172, 177n3
van Beethoven, L: 110n44
Belkin, A: 230nn6,8
Bell, C: 17n26
Bell, J: 5n3, 171, 308
Bereiter, C: 178f
Bergson, W: 10
Bernard, H.R: 161n27
Berthoff, A.E: 176n2, 176, 178, 197n11
Bevins, A: 136
Beynon, H: 17n27
Biancini, F: 325n7
Black, E: 312n8
Blaxter, L: 5n3, 64n2, 86n4
Boden, M.A: 10, 10n15, 35n2, 38, 49, 50n41, 02n30
de Bono, E: 11n17, 129, 129n10, 224n5

Bandura, A: 205n15
Booth, W.C: 5n4, 64n2
Brannigan, A: xixn1
Brenner, M: 144n17
Bulmer, M: 151n21
Bunyan, J: v
Burgess, R.G: 22n33, 86n6, 145n19
Burnham, P: 6n10, 17. 218n2
Butcher, H.J: 5n2, 85,47n27

Cameron, J: v, 52n51, 101n29, 213
Cannon, W.B: 119n4
Carey, J: 9
Castle, B: 274n3
Charlesworth, M:
Christie, T: 5n2, 47n27, 85
Colomb, G.G: 5n4, 64n2
Colson, E: 155
Conrad, J: 51n46
Cox, C.M: 96n21
Crewe, I: 191, 226
Crick, F: 96
Cropley, A.J: 92, 92n14
Curie, P: 51n46
Czikszentmihalyi, M: xixn1, 43n20, 50n42, 52n50, 62n1, 70, 91n10, 106

Dane, : 61
Dellas, M: 86n2
Dennett, D.C: 18n29, 328n9
Dewey, J: 49n37, 67
Dexter, L.A: 144n18
Dilts, R.B: 51n47
Dilts, R.W: 51n47
Dogan, M: 239n15
Dorrill, S: 231n10
Duncan, J.K: 11n17, 87

Economic and Social Research Council: 5n7
Emerson, R.M: 151n21
Encel. S: 17n27
Entwistle, N: 5n2, 101
Epstein, T: 51n47
Eysenck, H.J: 39n11, 43n21, 86n3

Fadden, R.R: 151n21
Fearon, J.D: 230n8
Feldhusen, J.F: 43n22, 88n8, 92n14
Fender, B: 312n9
Fielding, N: 17n27
Finch, J: 145n19
Flanders, A: 281n5
Flowers, L: 178
Ford, C.M: 39nn11,12, 91n12, 99n23, 100n27, 102n31, 101n34, 105n36, 108n40, 325n4
Ford, D.Y: 33n1
Foster, G.M: 155
Freeman, J: 5n2, 47n27, 85
Freud, S: 44n24
Fryer, M: 325n4
Fryer, R: 15n23

Gaier, E.L: 86n2
Gallway, W.T: 101n28
Ganim, R: 38n9
Gardner, H: 110n46
Gedo, J.E: 86n4
Getzels, J.W: 62n1, 70
Ghiselin, B: xx, 6, 17n25, 23, 47nn28,30, 110n46
Giddens, A: 324, 325n6
Gide, A: v
Gigerenzer, G: 10n14

Gioia, D.A: 325n4
Gioia, E: 17n25
Glaser, B: 20n31
Goleman, D: 93, 95n19, 101nn28,29, 325
Gordon, W.J.J: 92n13, 237n14, 239ff, 295, 295n2
Gornick, V: 107n38
Gould, J.D: 230n8
Gouldner, A: 21n32
Green, B: 101n28
Greengrass, P: 231nn11,12
Gruber, : 49n36, 95n20, 240n17, 245n20
Guilford, J.P: 38nn7,8, 66n6, 88n 8, 99n24, 105n36, 129n11

Hall, P: 325n7
Hammersley, M: 245n22
Hammond, P: 11n16, 17n26
Haggis, J: 64n2
Harris III, J.J: 33n1
Harris, M: 323n1
Harrop, M:191, 226
Haseler, S: 248
Hausman, C.R: 37n5, 39n11, 47n28
Hawthorne, G: 230n8
Helson, R: 104n34
Hennessey, B.A: 41n16
Hill, S: 102n32
Hill, T: 312n8
Hockey, J: 86n6
Horowitz, I.L: 24n36
Howard, K: 5n5, 64n2
Hudson, L: 85n1. 117n1
Hughes, C: 5n3, 64n2, 86n5

Jackson, B: xxin3
James, H: 123n6
James, W: 267
James, J: 47
Jenkins, P: 126, 274n3
Jevons, W.S: 108n41
Jewkes, J: 2
Jones, R: 43n22, 237n14
Jorgensen J: 146n20
Jubak, J: 237n14
Jung, C.G: 110n46

Kanter, R.M: 70n8
Kaplan, N: 93n17
Kaufman, P: 93, 101nn28,29, 325
Kemper, R.V: 155
Kloos, P: 195n8
Koestler, A: 6n10, 38n9, 47, 239f, 240n16, 245, 245n24, 256n26, 329
Kogan, N: 39n11
Kynge, J: 325n5

Landry, C: 325n7
Langley, P: 43n22, 237n14
Lasswell, H: 65n4
Lee, R.M: 139n15
Leigh, D: 231nn10,12
Leytham, G: 50n41, 52n51, 245n21
Lieberman, J.N: 44n23
Lightman, A: 230n7
Lin, Hsin-Tai: 38n8
Lodge, D: 202
Lombroso, C: 86n4
Lowenthall, D: 172n1
Lubart, T.I: 50nn39,44
Lumet, S: 303

McClelland, D.C: 92n14
McHarry, J:: 325n6
McKenzie, R: 72f
MacKinnon, D.W: 40n13, 50n43, 85f, 88n7, 99n25, 104n35
McNay, I: 312n12
McReynolds, P: 237n14
Maddi, S.R: 47n29, 88n8, 95n20, 99n24
Malcolm, N: 312n11
Mantel, H: 50n40
Marquand, D: 219
Marsden, D: xxin3
Marshall, R: 324n2
Maslow, A.H: 33, 37n4, 38, 40, 52n50, 86n4, 93
Medawar, P: 9n12, 16, 205, 329
Mednick, S.A: 241n18
Melville, H: 24, 197n10
Merton, R.K: 66n5
Metzger, D: 52n51, 101n29
Michels, R: 72f
Mills, C.W: 6n11, 109, 128
Minken, L: v, 16, 18n28, 73n9, 77, 126ff, 134, 143, 148f, 154n24, 161, 162n29, 182,189, 191, 193, 219f, 223, 223n4, 226ff, 236f, 242, 248, 253, 276f
Morris, P: 245n23
Morris, W.T: 41n19
Mulkay, M: 245n25
Murdock, M.M: 38n9

Nettl. J.P: 205
Newby, H: 17n26
Newell, A. 12n18
Nickerson, R.S: 38ff, 40n15, 43, 50, 101n28, 117, 241

Oakeshott, M: 23, 24
Oakley, A: 145n19
Ochse, R: 34, 39n11, 51nn45,48, 88n8
Olson, T: 50n40, 51n48
Osborn, A.F: 38, 48n35, 49, 50n41, 224n5, 267, 267n2

Pahre, R: 239n15
Papanek, V: 325n6
Parnes, S.J: 38n8, 45n25, 48n35, 92n13, 108n39, 190n5, 195n7, 241n19
Perkins, D.N: 10n15, 38nn6,7,8, 38ff, 40nn14,15, 43, 47, 47n31, 48n32, 50, 50n41, 86n2, 99n24, 101n28, 104n34, 108n42, 117, 120n5, 155, 155n25, 215, 237n14, 241, 308
Pesut, D.J: 40n15
Phillips, D.L: 177n3
Phillips, E.M: 86n5
Pinch, T: 196n9
Pincher, C: 231n11
Platt, J: 17n26
Pole, C.J: 86n6
Polya, G: 11, 12n18, 66, 215, 222
Popper, K: 10
Poze, A: 241n19
Prensky, R.A: 86n4
Prince, G.M: 41n16, 66
Prout, A: 13n19
Pugh, D.S: 86n5
Punch, M: 151n21

Ramsay, R: 231n10
Ray, M: 101nn28,29, 325
Reanney, D: 245
Richards, D: 125n8
Richards, P: 5n9, 98n22, 172, 177n3
Richardson, L: 5n8, 260n27
Roberts, R.M: 47n26
Roe, A: 37n5, 88n8, 92n14, 95n20, 99nn23,24
Rose, L.H: 38n8
Rothenberg, A: 37n5, 39n11, 47n28
Runco, M.A: 37n3, 41n18, 328n9
Russell, B: 50n40, 97

Sacks, O: 307n5
Sandblom, P: 86n4
Sawyer, K: 43n20, 50n42
Scardamalia, C: 178f
Schaffer, S: xixn1, 48n34
Schatzman, L: 22n33
Scheffler, I: 3n1
Schon, D.A: 205, 237n14, 238, 303n3
Schonfield, A.H: 12n18
Scott, R.K: 325n3
Scudder, T: 155
Seldon, A: 125n8
Seyd, P: 189
Shakespeare, P:
Sharp, J.A: 5n5, 64n2
Shively, W.P: 6n10, 19n30
Simon, A.H: 12n18, 295n2
Simon, N: 101n29, 102
Simonton, D.K: 99nn14,15, 108nn39,43, 329n10
Smiles, S: 100, 241
Smith, E.E: 38ff, 40n15, 43, 50, 101n28, 117, 241
Sternberg, R.J: 47n30, 48n33, 50nn39,44, 92n14, 93n16, 95n20, 99n23
Stevenson, R.L: 17
Stimson, J.A: 304n4
Stoppard, T: vi
Storr, A: 38, 44n23, 51n45, 86n4, 89, 96, 110n45, 202, 214
Strauss, A.L: 20n31, 22n33
Stretton, H: 17n27, 135n13, 230n8
Sullivan, J.L: 23n34

Tardif, T.Z: 47n30, 48n33, 205n14
Taylor, C: 33n1
Taylor, I.I: 50n38, 92
Tetlock, P.E: 230nn6,8
Tey, J: 166
Thomas, G.V: 171, 222n3, 326n8
Thompson, C: xxin4
Thorne, B: 151n21
Thoughless, R.H: 267
Tight, M: 5n3, 64n2, 86n5
Tomalin, C: 295n1
Torrance, M.S: 38n8, 171, 222n3, 326n8
Tucker, M: 324n2

United Nations Development Programme: 324

Vincent, D: xix

Wallace, R.J: 151n21
Wallach, M.A: 39n11
Wallas, G: 6, 47n27, 50n41, 52n49, 266n1, 312
Wason, P.C: 172n1

Watson, J.D: 245n20
Walters, L: 151n21
Webb, B:140n16
Webb, S: 140n16
Weber, R.J: 47,47n31, 155, 215
Weick, K.E: 330n11
Weisberg, R: 47n28, 50n41
Weldon, F: 178n4
Welsh, G.S: 38n7, 39n11
Wertheimer, M: 230n7
Weschler, J: 245
Wettersten, J: 10
White, M 47n26
White W.F: 139n14
Whitfield, P.R: 65, 129n11, 221
Williams, Fiona: 13n20, 51n45, 103
Williams, Forrest: 13n22
Williams, J.M: 5n4, 64n12
Williams, P: 232
Williams, R: 24n35, 33
Willmott, H: 312n11
Wilson, J: 91n11
Winks, R.W: 119n4
Wolcott, H.F: 5n6, 9n12, 24n35
Wright, A: 312n11
Wright, P: 231nn11,12'

Ziman, J: 330

SUBJECT INDEX

Academic life: 3
Aesthetic(s): 35, 244, 279f, 284
Analogies (as stimulants of creativity): 237ff
Analysis (relations with chronology): 192ff
Anxiety: 96f
Apprentice to a "master": 205ff
Appropriate strangeness: 190ff, 194
Art of the researcher: 24
Association of ideas: 266ff
Auden, W.J: 178
Autonomy of the object: 295

Benn, A.W. (Tony): 277
Bevan, A: 232
Brown, G: 232
Browne (inventor of the suspension bridge): 241
Brunel, M.A: 241
Buber, M: 307

Callaghan, J: 233
Campaign for Labour Party Democracy: 77
Cannon, L: 231
Careful disorderliness: 197
Castle, B: 290 (note 3)
Chapple, F: 133
Chronology (relations with analysis): 192ff
Cornell University: 230
Community (of scholars): 97ff, 202ff
Confidence: 100ff
Conservative Party (GB): 228, 234, 284
Copernicus, N: 195
Counter-factual thought experiments: 230ff
Courage of the mind: 97ff
Creative
  altruism: 325
  city: 325
  collaboration: 325
  critic: 217
  mind: 211
  player, the: 34f
  process (and writing): 4ff, 99, 103, 171ff, 175ff, 243ff
  research culture: 326ff
Creativity
  applied: 41
  awareness of: 39
    and creativogenic culture: 323
  definition: 33f
  enhancement of: 37ff
  forms of: 36f
  intangible and mysterious: 10ff
  intellectual aspects: 85ff
  key attributes: 36
    and motivation: 88ff
    as patternmaking: 184ff
    and personality: 86ff
    and politics: 9
  psychological aspects: 85ff
    and the scientific: 8f
    and sleep: 214
    and the theatre of the mind: 117ff
Critical Examination: 64ff, 129f

Dangers (ethical): 151
Darwin, C: 240
Deakin, A: 236f
Deferment (of judgement) 194ff
Deferment (of project closure): 91ff
Democratic Party, U.S.A: 188
Discovery: 126ff

Edison, T.A: 47
Effort: 95f
Einstein, A: 49, 245
Electoral orientation: 183
Emotions: 93ff
Empathy: 136f
Engels, F: 1
Eureka moment: 46ff, 108
Exploring: 42f
Evasion, disgust at: 3

Failure in research: see research, failure in
Feminist social science research: 13
Finer, S: 2
Flow, the": xxviii, 52ff, 63, 106, 204, 214, 272, 319
Frameworks, construction of: xxix, ch6 *passim*
Functional differentiation: 183

Gaitskell, H: 143, 231f
Gershwin, I: 90

Heath, E: 228
Heisenberg, W: 245
Heuristics: 11f, 165f, 240, 251
Heuristic rule: 252
Heuristic strategies: 41
Heuristic thinking: 129f, ch7 *passim*, 265
Holism, holistic: 172

Ideological cleavage: 183
Industrial conflict: 183
In Place of Strife 126, 158, 182,
Interviewing: 138ff
  as conversation: 140ff
  as creative dialogue: 147ff
  as joint enquiry: 144ff
  and recording: 138ff
Introspection, philosophical: 13

Jenkins, C: 278
Jewkes, J: 1
Jones, J: 79, 275,
Joseph II, Emperor: 200

K.G.B: 231f
Kinnock, N: 143

Labour movement: iii, 287
Labour Party (British),
  Commission of Enquiry: 143
  comparison with European parties: 188
  comparison with old commonwealth parties: 73
  comparison with US Democratic Party: 188
  Conference: 73ff, 77ff, 127, 130f, 132, 134, 143, 159, 183, 193, 237f, 248, 277
  conference agenda management: 74ff, 143, 156ff, 193, 238f
  and crisis, 183

culture: 220ff
deals: 227f
death of leaders: 230ff
distribution of power: 65, 73, 80f, 235f, 248
funding by trade unions: 78f, 227, 273f
in government: iii, 2, 75
and industrial relations: 160
inflexibility: 222f
leadership: 73, 75, 131, 287
(New): xxvi, 135, 268
in opposition: 77f
National Executive Committee: 31, 159, 229, 280, 297
"Party into Power" project: iii
and public ownership: 127f, 248f
Review Group: iii
rules: 80f, 131, 193, 271f, 278ff, 282ff, 287ff¡
Special Conference: 277
and trade unions: iii, 77, 78ff, 126f, 160, 181, 191, 193, 201, 227ff, 233, 241ff, 271ff
Women's Conference: 160
Leeds Business School: vii
Leeds, University of: iii, 6
Leeds Metropolitan University: vii, xxv, 7
Lovell, A.C.B: 1
Lying, contempt of: 3

MacDonald, R: 135
Manchester, University of: iii, xxv, 1, 3, 7
Mao-Tse-Tung: 294
Masks, protective: 3f
Melville, H: 197
Metacognition: 12ff, 39f
Metaphors (as stimulants of creativity) 237ff
Metaphors (used by author)
Artist (or patternmaker-artist): 194ff, 223, 275
Awkward Sod: 118, 148, ch7 *passim*, 277
Battle of the Patternmakers: 194ff
Chattering Monkey: 118, ch7 *passim*, 267
Cluster effect: 268
Creative critic: 217ff
Destructive Critic: 101ff, 119, 213, 275
Detective: xxix, ch5 *passim*, 173, 180, 186ff, 190, 198f, 296
Devil's Advocate: 148
Drama: 183, 252f
Ecological balance: 258f
Explorer: xxviii, 42f, 118
Family: 242f, 282
Faust:110
Fiddler on the roof: 304
Helter-Skelter: 105ff
Juggler: xxix, 118, ch6 *passim*
Moving meditation: 213
Navigator: 118
Observer-Insider: 161
Overture (as a finale): 307, 321
Patternmaker: xxix, 118, 130, 133, ch6 *passim*
Pilgrim: 109f, 286
Pitfalls and Pratfalls: 137f
Player, 34, 44f, 118
Realist (or patternmaker-realist):

194ff, 275
Right-angle effect: 267
Roman candle effect: 269
Showbusiness: 97ff
Symbiotic relationship: 241f
Theatre of the mind: 117,
"Too many notes": 200
Vicious Circle (of critics): 119
Walter Mitty: 117f
Watcher in the wings: 118
Mind-games: 230
Mind, non-directed activities: xxix, ch7 *passim*
Modes of heuristic thinking 217ff
Monks, J: 191
Moods: 93ff
Motivation: 88ff
Mozart, W.A: 200

Naivety: 227f
National Union of Mineworkers: 278
"New Labour Party": see Labour Party (New)
Newton, I: 47
Northern College: iii
Northern Institute for Continuing Education: vii, xxv

Observational vigilance: 124f
Parliamentary Select Committee on Home Affairs: 227
Peculiarity, agenda management: 74ff
Peculiarity, block vote politics: 132f
Peculiarity, union leaders: 78ff
Peculiarities as a key to problems: xxviii, 66ff, 130f, 318
Persistence: 95f
Phillips, M: 132
Playing: xxviii, 44ff
Pluralism in research: 18f
Political funds (trade union): see Trade unions, political funds,
Prepared mind: 154ff
Problems, developing solutions: xxixf, ch8 *passim*
Problems, focus upon: 68ff
Problem generation: 298f
Problems, nature and distinctiveness of: 61ff
Problem seeking: xxviii, ch3 *passim*
Processes of empirical investigation: xxix, ch5 *passim*
Psycho-analysis: 1
Psychology of the creative mind: xxix, ch4 *passim*

Reflexivity: 12ff
Research
academic aspects: 4ff
asserting control over: 302ff
Assessment Exercise: 310, 312
as creative art: 25, 317¡
failure in: 2, 15ff, 37, 107f, 328ff
process: 15ff
purpose of: 71ff
shifting nature of: xxx, ch9 *passim*, 293ff
and university culture: xxv, xxvii, 3ff, 310, ch10 *passim*
and verification: 255
Resilience: 100ff
Risk taking: 92f, 100, 281f, 308ff

Rugby League: xxxi (note 4), 186
Rutherford, E: 1

Scanlon, H, 79, 274
Scargill, A: 133, 278
Second World War consensus: 219
Self-awareness: 21ff, 39f
Self-disciplined squigliness: 45
Self-image: 40f, 104f, 117ff
Self-management: 93ff
Serendipity: 154ff
Sheffield Hallam University: iii, vii
Social Democratic Party (GB): 281
Social Democratic Party (Germany): 188
Social Democratic Party (Sweden): 188
Social empathy: 183
Socialist Labour Party (GB): 278
Solitude: 51f
Space and distance: 191
Specialism in research: 19f
Strangeness, "strangeify": see appropriate strangeness
Strangeness and familiarity: 240
Symbolic representation: 184ff
Synectics: 239ff

Talking as thinking: 250ff
Thatcherism: 235
Theorising: 20, 30 (note 31), 74f,
Time, use of: xxviii, 46ff, 152, 289, 308ff
Trades Union Congress: 135, 191, 233, 247, 280, 283
Trade Unions: see also Labour Party and trade unions: 78ff
  National Union of Mineworkers: 278, 305
  and political communication: 226f
  political funds: 226f, 284f, 299
  Transport and General Workers Union: 127, 143, 237, 275
Transmutations and destabilisation: 293ff
Truth, love of: 3

Union leaders: see peculiarity, union leaders

Vienna panic, the: 257ff

Walpole, R: 155
Watt, J: 241
Weldon, F: 178
Wilson, H; 75, 126, 152, 156, 231, 2744
Winter of discontent: 233f, 277
Wittgenstein, L: 1
Wright, brothers O. and W: 42
Writing: see creative process and writing

York, University of: iii

LEARNING and SOCIETY

About the Series

As advanced industrial societies move into the 21st century, they are experiencing profound and widespread changes. These embrace their economies, labour markets, technologies and communications, international relations, the organisation of their communities, family forms, questions of social order and social policies. At the heart of these changes are located people's own changing aspirations and identities, as we shift towards what some commentators have termed a post modern world, shaped increasingly by global forces and the information revolution, and characterised increasingly by uncertainty, risk and indeterminacy.

Individuals, groups and whole communities are differently placed to meet the raft of challenges presented by these changes. It is essential that people be adequately equipped, as citizens, not only to respond to change, but also to be able to make their own choices in the world and contribute to the shape of their own lives and environments. Learning has a vital contribution to make to a process of resourcing people, throughout their lives and in relation to the whole panoply of their needs, concerns and interests.

This means that lifelong learning must rise to the top of agendas, as much for policy makers as for individuals, and must raise questions especially for those whose responsibility it is to secure educational opportunities for all. The extent of this challenge can scarcely be exaggerated, especially in the United Kingdom where, for far too long, education has been predicated upon a fatal combination of elitism, failure, exclusion and limited time horizons. Too few people achieve their full potential through current educational provision and too many exit from learning too soon. The evidence indicates that those who succeed initially in education are those who will continue to access and benefit from it throughout their lives, whether in employment, professional development or in their role as active citizens and private individuals.

Whilst there is welcome additional attention now paid to the importance of securing employability for individuals and contributing to greater competitiveness for economies through learning, the agenda for learning must be much wider than this. Learning should be one of those activities which enhance the opportunities for people to live fuller, more creative and more satisfying lives in every aspect of their experience. Citizens are not defined by, and should not be confined to, their labour market positions alone, and learning cannot be oriented simply to the needs of future employment, narrowly defined, even if we knew precisely what those needs might be.

The Northern College is a residential education college which stands in a long tradition of extending liberal education to a wider group of citizens than are conventionally given access to learning through mainstream educational provision in schools, colleges, universities and their place of work. The mission of the College commits itself both to widening participation and to contributing, through learning, to the strengthening of active citizenship - in communities, in trade unions, in voluntary organisations, in religious and secular groups of one kind or another, in families, employment and recreation. The College seeks to resource people in their own lives for paid work, community activity and personal development.

In 1994, the College signed a high-level partnership agreement with Sheffield Hallam University (formerly Sheffield City Polytechnic) to enable the two institutions to work more closely in extending learning and educational achievement to a wider constituency. As part of that partnership, the University and the College established a joint institute for research and development, The Northern Institute for Continuing Education (NICE). The brief of that institute is to undertake detailed and focused work on a wide range of empirical, developmental and conceptual concerns central to those linking learning and society as we move into the next millennium.

One of the initiatives taken by NICE has been to launch this new monograph series entitled 'Learning and Society'. We intend to produce a variety of publications in the series. This will include individual research monographs, whether based upon empirical study or critical review, accounts of new developments in the field, collections of papers and conference reports and studies of history, policy and method in relation to learning and society.

This volume, by Lewis Minkin, is the first in our new series of publications. It represents a major contribution to the important question of how we conduct research and refine the findings of our research through rigorous, systematic and creative analysis and interpretation.

Enquiry and creativity stand at the heart of learning and relearning: each is also essential in the twin processes of personal development and mutual education. Interpretations and understandings of the world, as well as programmes and policies to change or reform it, depend essentially upon thorough and imaginative research and the willingness of researchers to share their experiences and insights with us. Such research may be carried on in the most informal ways in institutions established especially for the purpose, whether in universities, colleges, research institutes, industry, government or the wider community. It may also be the job of specialist researchers working individually or in teams, whether as recognised scholars or experts or as students in training. But, a commitment for enquiry and creativity may also include individuals and groups who wish to examine more systematically for themselves, aspects of their world and their experience as active citizens.

Lewis Minkin's volume will be an invaluable resource for all of these groups and individuals. It is engaging, accessible, instructive, enjoyable and inspirational. It builds on Lewis' own extensive experience researching the world of politics and sets out a wide range of ways in which Lewis has sought to open up politics to a wider understanding through the application of creativity and new interpretations. In this sense the volume constitutes a 'resource of hope' for those who would engage in research, that they may too find ways, through their own learning and the application of rigour and imagination, to become creative themselves.

Bob Fryer
Series Editor
Learning and Society